HUMAN–COMPUTER FACTORS:

A Study of Users and Information Systems

INFORMATION SYSTEMS SERIES

CONSULTING EDITORS

D. E. AVISON BA, MSc, PhD, FBCS
Professor of Information Systems
Department of Accounting and Management Science
Southampton University, UK

G. FITZGERALD BA, MSc, MBCS
Cable & Wireless Professor of Business Information Systems
Department of Computer Science
Birkbeck College, University of London, UK

This series of student and postgraduate texts covers a wide variety of topics relating to information systems. It is designed to fulfil the needs of the growing number of courses on, and interests in, computing and information systems which do not focus on the purely technological aspects, but seek to relate these to business and organizational context.

INFORMATION SYSTEMS SERIES

HUMAN–COMPUTER FACTORS:

A Study of Users and Information Systems

ANDY SMITH
Principal Lecturer
Department of Computing
University of Luton, UK

THE McGRAW-HILL COMPANIES

London · New York · St Louis · San Francisco · Auckland
Bogotá · Caracas · Lisbon · Madrid · Mexico
Milan · Montreal · New Delhi · Panama · Paris · San Juan
São Paulo · Singapore · Sydney · Tokyo · Toronto

Published by
McGRAW-HILL Publishing Company
Shoppenhangers Road, Maidenhead, Berkshire, SL6 2QL, England
Telephone: 01628 502500
Fax: 01628 770224

British Library Cataloguing in Publication Data
The CIP data of this title is available from the British Library, UK

Library of Congress Cataloging-in-Publication Data
The CIP data of this title is available from the Library of Congress,
Washington DC, USA

McGraw-Hill

A Division of The McGraw-Hill Companies

Printed and bound in Malta by Interprint Ltd.

CONTENTS

6 Elements of human–computer interaction

7 The technical system: designing for interface usability

8 Supporting the user

SERIES FOREWORD

The Information Systems Series is a series of student and postgraduate texts covering a wide variety of topics relating to information systems. The focus of the series is the use of computers and the flow of information in business and large organizations. The series is designed to fill the needs of the growing number of courses on information systems and computing which do not focus on purely technical aspects, but seek to relate information systems to their commercial and organizational context.

The term 'information systems' has been defined as the effective design, delivery, use and impact of information technology in organizations and society. Utilizing this broad definition it is clear that the subject is interdisciplinary. Thus the series seeks to integrate technological disciplines with management and other disciplines, for example, psychology and sociology. These areas do not have a natural home and were until comparatively recently, rarely represented by single departments in universities and colleges. To put such books in a purely computer science or management series restricts potential readership and the benefits that such texts can provide. The series on information systems provides such a home.

The titles are mainly for student use, although certain topics will be covered at greater depth and be more research oriented for postgraduate study.

The series includes the following areas, although this is not an exhaustive list: information systems development methodologies, office information systems, management information systems, decision-support systems, information modelling and databases, systems theory, human aspects and the human–computer interface, application systems, technology strategy, planning and control, expert systems, knowledge acquisition and its representation.

A mention of the books so far published in the series gives a 'flavour' of the richness of the information systems world. *Information Systems Development: Methodologies, Techniques and Tools, second edition* (David Avison and Guy Fitzgerald) provides a comprehensive coverage of the different elements of information systems development. *Information Systems Development: A Database Approach, second edition* (David Avison) provides a coherent methodology which has been widely used to develop adaptable computer systems using databases; *Structured Systems Analysis and Design Methodology, second edition* (Geoff Cutts) looks at one particular information systems development methodology in detail; *Software Engineering for Information Systems* (Donald McDermid) discusses software engineering in the context of information systems; *Information Systems Research: Issues, Techniques and Practical Guidelines* (Robert Galliers, Editor) provides a collection of papers on key information systems issues which will be of special interest to researchers; *Multiview: An Exploration in Information Systems Development* (David Avison and Trevor Wood-Harper) looks at an approach to information systems development which combines human and technical considerations; *Relational Database Design* (Paul Beynon-Davies) offers a practical discussion of relational database design. Other recent titles include *Business Management and Systems Analysis* (Eddie Moynihan), *Systems Analysis, System Design* (David Mason and Leslie Willcocks), *Decision Support Systems* (Paul Rhodes), *Why Information Systems Fail* (Chris Sauer), *Transforming the Business: the IT contribution* (Robert Moreton and Myrvin Chester).

One missing link in our Series has been a text on human factors. Andy Smith's book fills this gap. Further, the emphasis placed on the human–computer aspects of information systems development gives the book a unique feature but one of direct relevance to readers. The author makes copious use of diagrams which illustrate the narrative material, and the case study in particular provides the reader with an understanding of the integrated nature of the approach in context. Thus the potential danger of texts in this subject—as only being merely a description of a number of techniques is avoided. Indeed, the book is exemplar in showing the high level of integration required for human topics in information systems. A glossary of terms is also provided. We welcome this addition to the Series as it provides a sound introduction to human–computer factors in information systems.

PREFACE

Aim

This study provides a co-ordinated and consistent coverage of the major user issues in information systems development.

Rationale

We may assume that all information systems aim to improve some area of organizational effectiveness. It is unfortunate that the success rate of such systems, in terms of achieving these aims, is so low. Studies show that only a minority of IT systems achieve full success as defined by fully meeting initial objectives. Many of the reasons for this lack of success relate to the ways in which the information systems designer attempted to meet the needs of the users of these systems; to what might generally be referred to as *human–computer factors*.

Over the last decade an increasing importance has been attached to the place of the user within the development of information systems. Much of the thrust behind this comes from the rapid expansion in the use of both interactive and end-user systems. Current developments in a wide range of new technologies are opening up computer systems to a much wider user population.

This book attempts to provide an overview of the major ideas and concepts underpinning the development and operation of computer-based information systems. It is founded on the premise that the underlying discipline behind a study of users and information systems is constituted from a number of areas. One of the most significant areas is that of human–computer interaction (HCI). User issues are, however, much wider than just interface design on which HCI concentrates. It is not possible to separate the technical nature of the IT system from the organization into which it is to be introduced or from the users who are going to use it.

Specifically the book aims to develop the reader's appreciation of the needs of different types of users of modern information systems, with particular reference to the attainment of usability of information systems within their organizational settings.

Objectives

Through a comprehensive study of the book the reader should be able to:

Develop a detailed understanding of the needs of computer users:
- Recognize the many characteristics through which users diverge
- Identify different types of user need
- Develop and evaluate user taxonomies
- Differentiate typical user populations
- Identify how human psychological and physiological characteristics may influence information systems design
- Perform a user analysis in an organizational setting
- Produce a user specification

Evaluate the contributions which the user can make to systems design:
- Appreciate the importance of the user contribution to successful systems design
- Advise on the involvement of users in systems design
- Recognize the essential elements of user-centred design
- Relate theory of user-centred design to current commercial practice
- Propose design teams
- Evaluate the user-centredness of software projects

Review and evaluate the contribution of information systems design methods:
- Appreciate the inherent socio-technical requirements of information systems
- Identify the different approaches taken by methodologies
- Outline the activities involved in a number of methodologies
- Evaluate the role of the user in different methods
- Compare methods in their approach to usability criteria
- Select a methodology to meet specific user and system needs

Recommend outline social systems designs to ensure organizational acceptability:
- Appreciate the relationship between information systems and organizational change
- Define organizational acceptability and rejection
- Evaluate the user and organizational effects of proposed information systems solutions
- Propose social system designs which lead to organizational acceptability
- Recognize the ingredients of successful change management

- Evaluate the user implications of different implementation strategies

Identify some essential elements within the arena of human–computer interaction:
- Place user interactions within a context of goals, activities and tasks
- Describe user tasks using basic techniques
- Recognize the factors that affect interaction design
- Apply design rationale techniques
- Specify interfaces using basic techniques

Demonstrate how a user-centred approach to interface design can lead to interface usability:
- Provide a comprehensive definition of usability
- Relate usability and evaluation
- Perform simple user-based interface evaluations
- Evaluate the user contribution to a range of interface design methods
- Describe the essential elements of a user-centred interface development approach

Describe the essential elements within a comprehensive user support system:
- Identify levels and domains of user understanding
- Appreciate the need for, and nature of, user-support systems
- Design outline training programmes to meet user needs
- Describe the types and distinguishing features of support materials
- Recognize the reasons for the growth of end-user systems and identify the specific support requirements of those who implement such systems
- Understand the issues associated with the organization and management of training and user support

Recognize the practical problems experienced in commercial development situations:
- Relate the theory and practice of human–computer factors
- Identify problems experienced in practice
- Describe the major influences on user-centred design
- Recognize the growing importance of human-factor specialists within and external to user organizations

Evaluate the way in which new technological developments are leading to new types of information systems and continuing to affect the user role:
- Appreciate the implications of data communications on the user role

- Evaluate the contribution of, and recognize the difficulties associated with, computer supported co-operative working systems
- Assess the potential applications of virtual reality to information systems

ACKNOWLEDGEMENTS

It should be admitted at the outset that I take full responsibility for the rationale for, and structure and content of, this study of users and information systems.

The book would, however, not have been possible without the contribution of a considerable number of individuals. Some of these *contributors* have provided text which has been directly integrated into the main body of the study, while others have undertaken underpinning research for particular aspects of the book.

Specifically I would like to acknowledge and thank:

Dr Lynne Dunckley for providing a supportive and collaborative research environment that has enabled much of the research that has underpinned the user-centred design elements of this study. I am also pleased to acknowledge both the many helpful comments on various aspects of the book and the specific collaboration and partnership that has led to the development of Chapter 4.

Professor Ken Eason for introducing me to the study of user-centred design, for providing a major input to the development of the Plumbest case study, for the very many references throughout the text, and for his specific input to Chapter 5.

Andrew Tinson for providing the basis for the telematics elements of Chapter 10.

Sunila Modi both for working with me in the development of a module titled *Users and Information Systems* at the University of Luton which formed the basis for the book, and also for providing the underpinning research for Chapter 8.

Mick Baldwin for providing the basis for the virtual reality elements of Chapter 10.

Laurie Smith, and Chalfont Software Ltd, for providing access to the minor case study: Acadmin.

I would also like to thank my mother for undertaking much of the proof-reading, Alfred for being so patient and someone else without whose actions in 1991 none of this would have happened.

Andy Smith
October 1996

INTRODUCTION

Chapter aims

Through study of this chapter the reader will develop a broad overview of the role of human factors within the development of an information system (IS) and in particular should be able to:

- Appreciate the growing importance of information systems to today's society
- Perform a basic classification of information systems
- Distinguish between organizational and end-user systems
- Appreciate the significance of the user role within information systems
- Relate the information systems development life cycle to the user role
- Comprehend the importance of human-factor issues in information systems development
- Define systems success in terms of usability characteristics

1.1   A review of information systems

1.1.1   What is an information system?

The British Computer Society, in a definition agreed with the Engineering Council in 1989, defines an *information system* (IS) as:

> an application of computing and communications technology to meet a defined need . . .

Most readers embarking on this book will, no doubt already have some idea in their minds about the constituent elements of an information system. Such ideas will probably include the use of information technology (IT) equipment to solve and/or computerize problems in business, commerce and industry. There are, of course, many types of such systems, and many ways in which such systems can be classified.

One way to categorize information systems might be to investigate the uses to which they are put. Information systems exist today in a vast range of areas from applications in the home environment, through day-to-day business systems, to complex real-time manufacturing and control systems. Even if we restrict our analysis to information systems used in business and commerce we cover a wide spectrum from relatively simple *transaction processing systems* (such as payroll and stock control) through *management information systems* (such as those to assist in financial management) to *executive information systems* and *decision support systems* which can help in decision making and strategic planning within the organization.

This book is a study into the way in which users interact with a variety of information systems. The focus, however, is clearly on the user, and associated human factors, rather than the details of the information system itself. The reader will have access to a wide range of literature outlining the details of, and development methods for, information systems. For our needs the intricacies of the domain application itself will also be largely irrelevant.

It will be useful to start our analysis by comparing three different definitions related to information systems and management information systems:

Definition 1   Kroenke (1989) defines a management information system as:

> a system using formalised procedures to provide management at all levels in all functions with appropriate information based on data from both internal and external sources, to enable them to make timely and effective decisions for planning, directing and controlling the activities for which they are responsible

Definition 2   Lucey (1991) says that:

> an MIS is an integrated, computer based, user machine system that provides information for supporting operations and decision making functions

Definition 3   Carver (1989) has a slightly different approach and gives an interpretation of an information system that includes:

> the man, the computer, the task, and the interaction between them, within an environment which may include the immediate workspace, the physical environment, the social environment, and the organizational environment

There is a clear shift in emphasis in these three definitions of an information system away from the *product* of the management support process, as shown in definition one, to the *processes* and *environments* involved as emphasized in definition three. It is the latter definition that should interest us in our study of users and information systems, and we should use this definition as a starting point for our analysis.

1.1.2   Development of information systems applications

When computers were first developed in the 1950s predictions concerning their spread were vastly under-estimated. In only four decades information technology has pervaded almost all aspects of life. In the final chapter of this book we will study in more detail a number of ways in which information systems are changing society today.

In business, information systems have evolved to meet the needs of, and in many cases to modify, the working environment they serve. Early computerized information systems were introduced to increase the efficiency or productivity of routine procedures. Initially the computation focused on processing numerical data and solving mathematical equations. The first business oriented application involved the analysis of data from the 1951 US Census. Nowadays information systems serve higher level activities such as providing integration across and within organizations and providing management information and decision support to senior managers. In industry information technology is used to automate physical processes in process control, computer aided design and computer aided manufacture. Expert systems across a wide range of applications are beginning to bring the skills of the expert to a wider range of personnel.

1.1.3   The IT revolution

The massive spread in the use of information technology/information systems has been described as a *third revolution*, following on from the earlier agricultural and industrial revolutions. In his book *The Third Wave*, Toffler (1980), examines the forces for change within the world and concludes that we are leaving the industrial society for a world of 'electronic cottages'. The ability of microelectronics to store and communicate vast amounts of information quickly and cheaply has already prompted significant changes in society. Predictions about the future impact of IT are just that: predictions. The interesting question is how far we will be able to control the future impact. To what extent is the spread of IT under society's control and will such spread determine the nature of tomorrow's society?

Effects of the IT revolution as far as the user is concerned can be summarized under the changes they make to individuals, to the organizations in which they work and to society in general. Some of the individual, organizational and societal changes that have been predicted are summarized in Fig. 1.1.

	Effect	**What is causing the effect?**
Individual	Demise of the expert	Expert systems
	Leisure society/unemployment	Automation of manual processes
	Dehumanized work	Deskilling in the workplace
	Job enrichment/empowerment	IT/IS support at work
Organizational	Unmanned factory	Automation and robotics
	Paperless office	Networking and communications
Societal	Collapse of the city	Communications
	Global village	Communications
	Electronic cottage	Communications
	Leisure society	Automation

FIGURE 1.1   *Effects of the IT revolution*

Contradictory predictions are made concerning effects on the individual. At one extreme the introduction of automated systems and expert systems could be seen as having a deskilling effect and a resultant downgrading or dehumanization of work. The contrary view is that appropriate use of IT/IS can enrich the jobs of individuals and that through access to information sources and processing methods not previously available, it can increase the independence and empowerment of the individual.

At the organizational or business level, office and production automation is already having considerable effects, some of which will be taken up in depth in Chapter 10. The unmanned factory, totally controlled by robotics and the paperless office, dominated by electronic communications, is to a large extent already with us.

Changes to society are probably harder to predict. There have been many predictions of mass unemployment resulting from the automation of functions and processes within administrative and manufacturing procedures. Studies in the late 1970s in the USA suggested in excess of a 30 per cent loss in office jobs by 1990. However, by the mid-1980s there was only a slowdown in the growth of office jobs. While savings are often made by centralizing personnel resources (for example by relocating typists to secretarial pools) the growth in information being processed, and associated new jobs, has been shown to mitigate against any negative effects. The situation has been further confused as in many countries it has been difficult to distinguish the effects of recent economic recessions from the growth of IT applications.

If the IT/IS systems currently being introduced are designed to aid people in the workplace, rather than overtly to replace them, then the doomladen predictions of the 1970s will probably not come true.

1.1.4   Classifying information systems

So far in our introduction we have looked at how the spread of IT is changing the role of society, organizations, and the individual. It is now possible to undertake a limited analysis of the different ways in which information systems that are currently in operation in business today can be classified. It will indeed be only a limited examination; the reader will find much more detail in references focusing on management information systems themselves. Some references are provided at the end of the chapter.

Levels of planning

Within the arena of business information systems probably the most significant classification of information systems is the one provided by Anthony (1965). The model shown in Fig. 1.2 focuses on the management process, dividing it into three levels: *strategic, tactical,* and *operational*, in a hierarchical model of the organization. At each level we can place a distinct type of information system, each with a particular user type undertaking a specific work role. At the strategic level the user is likely to include senior managers using a decision support or executive information system thereby gaining automated support during the decision-making process. Within the middle, tactical level, middle mangers may be using management information systems to enable the organization's planning, control and operational functions to be carried out effectively. At the operational level end users will be using transaction processing systems to *process* the routine activities of the organization.

Although useful as an initial structuring tool the model shown in Fig. 1.2 hides a wide range of other types of information system such as expert systems and computer supported co-operative working (CSCW) systems. CSCW systems enable groups of workers to communicate and work together (refer to Chapter 10 for details). Both these types of system could conceivably operate at any of the three levels depending on the user and task.

Management hierarchy

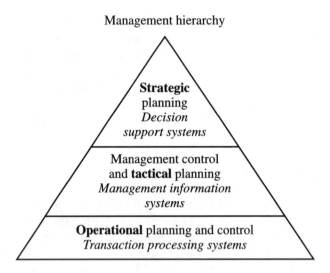

FIGURE 1.2   *Anthony's model of levels of planning and associated types of IS* (adapted with permission of author from Anthony, R. A. (1965), *Planning and control systems: a framework for analysis;* Boston: Division of Research, Harvard University)

Organizational vs. end-user systems

The majority of the information systems outlined above are bespoke organizational systems in that they have been designed and implemented centrally, and exist to meet overall organizational aims and objectives. Such systems will have been developed by the organization's own IT or data processing (DP) department, with or without support from external consultancies such as software houses. There is, however, another whole class of information system that includes what we might refer to as *end-user* or *personal information systems*. The growth of both these types of information system is largely as a consequence of the spread of the personal computer and has come about for the following reasons:

- Low cost of hardware
- Easy access to a range of off-the-shelf software packages
- Enhanced ability of users to customize and even develop their own systems

Personal information systems enable individuals to adopt relatively simple software solutions to the management of everyday activities such as personal information retrieval (names, addresses), personal budgeting, time management (calendars, etc.) and document management. By using off-the-shelf packages the user is able to set up systems to meet individual perceived needs. At a simple level these end-user systems include basic data processing facilities. However, the increasing sophistication of spreadsheet and database applications is providing end users with the ability to provide, independent from the wider organization, much more of the information systems support that they need. There are, however, a number of problems with the end-user systems approach. These will be analysed in much greater detail later but can be summarized as follows:

- The quality of such applications is questionable
- Data is duplicated throughout the organization and is likely to be incompatible
- Providing support in cases of failure is problematic

A domain taxonomy

As we have seen, information technology is pervading all aspects of the social and working environment. There are very few occupational areas in which there are no procedures or processes that are not open to computerization. There are a number of methods that we could use to categorize these application areas or user domains. In the UK we have a number of possible classifications provided by government. Other countries will have similar systems. One approach might be to use the SIC or Standard Industry Classification. For our purposes, however, we can do no better than use the Association for Computing Machinery (ACM) Guide to Literature (1991 version) which provides seven general application areas. These are presented in Table 1.1 together with the detailed domain areas and some example user groups.

There is yet another, and for us final, way of classifying information systems. Independent from the type of system or its application areas, Land (1989) describes four *classes of interaction* between a system and its environment (refer to Fig. 1.3). The move from class one to class four represents an increase in both *complexity* and *uncertainty* within the system. These four classes are very useful to us in our study of users and information systems as they involve some important user issues that will affect the nature of human–computer interaction. These issues are:

- Stability and degree of understanding of the real world in which the system operates
- Ability to derive an accurate functional specification
- Degree of emphasis on flexibility and ability to change
- Degree of applicability of prototyping approaches
- User responses and user involvement

TABLE 1.1 *ACM computer applications and example user groups*

Application area	Domain areas		Example user groups
Administrative data processing	Business Finance Law Marketing	Education Government Manufacturing Military	University administrators Accounts clerks Lawyers Tele-sales staff
Physical sciences	Aerospace Chemistry Electronics Maths./Stats.	Astronomy Earth sciences Engineering Physics	Aeronautical engineers Environmental scientists Structural engineers Research scientists
Life and medical sciences	Biology Medical IS	Health	Doctors Hospital administrators
Social and behavioural sciences	Economics Sociology	Psychology	Economists
Arts and humanities	Fine arts Language Literature	Performing arts Linguistics Music	Curators Translators Musicians
Computer aided engineering	CAD	CAM	Designers
Other systems	Command and control Industrial/consumer products Real time and process control Publishing		Armed forces personnel Consumers Flight simulator users Writers and publishers

1.2 Do information systems work?

1.2.1 Systems success rates

A major problem with the introduction of information systems, and indeed a major thrust for the production of this book, is the fact that a very large proportion of information systems fail. A recent UK newspaper headline (Fig. 1.4) clearly illuminates the problem.

By saying that so many information systems fail we do not necessarily mean that they do not work; rather that they fail to meet initial aspirations. In this context success can be described as *being used effectively for the uses for which it was commissioned*. Often these uses are high-level ones and relate to how closely strategic

Class	Characteristics
1	Real world is well understood and stable
	Functional specification is a good representation of that world
	Emphasis is upon error-free code and upon an accurate transform of specification
2	Real world is dynamic
	Information system itself changes
	Specification is valid for limited period only
	Emphasis is on flexibility and the ability to respond to change
3	Designers unsure of the real-world requirements or user responses
	A highly turbulent environment makes confident specification difficult to produce
	Emphasis is on experimental methods including prototyping
4	Intense interaction between system and environment
	Process of system's operation itself changes the environment
	Emphasis is on constantly changing specification and adaptive code

FIGURE 1.3   *Four classes of information systems* (Land, 1989)

business objectives are met. Many factors can inhibit an information system from achieving its objectives, but the degree of acceptance or rejection by individual and organizational users is often important.

At this stage in our study it will be useful to emphasize the results of studies of the success of IT/IS applications. A variety of studies from the 1970s onwards have demonstrated largely similar results. In 1994, for example, *Scientific American* (Gibbs, 1994) reported that three-quarters of all large systems are 'operating failures' that either do not function as intended or are not used at all. Some additional data is presented in Table 1.2. Overall it would seem that roughly only 30 per cent of IT systems are fully successful and that some 70 per cent either fail or only produce some marginal gain to the organization.

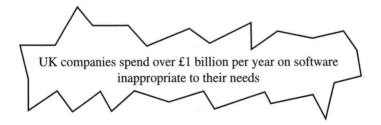

UK companies spend over £1 billion per year on software inappropriate to their needs

FIGURE 1.4   *A recent UK newspaper headline* (source: *Computing*, 16 November 1995)

TABLE 1.2   *Systems success rates*

	Success (%)	Marginal gain (%)	Failure/ rejection (%)
USA 1976	20	40	40
UK Office Automation Survey 1986	37	30	33
UK Small Medium Enterprises 1986	40	20	40
Typically	30	30	40

1.2.2   Why do systems fail?

If these failing systems do not represent inoperative or incorrect systems, what is it that they are failing to do? We need to have a greater understanding about what constitutes success for information systems. Possible success criteria will include reductions in resourcing costs (e.g. staffing costs), increasing output (e.g. on automated production lines), making processes easier to perform (e.g. by providing expert systems support) and improving accuracy (e.g. by the use of a decision support system). Broadly speaking the success criteria can be grouped under the two categories of *increasing productivity* and *improving efficiency.*

A number of different system success criteria are set out in Fig. 1.5. Those on the left-hand side of the diagram represent criteria oriented more towards increasing productivity, while others relate more to the improvement of efficiency. Central to the achievement of all criteria are users operating in organizations seeking IS success. Almost all information systems have a human element and it is often the way in

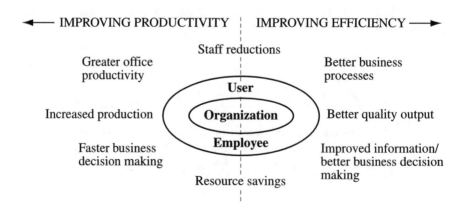

FIGURE 1.5   *System success criteria*

which this human, or user, element is handled that can determine success or failure.

Broadly speaking we can identify three ways in which failure might occur:

1. **Technical failure**
   Failure may occur at the technical level, through either a hardware, software or communications fault. Technical failure is outside the scope of this study in human–computer factors.

2. **Utility failure**
   The IBM Dictionary of Computing (1993) defines *utility* as:

   the capability of a system, program or device to perform the functions for which it was devised

   A software system may be correct in that it does not suffer technical failure, but it may not meet the real, or full, task-related needs of the organization and the individuals within it. In this situation of poor utility, failure may have occurred in the requirements capture stage of the analysis and design process. Utility is also often equated to *functionality*. Information systems that suffer poor utility are highly likely to result in a lack of acceptance by the user community.

3. **Usability failure**
   The IBM Dictionary of Computing (1993) defines *usability* as:

   the quality of a system, program or device that enables it to be easily understood and conveniently applied by the user

   Systems that are both technically correct, and meet the fully specified utility requirements may still fail as a result of a lack of user *acceptance* or even positive user *rejection*. For some reason the people for whom the system is designed are unable to make full, or appropriate, use of the end product. Reasons for this might relate to the lack, or inappropriateness, of training, or to a poorly designed software interface. Alternatively the way in which the overall software systems matches, or fails to match, the organizational culture, ethos or management style may be significant.

Usability and human–computer factors

With the exception of the technical failure category, many of the detailed reasons for failure are caused by the way in which users are involved, or more specifically insufficiently involved, in the whole analysis and design process. The methods in which users are involved might loosely be called human–computer factors and it is these that will form the basis of our study in users and information systems. Usability will be a central issue within our study and it therefore deserves a greater coverage, even within this introduction.

1.2.3   Usability

According to Eason (1988), studies have shown that users operate on an implicit cost-benefit analysis basis when it comes to establishing whether and how they will use a system. The *benefits* that they get from the system are supplied through the functionality provided. If the functionality is poor then the benefits will be limited. The costs involved in using a system is a mixture of the effort, time, risk and financial penalties involved. The cost side of the equation is dependant on two features: usability and acceptability. Functionality can therefore be seen as an end *product* of an information system whereas usability and acceptability are part of the *process* in achieving the required functionality.

Usability is often merely equated to ease of use. The IBM definition quoted above goes slightly further. However, usability is often considered to be an even wider concept and includes issues such as ease of learning, the degree to which it is effective in supporting users in their jobs, together with user system satisfaction. We will return to a detailed exploration of usability in Chapter 7, but for now it is important to emphasize that usability is only meaningful within a certain context. Normally this *context of use* includes aspects relating to the users themselves, the tasks they are undertaking, the equipment they are using and the environment in which they are working. One particular system placed in one context will probably display different usability characteristics when placed in a second context. The International Standards Organization defines usability (ISO 9241-11.3) as:

> the effectiveness, efficiency and satisfaction with which specified users can achieve specified goals in particular environments

Within their definition:

effectiveness is

> the accuracy and completeness with which users achieve specific goals

efficiency is

> the accuracy and completeness of goals in relation to resources expended

and *satisfaction* is

> the comfort and acceptability of the system

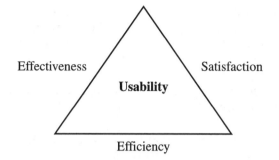

Effectiveness

Usability

Satisfaction

Efficiency

FIGURE 1.6   *Usability success characteristics*

Acceptability is one determining factor in user satisfaction and as a result is considered to be a subset of usability. However, it is often necessary to take a wide view of acceptability and relate it to both the user and to the organization. In our study we will adopt the ISO definition of usability as the main determining factor in systems success and will emphasize that satisfaction relates to the individual user *within the organizational context*. Assuming therefore that the software solution is technically correct we can identify three characteristics (see Fig. 1.6) that determine the success of the system: effectiveness, efficiency and satisfaction.

1.3   Introducing the user role

1.3.1   The socio-technical context

We may assume that all information systems aim to improve some area of organizational effectiveness (efficiency or productivity). Many of the reasons for the lack of success in achieving the improvement relate to the inherent socio-technical nature of IT systems and, until recently at least, to the often only marginal importance given to this fact by systems designers. An effective socio-technical system is one in which the technical nature of the solution (hardware and software) is in balance with the social system (people and procedures) in which it operates. It is not possible to separate the technical nature of the IT system from the organization into which it is to be introduced, or from the users who are going to operate it.

1.3.2   The crucial user element

This study aims to explore the central user issues within the successful development and implementation of such a socio-technical information system. In Chapter 2 we will explore in much more detail a range of different types of users of information systems. For now it will be sufficient to establish two main categories of user:

1. *Individual user,* any person using information technology equipment in support of specific work-related or leisure-oriented tasks.
2. *Organizational user,* any organization using information systems in support of organizational objectives.

To a number of IS specialists many of the individual user issues come under the general heading of human–computer interaction (HCI), and many of the organizational issues are often regarded as part of business or management studies. The premise within our study is that the crucial user issues cannot be compartmentalized and that a co-ordinated view of all user issues within information systems development is necessary.

1.3.3   Who is the user?

Within any information system application there may be a wide range of different users: manager users, end users, customers. The term *stakeholder* has been introduced to encompass all those who have an interest in the system that is being implemented. System designers are also stakeholders as they have an important stake in the success of the project. Lodge (1989) defines six distinct types of user: the governing body, the sponsor, the user specifier, the end user, the input generator and the output receiver. When looking at any particular information system it is usually possible to identify a number of distinct user groups such as those shown in Table 1.1. A much more detailed coverage of user classifications will be provided in Chapter 2.

For the purpose of our study a user is defined to be:

> any employee or customer of the organization who will be directly or indirectly affected by the system.

1.3.4   Why consider users?

Users are, of course, the source of functional requirements. How else would information systems designers be able to provide IT solutions? Given, however, the socio-technical nature of IT systems, and the dynamic nature of the real world in which systems interact, users have a much wider role. As we have already mentioned, success or failure in an IT application often depends upon acceptance by the user community. If the likelihood of success is to be maximized, and for resistance to change and the introduction of counter-implementation strategies to be minimized, the socio-technical design process needs to engage the users in issues that are far wider than just the domain of functional requirements. Considerations relating to task performance, job design, organization design, user satisfaction and even organizational power and influence are necessary. Neither the dynamic, nor the social-technical nature of the system, can be adequately addressed without the active involvement of users.

1.4 The importance of human factors

1.4.1 Systems and human factors

Human factors constitute a discipline that covers the human interaction with a whole range of artefacts, not just the computer or information system with which we are interested. Through the study of human factors, and the adoption of appropriate techniques, it is possible to analyse and optimize the human element within a total system.

It will be useful, at this stage, to pursue what we mean by a *system*. The Oxford Dictionary provides a number of alternative definitions of which the most appropriate is:

> a complex whole; a set of connected things or parts; an organized body of material or immaterial things

There are a number of different types of system. At the first level we can distinguish between *natural* systems (for example the solar system, a tree) and *man-made* systems. The latter category include the following:

- Engineered/physical systems (e.g. a bicycle, a bridge)
- Social systems (e.g. a democratic system of government)
- Human activity systems (e.g. playing a game of football, marketing a product or organization)

Man-made systems are designed by engineers (a person who *designs* or *constructs* according to the Oxford Dictionary). Systems engineers operate in a variety of domains such as structural engineering (the construction of buildings and bridges), automobile engineering (the design of cars), and software engineering (the writing of software for use within some form of information system). The majority of systems engineers have to include and consider the human element within the boundary of the system that they are analysing and/or designing. The degree to which human factors pervades their work will vary. A structural engineer designing a new suspension bridge will be aware that drivers will be using his bridge. The automobile engineer, however, will be far more concerned about the human element; if the brake pedal is too far away from the driving seat there could be severe safety problems.

An information systems engineer is involved with both human activity and engineered systems and according to the British Computer Society:

> applies engineering principles, founded on appropriate scientific and technological disciplines, to the creation, use and support of information systems for the solution of practical problems

Systems that have a significant user element are best analysed and designed by including well-known human-factor techniques. Through the study of human factors we attempt to optimize the effectiveness of the human–machine interface. This is done not only for reasons of efficiency and productivity within the system, but also for reasons relating to the improvement of the physical and mental well-being of the human element within the system.

According to Singleton (1974):

> an interface is an imaginary plane across which information and power are exchanged

In the case of a human–machine system the exchange is primarily of information (Fig. 1.7). This information is of two types. First *display* information is passed from the hardware to the human operator; for example the speedometer on a car will alert the driver that he or she is exceeding the speed limit. Secondly *control* information will pass from the user to the hardware; for example by pressing the brake pedal the driver will slow the car with a resulting change in the display information.

1.4.2   A short history of human–computer factors

The generic discipline of human factors is rooted in the sciences of physiology and psychology, with contributions from philosophy,

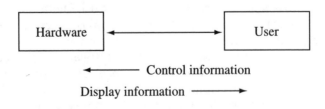

FIGURE 1.7   *The human–machine interface*

together with systems and information theory. It is closely related to the study of ergonomics. The development and growth of generic human factors (as opposed to specific human–computer factors) as an independent area of study has been strongly influenced by both war and industry.

During the First World War, for example, the need to expand the production of armaments in the UK led to ever increasing working hours to a point where production actually declined. After considering basic human-factor issues the government of the time introduced the standard working day with which we are all now familiar. At this time, however, there was little active consideration of human-factor issues within the design of artefacts. Any changes in design came about as a result of product failure in the field. After the First World War studies were undertaken in the USA in what was referred to as *scientific management* that included aspects of work study and psychological selection testing.

Human factors did not develop into a recognized field until during the Second World War (Dul and Weerdmeester, 1993). Simple design flaws were found to have serious effects, such as poorly engineered aircraft escape hatches causing the deaths of over 10 000 British airmen (Baecker *et al.*, 1995). The need to win the war also led to a much more technological approach, with the development of radar, sonar and guided missiles. The role psychology played in interface design increased significantly. Through war-time collaboration between natural scientists and engineers came major advances, such as a methodology for the design of cockpit instrument displays. The increasing sophistication in the equipment being used, under extreme war-time situations, required an analysis of the total system (user and machine) being implemented. As a result the new science of ergonomics was born. The first national ergonomics society was set up in England in 1949. The word *ergonomics* itself comes from the Greek words *ergon* meaning work and *nomos* meaning law. In the USA ergonomics is referred to as human factors.

Since the war the generic application of human-factor knowledge has enjoyed varying degrees of success. Greater importance has been placed on human factors in the USA, Japan and Russia than in the UK. The USA and ex-Soviet space programmes have benefited significantly from human-factor knowledge.

Licklider (1960) was one of the first researchers to undertake specific study in human–computer factors and noted the potential for optimizing performance within such an arena. He identified the concept *of man-computer symbiosis*. Later together with Clark (Licklider and Clark, 1962) he reported on some early experiments and prototype systems, outlined applications of human–computer communication to a number of domains including military command and control, mathematics, programming, planning and design and education, and listed, with considerable insight, a number of problems that needed to be solved for true human–computer symbiosis. Some of these, such as the need for 'interactive, real-time systems for information processing' have clearly been solved, but others, for example the 'recognition of the speech of arbitrary users' are still not fully addressed.

In the 1960s psychological research began to have a considerable influence on the design of interactive computer systems and software. At this time the focus was on the computer programmers as these were the only people with direct computer access. In the early 1970s Weinberg (1971) focused on the human factors of programming and encouraged programmers to improve the interfaces to their own systems. During the 1970s the shift from programmer user to end user began, and although there was little priority to human–computer interaction in commercial environments, a number of researchers and consultants were influential (e.g. Shackel, 1969; Hansen, 1971 and Martin, 1973) in establishing the ground rules for interactive systems design.

Also in the 1970s a greater emphasis on scientific and behavioural studies of interfaces was developed including a group formed by Gould at IBM Research and one containing Card, Moran and Newell at Xerox PARC. The latter group has made a significant contribution to the underlying *applied science* of human–computer interaction (Baecker *et al.*, 1995) and have described how humans can be viewed as *active processors* of information (Card, Moran and Newell, 1983).

Today, as we are now aware, great importance is placed on the contribution human factors can make to enhancing the design of the human–computer interface. Although by no means universally adopted, the graphical user interface (GUI) is fast becoming the standard interface style and its implementation is generally seen as providing a significant enhancement to human–computer interaction. Although the groundwork for its development can be traced back to the 1960s and 1970s, two major innovations were the Xerox Star machine, which was developed in 1981, and the Apple Macintosh, which was introduced in 1984. Since then it has become the standard means of interaction on personal computers (e.g. Microsoft Windows) and other workstations (e.g. X Windows). A detailed coverage of the history of personal computer hardware and software is outside the remit for our study but is discussed by Ranade and Nash (1994).

The rapid growth in research relating to human factors in computing has been demonstrated by Nickerson (1992) who shows that while in 1975 only 2 out of 62 articles in the journal *Human Factors* were on the topic of human–computer interaction, by 1985 the proportion had grown to over one-third. We now have a whole series of publications and conferences that cover human-factor issues in IT including:

Journals
Behaviour and IT
Human–computer Interaction
International Journal of Human–computer Interaction
Interacting with Computers

Conferences
People and Computers (BCS—British Computer Society)
INTERACT (IFIP—International Federation of Information Processing)
CHI—Human factors in Computing System (ACM—Association for Computing Machinery)

The interested reader will be able to locate a wide range of journal articles that look at user issues in even more detail that we will be able to in this study.

1.4.3   Human vs. computer

In designing a total system, one containing both the human and computer elements we need to investigate the differences, and provide for an optimization, between the two elements. Some issues relevant to the relative performance of human and computer within an information system are shown in Table 1.3, which has been developed from Singleton (1971). It is clear that the human and machine elements have very different performance characteristics. It

TABLE 1.3   *Relative performance of human and computer within information systems*

Property	Computer	Human
Speed	Fast response possible	Delays involved
Processing power	Large	Limited
Consistency	Strong for numerical activities	Not reliable: depends on fatigue, training, etc.
	Variable for presentation issues	
Reasoning	Strong deductive powers	Good inductive powers
Overload reliability	Sudden breakdown	Graceful degradation
Intelligence	Limited (expert systems, neural networks)	Considerable: can anticipate and adapt

is this underlying issue that is one reason why an understanding of human–computer factors is so important to successful systems design.

The rest of this study is devoted to issues related to human–computer factors. Studies in human factors in other domains would lead us to expect that we will need to look at to the following generic issues:

- Task analysis
- Job analysis
- Training
- Interface design
- Ergonomics

All of these, and many more will be addressed.

1.5   The development of successful systems

1.5.1   Systems development life cycle

The process of analysing, designing and implementing an information system involves a number of distinct stages. These stages in systems and software development are often referred to as part of a *systems development life cycle (SDLC)*. In our study of human–computer factors we will need to span the whole life cycle of information systems development. Human factors in general, and human–computer interaction in particular, cannot be treated as a separate add-on to the techniques and procedures normally adopted. Instead all phases of the life cycle need to be modified to take account of human-factor and user issues. Figure 1.8 gives a diagrammatic representation of the systems development life cycle in what is known as a *waterfall* model. The interested reader will be able to identify a number of other life cycle models from sources detailing software development, software design (e.g. Budgen, 1993) or software engineering (e.g. Sommerville, 1992). While in our study of human–computer factors we will be highly interested in non-waterfall approaches, particularly iterative and evolutionary methods that lead to far greater flexibility within the life cycle, it remains a useful framework for analysis.

During the various stages of the life cycle a range of outputs are produced. As an end product of the design stage a fully functioning software product will be available for use in the next stage referred to as implementation. Earlier on, however, a number of reports are produced which are required as input to future activities. A number of these will be relevant to our future study and some are outlined below:

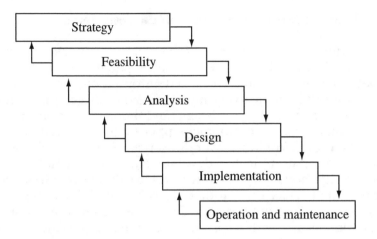

FIGURE 1.8   *Systems development life cycle*

- *Strategic plans*, a variety of strategic plans from those describing overall business strategic objectives to more detailed specification of hardware and software policies are relevant to future systems development.
- *Feasibility study*, in which an estimate is made as to whether the identified needs can be met by a proposed system within given constraints of physical resources, time and budget.
- *User specification*, a specification of the user groups involved within an information system and their associated characteristics and needs.
- *Requirements definition*, a statement in natural language that is understandable by both the client and technical specialists and which specifies the services that the proposed system will provide.
- *Requirements specification*, also called a functional specification this is a more precise document that can be used as a basis for a contract between developer and client.

Throughout the life cycle the design must be checked for validation and verification. Validation focuses on the need to satisfy the requirements (to do the right thing) whereas verification ensures completeness and internal consistency (doing the thing right). Various techniques are used throughout software design to specify validation and verification from the use of natural language to the application of mathematical formal methods. In human–computer interaction terms validation is often referred to as *evaluation*. We will see in Chapters 5 and 7 how a number of human-factor validation and verification techniques can be performed.

1.5.2   Placing the user at the centre of the design process

In our study we shall place a great deal of importance on *user-centred design*. By this we mean a development approach in which all potential users of the proposed information system have the opportunity of being actively involved, either directly or indirectly, in all aspects of analysis, design and implementation. It is our premise that such a development philosophy will lead to greater systems success. Within an overall user-centred approach there is a special role for users in the development of the human–computer interface. Effective user-centred interface design requires users to take part in interface evaluation exercises so that the usability of the end product can be determined. There are therefore two important roles for users within a user-centred information systems development process:

1. *Users as designers,* working with technical specialists as members of the design team (Chapter 3).
2. *Users as subjects,* in real life and simulated situations providing usage information required for evaluation studies (Chapter 7).

1.5.3   Design methods

When designing a new, or updating a current, computerized information system the designer has a very wide number of tools and techniques at his or her disposal. In some cases these tools are generic in that they are used by a great number of designers and have an international usage. Most readers will, for example, be familiar with data flow diagrams as a way of describing the flow of information within an organization. Often these tools and techniques are brought together into a prescribed methodology. Systems analysis and design methodologies such as Jackson Structured Design (JSD) have world-wide usage while others (e.g. SSADM in the UK and MERISE in France) are national in context. We will study the implications of various design methodologies to the user in much greater detail in Chapter 4.

At this stage it will be sufficient to introduce two broad ways in which design methodologies may be classified. One way is to split them into either hard or soft approaches, while the alternative is to distinguish between technical and socio-technical methods. Essentially hard systems analysis methods focus on implementing a well-understood problem while soft methods emphasize understanding the underlying problems within an organization. Technical design methods deal exclusively with the hardware and software solution to a problem, whereas socio-technical analysis and design involves the detailed needs of the user and the organization in which he or she operates. The choice, or lack of choice of a systems analysis and design method can have significant effects (either positive or negative) on the final user of the system and will be a significant element within our study.

1.5.4   Designing for organizational acceptability

A major premise of this study is that the majority of information systems projects are not solely technical problems. The system is inherently socio-technical and the user (human and organizational) element must be addressed. In terms of the organization itself, a number of aspects will need to be considered including:

- The design of the social system (the design of the organizational structure, individual job designs and the allocation of tasks between the man and machine)
- Systems implementation (changeover from one system to another)
- Organizational change

We will focus on the design of the social systems element and on ensuring acceptability within the organization in Chapter 5.

1.5.5   HCI: designing for interface usability

The last decade has seen a great increase in what we refer to as *interactive* systems.'' The Oxford Dictionary provides us with a definition of interactive:

> acting upon or influencing each other, allowing a two way flow of information

In terms of interactive computer systems (Fig. 1.7) the medium for this interaction is the software interface comprising a number of screens of information displayed on the visual display unit together with an appropriate input mechanism (e.g. keyboard). Surveys show that about 50 per cent of software designers' time is spent on devising programming code for the interface part of the whole software system. Given that so much time and effort is being spent by developers on the interface, even without considering the effect on the users themselves, it must be important to understand, structure and improve the overall interface design process. The aim of good interface design is to improve the accessibility of the user to the underlying functionality of the software; i.e. to increase the *usability* of the software. An effective software interface is crucial in determining the usability of the software component of an information system and is therefore an important element in ensuring overall systems success. We will explore human–computer interaction and designing for usability in Chapters 6 and 7.

1.5.6   Supporting the user

Human–computer factor considerations do not finish with the delivery of an apparently usable product; users need to be supported in its future use. In Chapter 8 we will focus on ways in which training can be offered, and how both on- and off-line help can be provided. While the major assumption within our study is that information systems are provided with support from technical specialists, as we have seen there has been a considerable expansion in end-user systems. Organizational support and co-ordination is necessary if end-user systems are to be fully effective.

1.6   Pulling it all together

Overall, having introduced a variety of information systems, we can provide the following broad classification of information systems:

- Decision support systems
- Executive information on systems
- Management information on systems
- Transaction processing systems
- Expert systems
- CSCW systems
- Production and real-time systems
- End-user systems including personal information systems

In addition, this introduction to our study of users and information systems has identified a number of issues that are significant to the user role:

- Planning levels of information systems
- User groups
- Success rates and criteria
- Usability
- Socio-technical nature of systems
- Methods of information systems development

Table 1.4 provides a summarizing framework whereby the various issues that we have explored so far can be related together.

1.7   Acadmin: introducing the minor case study

At various places within our analysis we will attempt to relate a number of human–computer factor considerations to an example information system: our minor case study focuses on Acadmin (copyright Chalfont Software Ltd.). Now fully developed Acadmin is available as a commercial off-the-shelf academic administration system that can be customized for use in a range of UK further and higher education institutions. However, it was initially developed for use in one specific institution. Acadmin's main purposes are to:

• Maintain and organize a student record system
• Input and process basic student data

TABLE 1.4   *Types of information system*

| IS type | Planning level | System level issues | | |
		Software base	Development methods	Success criteria
Decision support Executive IS	Strategic	Specialized languages/ packages	Use of DSS generator	Improved efficiency
Management IS	Tactical	3rd and 4th	Structured soft	Improved efficiency
Transaction processing	Operational	3rd and 4th	Structured	Increased productivity
Expert system	Operational/ strategic	Rule-based systems	Use of ES 'shell' declarative languages	Improved efficiency/ productivity
CSCW	All	3rd generation	Specialized development	Improved efficiency
Production/ real time systems	Operational	3rd generation	'Hard'/structured real-time systems design	Increased productivity
End-user systems	Operational/ tactical	4th generation/ PC packages	No formal methods	Improved efficiency

Table 1.4 continued overleaf

TABLE 1.4 continued   *Types of information system*

IS type	User group	User level issues		Importance[1] of usability
		Usage level	Socio-technical	
Decision support Executive IS	Senior mgr.	Low	Largely technical	High
Management IS	Middle mgr.	Moderate	Socio-technical	Moderate
Transaction processing	End user	High	Socio-technical	Low
Expert system	All	Low	Largely technical	High
CSCW	All	Moderate	Highly socio-technical	High
Production/ real-time systems	End user	High	Largely technical	Low
End-user systems	Middle mgr. senior mgr.	Low to moderate	Unlikely to cover social issues	Low: lack of skills

[1]Importance relates to that usually given to usability

- Maintain a profile of individual students (grades, etc.) as their courses continue
- Produce a variety of reports for lecturers and administrative staff

Acadmin operates largely at an *operational* level and aims to improve *efficiency* within the educational environment. It can be considered to be *a transaction processing system*, being operated by university administrators (the main *end-user* group). However, some of the reports that it produces are of use by management in making *tactical* decisions, and it can therefore be seen to contain a *management information systems* element. Although it can be customized to individual client needs, it is effectively an off-the-shelf package and can be considered as an *organizational* system. It has been developed to operate through a graphical user interface (GUI) and therefore considerable effort was put into ensuring *usability*. Before continuing with your study make sure that you understand all of the words in *italic*. Refer back if necessary.

1.8   Plumbest plc: the major case study, an analysis of information systems

1.8.1   Introducing the major case study

In order to provide practical examples of human–computer factor techniques a major case study has been provided. The case study centres around a company that provides plumbing services to the eastern region of the UK; Plumbest plc. Background information concerning Plumbest can be found in the Appendix. Most chapters will make reference to the case study towards the end of the chapter where a number of tasks will be set out. In the majority of cases solutions to the tasks are provided. The reader is advised to carefully read the case study before proceeding further with this book.

While the case study itself does not directly represent a single real-life organization, it is based upon a number of real-life situations and has been strongly influenced by the work of Ken Eason as documented in Eason (1996) and Eason and Olphert (1996).

1.8.2   Tasks

Plumbest Task 1.1

At Plumbest a number of information systems already exist. It will be useful to perform an analysis of all current and proposed systems. In order to do this place all current systems, together with the proposed job allocation system (JAS), on a grid similar to that provided in Table 1.4. Use the systems and user issues shown below:

- Planning level
- Success criteria
- User groups involved
- Usage level experienced
- Socio-technical nature
- Importance of usability

Plumbest Task 1.2

Make a list of all the current issues and/or problems that you see operating within Plumbest.

1.8.3   Solutions

Plumbest Solution 1.1

A summary of all of Plumbest's systems is provided in Table 1.5.

Plumbest Solution 1.2

Problems:
* Safety critical nature of gas work
* The MOs are currently inefficiently utilized
* There are delays in communicating with MOs as they are often 'on a job' and cannot be contacted by telephone
* The system will certainly not be able to cope with the extra demands of the new UK Gas contract
* More efficient utilization of staff
* Inappropriate customer service

Issues:
* Attention to employee participation

TABLE 1.5   *Information systems at Plumbest*

IS type	Planning level	Success criteria	User group	Usage level	Socio-technical	Import-ance of usability[2]
Marketing decision support	Strategic	Improved efficiency	Marketing director	Low	Largely[1] technical	High
MIS	Tactical	Improved efficiency	Directors Operations manager	Moderate	Socio-technical	Moderate
Inventory	Opera-tional	Improved efficiency	Foremen Depot staff	High	Socio-technical	Low
Invoicing/ accounting	Opera-tional	Improved producti-vity	Service ad. Finance staff	High	Socio-technical	Low
Job allocation	Opera-tional	Increased producti-vity	MOs Service centre staff	High	Socio-technical	High

[1]Single user
[2]Answers are relative to each other

- Recognized trade unions
- Operations manager's 'pet plan'
- Concern over redundancies
- Conflicting views concerning inadequacies in current set up

Summary

In this chapter we have been able to develop a broad overview of information systems and the role of human factors within their development and operation. In particular we have seen:

- Some basic classifications of information systems
- The significance of the user role in relation to IS success
- The importance of the human-factor side of IS development
- A definition of usability and its relationship to systems success
- The crucial role that the interface can play in systems design
- The implications of the software development life cycle and associated techniques to users and developers
- The distinction between organizational and end-user systems

Questions

1.1 You are asked to discuss and propose answers to the following questions
   (i) Give three reasons why we need to study the users of an information system
   (ii) Give three ways in which the IS designer can address the needs of the user

1.2 The following terms have been used to predict the effects IT/IS will have on society and individual users:

   paperless office   unmanned factory   electronic cottage
   collapse of the city   global village   demise of the expert
   leisure society

   (i) What is causing the effect?
   (ii) What are the detailed effects on the user? Do you see these effects, should they occur, as advantages or disadvantages?
   (iii) To what extent do you think the predictions will come true?

1.3 *What are the measures of success for an information system?*Before we can analyse systems failure we need to know what constitutes success. Try to identify a range of specific success criteria for information systems (e.g. more words processed per hour might be one measure of success for a word-processing system) and then group them under broad and named categories (productivity might be one).

1.4 *What are the ways in which information systems failure manifests itself?*Try to identify, from academic and trade journals, specific examples of information systems failure and from these develop broad categories.

1.5 *How can the IS designer address the issue of failure?*Try to identify six separate areas within the analysis, design and implementation phases of information systems development.

1.6 Make a list of artefacts in which you consider that there is a significant human-factor element. Describe how the human–machine interface operates. What information passes across the interface?

1.7 Identify a number of information systems within the organization in which you work. Create a grid similar to that provided in Table 1.4. Use whichever systems and user issues you deem appropriate.

References

Anthony, R. A. (1965), 'Planning and control systems: a framework for analysis', Division of Research, Harvard University, Boston.

Baecker, R. M., Grudin, J., Buxton, W. A. S. and Greenberg, S. (1995), 'A historical and intellectual perspective', in *Human–computer Interaction: Towards the Year 2000*, Morgan Kaufman, San Francisco.

British Computer Society (1994), Guidance notes on the application process for professional membership of the BCS.

Budgen, D. (1993), *Software Design*, Addison-Wesley.

Card, S. K., Moran, T. P. and Newell, A. (1983), *The Psychology of Human–computer Interaction*, Lawrence Erlbaum, New Jersey.

Carver, M. K. (1988), 'Practical experiences of specifying the human–computer interface using JSD', in *Contemporary Ergonomics, Proceedings of the Ergonomics Society's 1988 Annual Conference*, Taylor and Francis, London.

Dul, J. and Weerdmeester, B. (1993), *Ergonomics for Beginners*, Taylor and Francis.

Eason, K. (1988), *Information Technology and Organisational Change*, Taylor and Francis, London.

Eason, K. (1996), 'Division of labour and the design of systems for computer support for co-operative work', *Journal of IT*, 11, 39–50.

Eason, K. and Olphert, W. (1996), 'Early evaluation of the organizational implications of CSCW systems', in P. J. Thomas (ed.), *CSCW Requirements and Evaluation*, Springer, London.

Gibbs, W. W. (1994), 'Software's chronic crisis', *Scientific American*, September, 271(3), 72–81.

Hansen, W. (1971), 'User engineering principles for interactive systems', *AFIPS Conference Proceedings 39*, Fall Joint Computer Conference, AFIPS Press.

IBM (1993), *IBM Dictionary of Computing*, McGraw-Hill, New York.

ISO 9241-11, Ergonomics Requirements for Office Work with Visual Display Terminals: Guidance on Usability.

Kroenke, D. (1989), *Management Information Systems*, McGraw-Hill, London.

Land, F. (1989), 'From software engineering to information systems engineering', in K. Knight (ed.), *Participation in Systems Development: UNICOM Applied IT Reports*, Kogan Page, London.

Licklider, J. (1960), Man-computer Symbiosis, IRE Transactions of Human factors in Electronics HFE-1(1).

Licklider, J. and Clark W. (1962), 'Man-computer Communication', *Annual Review of Information Science and Technology*, 3, 201–240.

Lodge, L. (1989), 'A user led model of systems development', in K. Knight (ed.), *Participation in Systems Development: UNICOM Applied IT Reports*, Kogan Page, London.

Lucey, T. (1991), *Management Information Systems*, 6th edition, DP Publications, London.

Martin, J. (1973), *Design of Man-Computer Dialogues*, Prentice-Hall, Englewood Cliffs, NJ.

Nickerson, S. N. (1992), *Looking Ahead, Human Factors in a Changing World*, Laurence Erlbaum, New Jersey.

Ranade, J. and Nash, A. (eds) (1994), *The Best of Byte: Two decades on the leading edge*, McGraw-Hill, New York.

Shackel, B. (1969), 'Man-computer interaction—the contribution of the human sciences', *IEEE Transactions on Man-Machine Systems*, 10, Part II (4), 149–163.

Singleton W. T. (1971), 'Current trends towards systems design', *Applied Ergonomics*, 2(2), 150–158.

Singleton, W. T. (1974), *Man-Machine Systems*, Penguin, Harmondsworth.

Sommerville, I. (1992), *Software Engineering*, 4th edition, Addison-Wesley, Wokingham.

Toffler, A (1980), *The Third Wave*, Collins, London.

Weinberg, G. (1971), *The Psychology of Computer Programming*, Van Nostrand Reinhold.

Further reading

Avison, D. E. and Fitzgerald, G. (1995), *Information Systems Development: methodologies, techniques and tools*, McGraw-Hill, London.

Eason, K. (1998) *Information Technology and Organisational Change*, Taylor and Francis, London.

Long, L. (1989), *Management Information Systems*, Prentice-Hall.

Robson, W. (1994), *Strategic Management and Information Systems*, Pitman, London.

Sauer, C. (1993), *Why Information Systems Fail: a case study approach*, McGraw-Hill, London.

Chapter 2

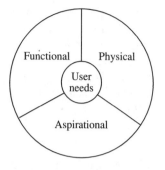

THE USER

Chapter aims

Through study of this chapter the reader will develop a detailed understanding of user needs and in particular should be able to:

- Recognize the many characteristics through which users diverge
- Identify different types of user need
- Develop and evaluate user taxonomies
- Differentiate typical user populations
- Identify how human psychological and physiological characteristics may influence information systems design
- Perform a user analysis in an organizational setting
- Produce a user specification

2.1 User characteristics: a multidimensional situation

We have seen (Chapter 1) that Carver's (1988) definition of an information system was appropriate for our study:

> the man, the computer, the task, and the interaction between them, within an environment which may include the immediate workspace, the physical environment, the social environment, and the organizational environment

In this section of our study we will look at the user (Carver's *the man* aspect) as part of a system and focus on the needs and the many characteristics of users which inform the design of information systems. We will also see some of the ways in which researchers have attempted to classify users of information systems and note the limitations of such an approach.

It will be useful to start our analysis of users by repeating the definition of what we mean by a user of an information system:

> any employee or customer of the organization who will be directly or indirectly affected by the system

We have already begun to explore the many dimensions which underpin the user role. To continue with our analysis in the following sections we will look at how some of these dimensions can help us begin to classify users and thereby assist us in the identification of user needs. To start with we will look at one useful generic classification of users of computer systems proposed by Eason. In his book, he identifies three criteria by which a user interaction with a system may be investigated:

- *Task complexity,* some computer usage tasks are relatively easy (e.g. data input) while others are more complicated (e.g. computer programming).
- *Frequency of use,* different users will perform their tasks more or less often; a doctor may use an expert system quite rarely whereas a word-processing operator will be performing the task throughout the working day.
- *Adaptability,* individual users will differ in their inherent adaptability to perform their task; the home computer enthusiast is likely to be highly adaptable while the busy doctor using the expert system may not be as adaptable.

By associating a high or low value to each of the three criteria Eason has produced a *taxonomy* of eight different user types as

TABLE 2.1   *Comparative analysis of the needs of computer users (adapted from Eason)*

User type	Task complexity	Frequency of use	Adapt-ability	Example occurrence
Professional	High	High	High	Computer programmers
Enthusiast	High	Low	High	Engineers, designers
Servant	Low	High	High	Data input clerks
Malleable user	Low	Low	High	Supervisory roles in industry/commerce
Needful user	High	Low	Low	Doctors, lawyers
Demanding user	High	High	Low	Manager in decision support
Habitual user	Low	High	Low	Public using computer-based equipment
Forgetful user	Low	Low	Low	Public using automatic bank till

shown in Table 2.1. It must be emphasized that this taxonomy is just one approach to the identification and documentation of user needs, as it is based upon just three user characteristics. It does, however, illustrate in a clear way a variety of user types. Each user type will have different needs. If a similar taxonomy was applied to the development of information systems in a large organization it would assist in the identification of user needs.

Before continuing we should emphasize that each of the following initial user classifications, while interesting in their own right, are only fully useful when put in the whole context of the complete range of user characteristics. Through a study of this chapter it is expected that the reader will gain an appreciation of this multidimensional situation.

2.2   Initial user classifications

Within any IT application there will be a wide range of different users: management, end users, customers, etc. All such individuals have some form of stake in the success, or otherwise, of the project, and are often referred to as stakeholders.

2.2.1   Users by function

Users can exercise their stake in the system in a number of ways. The four most obvious stakeholding groups are end users, managers, customers and system users. Taken together the four groups constitute a classification of users by the *function* which they perform within the overall information system.

End users

End users are the people who are required, or decide, to use directly the information system in order to complete the tasks they have as part of either their work or leisure activity. End users clearly have a stake in the system as it will either enhance or inhibit the way in which they complete their tasks. The end user is a crucial element in the successful acceptance of information systems within the organization. They are the people who are involved at the interface between the human and computer aspects of the information systems, and will therefore deserve by far the greatest emphasis within our study of human–computer factors.

Manager users

Organizational systems operate within a business or industrial environment with specific objectives (refer to Fig. 1.5). While end users represent the primary interaction with the information system it is the manager user who will benefit from the success of the system, for example through increases in efficiency within the organization. Manager users are also usually responsible for identifying the need for new or revised systems and for their initial specification.

Customer users

Customers of information systems are those who are immediately affected by the inputs to, and outputs from, an information system or part of a system. Customer users may, or may not, be customers of the organization as a whole. Customers of an electricity company's billing system are individual electricity consumers (organizational customers) as they receive quarterly bills, whereas the customer of a computerized hospital drug administration system is probably a nurse (organizational employee). In the latter case, although the patient (organizational customer) may receive the actual drug, he or she will have no interaction with the information system.

System users

The system user is the person who either generates or manages the application itself rather than using the software system to support an organizational role. Within a database environment a database administrator will have overall responsibility and 4GL programmers will develop and modify applications. In a sense the system user is also an end user. The 4GL programmer is the end user to the database development package while the clerk is the end user to the product produced by the 4GL programmer.

In many cases an individual may take more than one role. The owner of a one man small business, to take an extreme case, may well develop a simple accounting system using an off-the-shelf PC application, input data to the system, and experience the benefits from a more efficient accounting process. The owner is system user, end user, manager user and customer user.

These four user types do not operate in isolation. The primary interactions are as shown in Fig. 2.1. The end user is potentially closely involved with both his or her manager and with customers of the system. The diagram will also form a basis of our study of the user-centred design process (Chapter 3). Note that the system user

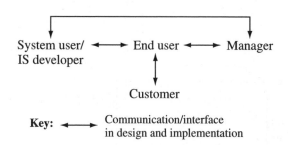

FIGURE 2.1   *Roles/functions in a user-centred system*

role has been extended to include the information systems developer who will need to work closely with both the manager and end user in order that a fully effective user-centred system is produced.

2.2.2   By nature of use

Another way to investigate classifications of users is to study the nature of the *use* and decide whether it is *direct* or *indirect*. Direct users will have physical contact with some physical artefact within the information system; often some form of input and output device (keyboard, visual display unit (VDU)). Examples of direct users include word-processing operatives, accounts clerks and members of the general public as they try to obtain cash from a 'hole in the wall' bank telling machine. Indirect users will benefit, or perhaps suffer, from the results of the system, but will not be involved in the creation of input to, or output from, the system. They may, however, be affected by the output from the system. The manager who receives high quality documentation from his or her secretary's word-processing system will benefit from the system, while the customer of a banking system who receives inaccurate monthly statements could suffer as a consequence.

2.2.3   By skill level

The role which the user performs within the system does not, by itself, provide sufficient information to enable successful usable systems to be produced. A further significant aspect is the individual *skill level* of users. At the simplest level we can identify *expert* (skilled) users and *novice* (unskilled) users. While it is clear that novice and expert users have different needs there are two underlying issues that need to be explored before we can move to meeting such needs. First a novice user becomes an expert user over time: frequent, initially novice,

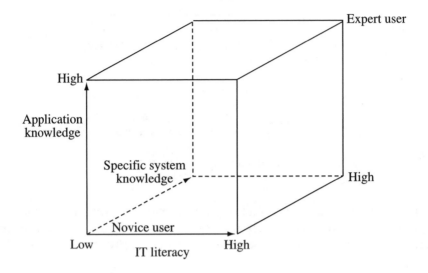

FIGURE 2.2   *The skill level user cube*

users will soon tire of a system designed for their early needs. Secondly a novice user for one system may be an expert user at another.

We need to know more about what is determining the lack of skill. Possibilities include:

• The knowledge/skill of the underlying application domain
• The knowledge/skill of the specific software system
• IT literacy and general computer knowledge/skill

Carey (1982) has suggested a two-dimensional model of skill level which uses the first two of the above factors. She describes a *naive* user as someone with little knowledge of both the application area and the system itself. A *novice* user has little application knowledge but considerable system knowledge. A *casual* user, however, has considerable application knowledge but limited system knowledge, whereas an *experienced* user has considerable knowledge of both the application area and the system itself.

If we include the third skill area of general IT literacy and computer knowledge then, by placing these three skill characteristics on the *x*, *y* and *z* axes, we can generate *a skill level user cube*, as shown in Fig. 2.2, onto which all users can be placed. Individual user skill levels can then be evaluated and compared so that appropriate support (including training) can be provided.

Two corners of the cube have been named. Evidently a *novice user* has a low skill level in all three aspects and an *expert user* the

TABLE 2.2   *User types by skill level*

IT literacy	Application knowledge	System knowledge	User type
Low	Low	Low	Novice
Low	Low	High	Parrot
Low	High	Low	Casual
Low	High	High	Specific
High	Low	Low	Literate
High	Low	High	Trained
High	High	Low	Transferring
High	High	High	Expert

complete opposite. If we extend the analysis to all vertices we can identify an eight member user taxonomy based upon skill level as shown in Table 2.2.

A parrot user, for example, is someone who is able to learn, or who has been trained, how to use one specific system in order to perform specific tasks but has little understanding of the underlying application domain or other computer systems. Many VDU input clerks operate in parrot fashion mode and come into this category. Try to describe the other members of this taxonomy.

2.2.4   By discretion

When trying to develop a full picture of the users of a system it is important to note the discretionary nature of the usage. Senior managers often have the choice whether to use a system or not, but some users, such as data input clerks, have no discretion in their usage situation. While it is important to address usability (effectiveness, efficiency and satisfaction) issues for all computer users, if it is not achieved for discretionary users then rejection of the system will certainly follow.

2.2.5   By development role

Users in the systems development life cycle

Having looked at a number of different factors which will assist in producing user classifications and thereby understanding user needs, we may now begin to look at the roles users might have within the development of new systems. If we take the systems development life

TABLE 2.3   *User roles within the systems development life cycle*

Life cycle stage	User roles
Strategy	Managers commission project Managers provide strategic requirements
Feasibility	Managers/end users provide functional requirements
Analysis	Managers/end users provide functional requirements Possible role for managers and end users in participative design (users as designers)
Design	Possible role for managers and end users in participative design (users as designers)
Implementation	End users take part in trials (users as subjects)
Operation and maintenance	All users are an integral part of operational system

cycle, which was introduced in Sec. 1.5.1, as a basis we can see, from Table 2.3, that a wide variety of different users are involved in all stages.

As we noted (Chapter 1) there are important roles, both for *users as designers* and *users as subjects* within a user-centred development process. At the early stages in the life cycle the project will be commissioned and the requirements will be set out by a range of personnel. If the design follows a user-centred approach then users may themselves be involved in the design of the system. Once all, or part, of the system is developed a number of trials may be conducted. Again a user-centred approach will require direct end-user involvement. Once the system is complete, and up and running, day-to-day operational use will be under the control of users.

Lodge's user classification

The relatively crude classification of users into direct or indirect, and end user, manager user or customer user has been expanded by Lodge (1989) who has defined six distinct types of user which are described detail as shown below:

Governing body

That part of the company that determines and promotes business strategy. It is likely to have influence on the amount of money available to new systems and on how it should be used.

Sponsor

Usually an individual in the organization who, within the strategy imposed by the governing body, can be said to have commissioned the development of the system and, therefore to have authorized the necessary funds.

User specifier

The key user practitioner who has in-depth professional knowledge of the functional area involved and significant practical experience. The 'user specifier' is likely to be the head of a business unit—a middle or line manager or supervisor. There will be as many 'user specifiers' as there are business units involved in the system.

End user

The member of staff who physically operates the user end of the system and thus deals with input and output directly.

Input generator

Those members of staff, or others, who may never see the system as such, but who generate input documents. The salesforce is perhaps the most obvious example.

Output receiver

Those staff, or others who may never see the system but who will receive documents from it for action. Warehouse staff receiving picking lists are an example within the company while customers receiving invoices are an example outside.

2.2.6   Summary of initial classifications

One of the first stages in the successful development of usable systems is the detailed analysis and documentation of the user population. There is no single way to do this and the approach adopted should be system specific. So far, however, we have identified five factors which can be used in a user analysis and classification:

1. Users by function
2. Users by nature of use
3. Users by skill level
4. Users by discretion
5. Users by development role

2.3   Human characteristics: deepening the analysis

There are a great number of complex human characteristics which are important to our understanding of how humans interact with computerized information systems. An appreciation of these individual characteristics is necessary to highlight the limitations in the classification approach adopted above, and to develop a full understanding of the richness of the complete user role. Although these human elements can be broken down into factors relating to physiology or psychology, the boundary between the two can often appear to be somewhat blurred.

The Oxford Dictionary defines physiology as:

The science of the functions of living organisms and their parts.

and psychology as:

The scientific study of the human mind and its functions especially those effecting behaviour in a given context.

Human physiological characteristics generate a whole range of concerns based upon human anthropology and they generally result in a number of design issues which are often referred to as *ergonomics*.

Human psychological considerations include perception, cognition personality and attitude. Here we are studying the way in which individuals behave within a given context. Humans differ, for example, in the way in which they perceive visual information. There are a number of well-known cases of visual ambiguities, such as the one provided in Fig. 2.3 where individuals given the same visual input demonstrate different perceptions. Users also differ in their cognitive abilities; i.e. the way in which they interpret their perceptions and

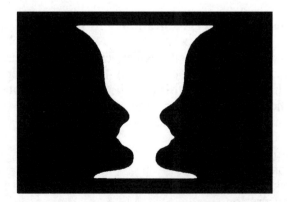

FIGURE 2.3   *An example of visual ambiguity: two faces or a vase?*

decide upon appropriate courses of action. Humans differ in inherent aspects of behaviour which in turn can affect attitude to, and behaviour with, computer equipment. An understanding of a variety of human characteristics is important for the development of information systems. In particular, physiological considerations will influence how we design the physical workstation whereas psychological factors will determine detailed aspects of the software interface.

2.3.1 Physiology, ergonomics and health and safety

A study in users and information systems should make reference to the important physiological characteristics of the human user. Ergonomics, as this area of our study in the UK is called, is becoming an increasingly important aspect of the design of computerized systems. Dul and Weerdmeester (1993) provide the following definition of ergonomics:

> ergonomics aims to design appliances, technical systems and tasks in such a way as to improve human safety, health, comfort and performance

We can see from this definition why the terms human factors and ergonomics are often considered to be synonymous, especially in the USA. According to Dul and Weerdmeester a large number of factors play a role in ergonomics; these include body posture and movement, environmental factors, information and operation as well as tasks and jobs. An important aspect of ergonomics is a sound understanding of human physiology and anthropology. In our study, however, we will not include the anatomical details of the brain, the eye or the ear although they do, of course, inform the ergonomic design of the technology used within information systems.

Ergonomics can contribute to the solution of a large number of social problems related to efficiency, comfort, safety and health. A number of possible health hazards resulting from the use of computer-based equipment have been identified. It is because of these that ergonomics is covered by national and international standards such as those issued by ISO (International Standards Organization), CEN, (the Comité Européen de Normalisation), ANSI (American National Standards Institute) and BSI (British Standards Institute). Within the European Union a directive has been issued (90/270/EEC) concerning the usability of computer systems and there is a relevant international standard (ISO 9241, Ergonomic Requirements for Office Work with Visual Display Terminals). Many of the requirements are being embedded into national standards and health and safety legislation. Particular examples of health hazards include muscular and skeletal problems, of which perhaps the most well known is RSI (repetitive strain injury) to the hands and upper limbs caused by repetitive keyboard actions. Visual problems, such as sore eyes and headaches brought on by spending too much time viewing VDTs, are also important. Not all health issues are fully agreed upon. Some people have claimed that cataracts and risks to pregnancy can be caused by screen emissions, and that skin rashes can result from the electric field caused by computer equipment. In the UK, the Display Screen Equipment Regulations, issued in 1992, required employers to perform a suitable and sufficient analysis of workstations for the purpose of assessing the health and safety risks of users, and required all workstations to meet the required standards by 31 December 1996. The regulations also provide for the entitlement of employees to eye and eyesight tests, when they first become users of display screen equipment, and at regular intervals thereafter. The costs of such tests and any corrective appliances required for screen viewing (e.g. spectacles) must be paid for by the employer. When describing a systematic approach to the assessment of display screen work and equipment to enable compliance with recent legislation, Woods (1993) provides a checklist of 42 issues to be investigated. A selection of these are summarized in Fig. 2.4. It can be noticed that one of the items requires software to be *easy to use*. This phrase is also used in the EU directive. Usability is not, therefore, a matter of choice, but a requirement put upon the IS developer.

2.3.2   Psychology and human memory

Psychology has made a significant contribution to the development of the discipline of human–computer interaction. Later we will see how it can inform a number of formal and semi-formal techniques in task analysis, interface design and interface evaluation. Many of these are based upon a sound psychological analysis of the user, upon an understanding of the user as *a human information processor* and upon models of *human information processing*. A comprehension of how human memory operates is central to much of this work.

Discrete models of human memory

A large number of researchers, over many years, have proposed models of the way in which the human brain manages the memory and recall processes. Until recently these models all focused on a series of discrete stages although nowadays alternatives to the

Furniture

Chair
- Is the chair stable, comfortable, adjustable and allows easy movement at the workstation?
- Are arm rests and foot rests provided?

Desk
- Is desk surface space sufficient and allows adequate space for movement and comfort?
- Is desk surface matt?
- Is a document holder provided?

Hardware

Keyboard
- Is keyboard, separate from the screen, tiltable, with space in front to rest the wrists and does it have a matt surface?
- Is the key layout suitable and are the keys acceptable in terms of size, shape, noise and force to press them?

Screen
- Are contrast and brightness adjustable?
- Are characters well defined, of adequate size, with adequate spacing between characters and lines?
- Is screen easy to pivot and tilt?

Software
- Does software allow easy task completion, with adequate pace and with a quicker or easier way of working?
- Is software easy to use, offering feedback, suiting user's ability?
- Was training offered?

Environment
- Is lighting satisfactory?
- Is equipment noise distracting?
- Is temperature controllable?

FIGURE 2.4   *Compliance with health and safety legislation* (summarized from Woods (1993))

discrete stage approach are being proposed. Examples of discrete models include the Atkinson–Shriffrin (1971) model of memory and the duplex model. The latter identifies three elements within the memory system: sensor memory, short-term memory and long-term memory.

The model human processor is a further instance of this discrete stage approach to memory. Common to many of the discrete stage models is the identification of a number of distinct aspects to memory as shown in Fig. 2.5 and explained below:

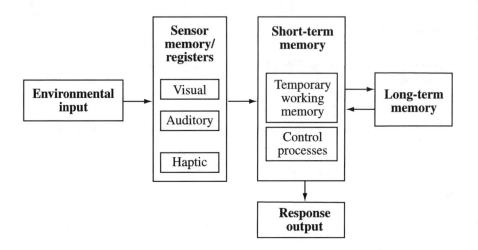

FIGURE 2.5   *A discrete model of memory*

- S*ensor memory/registers*
  The proposition is that there is an aspect of memory which handles the receipt of all stimuli from the human sensors (sight, hearing, touch, etc.). The vast majority of the input to sensory memory is never processed and is highly transitory. In our everyday life we experience a vast amount of sensory input. When walking down the high street we will capture a constantly changing visual image and hear a continuous stream of sounds. Only a very few of these are of any significance to the task that we are undertaking and immediately *decay* from sensor memory to be lost forever.
- *Short- and long-term memory*
  Some of the input to sensor memory will be of significance and will transfer to short-term memory (STM) and a proportion of this will later transfer to long-term memory (LTM). Models of memory differ in whether all information goes through short-term memory. One proposal allows for direct transfer for highly significant events. STM is highly limited in capacity. Miller (1956) has suggested that the capacity of STM can be characterized by the magic number of seven plus or minus two. STM, it is suggested, can handle between five and nine units or *chunks* of information. The questions at the end of the chapter include an exercise to verify Miller's proposal. The decay rate of short-term memory depends on the number of chunks currently stored but can be measured in seconds. Long-term memory is thought to be unlimited with no decay rate. Clearly humans are not able to remember all the information that transfers to LTM. A great amount appears to be forgotten. The problem here, it would seem, is related to the mechanisms we use for the

retrieval of the information, rather than permanent decay from memory.

- T*ransfer, rehearsal, elaboration* and *retrieval*

  In order to enhance the transfer of information to LTM a number of techniques can be implemented. Continual repetition of a list of items is an example of how *rehearsal* can assist in retention. Rehearsal is one of the few mental mechanisms of which we have control. *Elaboration*, on the other hand, provides a way of linking ideas together. Many students revising for an examination will use a mnemonic to aid the memorization of key ideas. It is easier to remember telephone numbers in groups rather than as individual digits (e.g. 27, 45, 12 rather than 2 7 4 5 1 2). *Retrieval* is the active act of recalling information from memory. We can differentiate between the recall (controlled retrieval) and recognition of information. Recognition is much easier as it is often visually based whereas recall involves logical processes. Much more of the brain is devoted to visual processing than to logical processing.

- *Closure*

  When STM is full a tension is created which prompts the clearing of short-term memory.

Model human processor

Card, Moran and Newell (1983) describe the user in terms of a model human processor which can be divided into three subsystems:

- Perceptual system
- Motor system
- Cognitive system

The user's perceptual system carries sensations from the physical world into internal representations in the mind. The motor system enables thought to be finally translated into action. However, before the action can be taken the cognitive system will need to perform tasks such as the retrieval of facts, the solution of problems and the selection of an appropriate course of action. The model human processor, simplified and represented in Fig. 2.6, provides a powerful model for applied research because it gives numerical values (typical and range values) for the parameters, such as capacity and time, which determine human performance. These values have been determined by empirical evidence and include, for example, a visual memory capacity of 17 letters and a perceptual processor cycle time (time to process the smallest unit of information) of 100 ms. These values can be used to predict human performance levels such as the time to complete detailed interface operations.

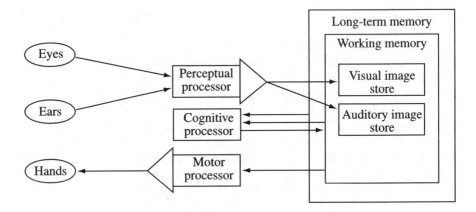

FIGURE 2.6   *Model human processor*

Alternative models and types of memory

It is important to emphasize that the descriptions of memory that we have analysed so far are only simple *models* of memory. Models are useful throughout science to help us understand a situation and predict how systems will behave. They are, however, only a simplified representation to assist in calculation and prediction, and are often only abstractions of the whole real-world situation thereby capturing only a limited view. The brain is a highly complex object and certainly is not compartmentalized as the discrete models indicate.

Discrete models tend to imply a serial process to memory. In reality humans are able to perform many activities which equate more to the ability to operate in a parallel mode. We are, for example, able to recognize large capacity patterns from thousands of alternatives (Eberts, 1994) at a far faster rate than any sequential processing model would allow. There is no support in discrete models for the process of learning or for the concepts of intelligence and intuition. More recently alternatives to the discrete stage approaches have been proposed. The most promising of these alternatives are neural network models (also called connectivist models) which emphasize the process of memory (rather than its structure) and the dynamic and learning aspects (Eberts, 1994). Discrete models do not help us analyse how information is logically arranged within memory or how it may be retrieved. The way in which memory works is still under debate. A number of alternatives have been proposed, two of which are illustrated in a highly simplified version as shown in Fig. 2.7.

- *Semantic memory* A semantic model uses a hierarchical structure of nodes together with additional associations or linkages. Information

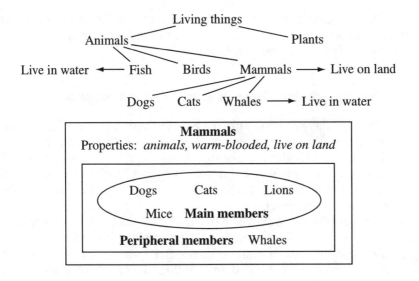

FIGURE 2.7   *Semantic and category memory*

is retrieved through the hierarchical structure from the top down or the bottom up.

- *Category memory* A slightly different approach takes the view that all objects exist within certain categories and that access is via the category often using the properties of the category. There is evidence that we allow overlap between the categories with main and peripheral members within each category. In the example provided the two approaches may help us understand why many people find it difficult to accept that whales are mammals.
- *Discourse memory* A third proposal is that memory is based upon a discourse or episodic approach. We are all able, to varying degrees of accuracy, to recall a story or series of events where associations are made in context. Individuals are able to extract the gist of a story, forgetting many details, and perhaps adding some things which were never there originally.

Relating memory to interface design

The major implications of the memory process lie within interface design. We will see in Chapter 6 how a number of design guidelines have been developed from an appreciation of human memory. For now it will be sufficient to highlight two examples:

1. An understanding of the differences between short- and long-term memory will assist in determining how much information a user can be assumed to retain, in STM, from one screen to another.

2. The knowledge that recognition is much easier than recall has prompted a major switch from command and text-driven interfaces to those using icons and graphics.

2.3.3   Social psychology, image theory and user perception

While the user classification approach described in the earlier sections can prove to be of considerable use, it does not on its own capture the full richness of individual users operating in differing situations. In particular it only provides limited support for describing why individual users generate different *perceptions* of the benefits and costs of information systems.

Social psychologists believe that while there is a great behavioural variation across people within a particular situation, there is also a significant consistency within a particular person across different situations (Vaske and Grantham, 1990). User classifications can attempt to describe some aspects of the variation within a situation, but a fuller understanding of social psychology is helpful in undertaking an analysis of individual actions across different situations. Social psychologists study the nature and causes of human behaviour within a social context. Allport (1969) describes the discipline of social psychology as:

> an attempt to understand how the thought, feeling and behaviour of individuals is influenced by the actual, imagined or implied presence of others

We are particularly interested in the last two categories as the computer can be seen as a technology through which imagined or implied presence can be experienced. One obvious example of this is electronic mail whereby human-to-human communication is mediated by the computer. Many mainstream transaction processing systems are also relevant here. A stock control clerk may no longer be in direct communication with the workers in the warehouse, but will still experience their presence through the computer system. Indeed a number of studies have looked at the degree to which users actually ascribe human-like qualities to computers.

We will investigate some of the individual social and psychological characteristics of users which might determine the perception that users have of new information systems, how their attitudes may be formed and how resultant behaviour may be enacted.

Social and psychological characteristics of users

Personality   Social psychologists have identified a number of different dimensions to individual personality of which the following may be of particular relevance to user interaction with information systems:

- *Locus of control*, the degree to which users believe they have self control; computerization can lead to considerable changes in work practices and thereby significantly modify individual locus of control.
- *Extroversion/introversion*, extroverts are more willing to explore computer systems, and therefore tend to learn more quickly than introverts.
- *Fear of failure/need for achievement*, success or failure in individual tasks strongly determines the manner in which future action is enacted.

Cognitive style   The way in which people differ in their individual generic perception and problem-solving skills is known as *cognitive style*. Contrasting with the process-oriented view adopted within the human model processor (Card, Moran and Newell, 1983), it is possible to identify a number of variables which help to describe individual differences. Cognitive style can, for example, be categorized as either *systematic* or *heuristic*; systematic individuals use abstract logical models and processes while heuristic people use past experience and intuition (Bariff and Lusk, 1977). A second approach is to identify the difference between *verbalizers* and *visualizers*; some people relate better to visual images whereas others prefer verbal structures. Overall users differ in their analytic cognitive abilities.

Demography and situation   A third group of elements underpinning the user response to information systems is related to issues specific to demography and situation. Demographic issues include gender and age. Certain patterns of behaviour, such as aggression are more associated with one gender rather than another. Older workers tend to be less receptive to computers than the young. Age and gender are, in themselves, not sufficient to predict performance as other factors are also significant. Newly appointed employees, for example, have been shown to be more receptive to computer systems than more established employees and those who have been educated and trained will also react differently.

User perception of information systems

While the individual social and psychological characteristics of users can be seen to affect the way users perceive information systems, and the way in which they react to them, we have yet to investigate the *process* by which user reactions may be determined. We will return to the discussion again in Chapter 5 where we will describe a behaviour model for users of information systems. At this stage in our study it will be helpful to introduce the concept of *image theory* which has been developed by Beach (1990) as a broad and comprehensive theory of decision making and provides a basis for decision making in personal and organizational contexts. Studies in decision making are relevant here as users, operating in both individual and group contexts, make decisions about the benefits and costs which they perceive to be associated with any particular information system.

Introducing image theory   Image theory accommodates aspects of classical decision theory and integrates many of the features of other decision theories. Even though most decisions are made in groups, *the decision maker* is viewed as having to make up his or her mind; then the various group members' decisions are integrated in a way that depends on the dynamics of the particular group. Image theory views a decision maker as possessing three distinct but related images of his or her situation with which reference is made when any decision is required. These three images are:

1. *Value image,* or set of principles, which defines how events should transpire in the light of the decision-maker's values, morals, ethics, etc.
2. T*rajectory image*, or goals which are about the kind of changes the decision maker wants for himself, herself or the organization, and constitutes an agenda for the future.
3. *Strategic image*, which describes the plans and tactics the decision maker has for accomplishing these goals.

Any decision, or course of action, is made in the context of these three images. Within the theory two distinct types of decision are identified:

1. *Adoption decisions*, which are about the adoption, or rejection, of courses of action with reference to the decision-maker's value, trajectory and strategic image.
2. *Progress decisions*, which are about whether a particular plan on the strategic image is producing satisfactory progress towards attainment of its goal.

When making a decision the decision maker engages in a process called *framing*, in which a subset of elements from his or her images are identified as being relevant to the decision at hand. Most decisions are made, and most attitudes are formed, in collaboration with others. In these cases the decision maker holds images which are, in part, common with others within the group. In some cases these shared images exist merely because there is an overlap between two individual user images, whereas in others the overlap has occurred as a result of shared experience within a common situation.

Image theory: user perception and attitude   Image theory provides us with a starting point for analysing how and why users take up particular initial stances (tendency towards acceptance and rejection) in response to new information systems. Essentially the user is making an *adoption decision* (as defined in image theory) which is made as a result of a *framing* process on the three *images*. Specifically:

1. The value image will be significant if any new information system is seen as being in conflict with the user's values, morals and ethics.
2. The trajectory image will determine whether the system is either in conflict with the personal goals of the user (for example systems which dehumanize or downgrade work practices) or in synergy with them (the empowerment ideal).
3. The strategic image provides a basis for mapping the functions and procedures of the system to currently established plans.

User attitude and resultant behaviour

By now it should be clear that a practising analyst needs to find out an awful lot of detail about the potential users of a computer system and about the many characteristics along which they may diverge. Taken together these many characteristics will determine the attitude that users take to the introduction of new technology. Individuals who hold negative attitudes are unlikely to make effective and efficient use of information systems. While effective user interface and social systems design may mitigate against inappropriate attitudes, systems success cannot be ensured without addressing attitudinal issues prior to implementation. We will return to these issues later in our study (Chapter 5).

2.4   User needs

The central focus of our study in human–computer factors is the attempt to provide an information system to meet all the needs of the different users. Far too often computer systems are implemented with only very limited user involvement and with, at best, only a cursory analysis of user needs. Often system developers may merely equate user needs with utility. Clearly users require systems to perform functions for which they were devised: but their needs are much wider. We will identify three types of user needs: functional, aspirational and physical which are illustrated in Fig. 2.8.

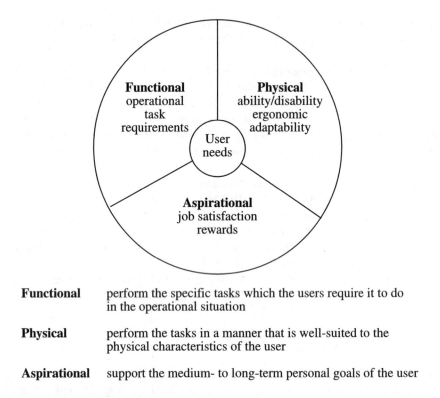

Functional	perform the specific tasks which the users require it to do in the operational situation
Physical	perform the tasks in a manner that is well-suited to the physical characteristics of the user
Aspirational	support the medium- to long-term personal goals of the user

FIGURE 2.8   *User needs*

2.4.1   Functional needs

In Chapter 1, when looking at the reasons for systems failure, we met a definition of utility which described the capability of a system to perform the functions *for which it was devised* and noted that utility and functionality are often assumed to be the same. We will take a wider view of functionality. While users plainly need a high level of utility in the system they use, it is possible that the functions for which it was devised are not the same as those that are needed when the system is operative. Sometimes not all requirements are captured and often requirements change. We may, therefore, define the functional needs of users to be:

> The requirement for the information system to perform the specific tasks which the users require it to do in the operational situation.

2.4.2   Aspirational needs

A useful starting point in a wider analysis of user needs is the work of Maslow (1943). In his *theory of human motivation* Maslow claims that all human motives can be viewed as components of a hierarchical system of needs as shown in Fig. 2.9. There has been much debate about the hierarchy of the needs that Maslow identified. Clearly the basic necessities of food and water need to be dealt with before others can be considered. The assessment of the relative importance of the higher level needs is a matter of opinion (Singleton, 1974). For us the identification of the various categories of needs is surprisingly informative. At first sight there might appear to be little relevance to the design of information systems, but after a more detailed inspection there are few categories which are not relevant. The implementation of information systems, for example, can affect the job *security* (level 2 need) of employees, the expansion in communications, for example the electronic cottage, may limit the ability of individuals to *affiliate* with colleagues (level 3 need), computer applications can reduce previously complex tasks to the more mundane thus diminishing the *prestige and status* of individuals (level 4 need) and the structure and order, or *aesthetic* nature of the interface can affect performance (level 6 need).

Level	Need	Example
1	Physiological	Food, water, sex, etc.
2	Safety	Freedom from threat, security, etc.
3	Belonging/love	Affiliation, acceptance, etc.
4	Esteem	Achievement, prestige, status, etc.
5	Cognitive	Knowledge, understanding, curiosity
6	Aesthetic	Order, beauty, structure
7	Self-actualization	Self-fulfilment, realization of potential, etc.

FIGURE 2.9   *Maslow's hierarchy of needs*

Many of the higher level needs are addressed in socio-technical and user-centred design methods which we will explore in later chapters. Some researchers cite job satisfaction to be a crucial element in information systems design. Mumford and Weir (1979) define job satisfaction as:

> the attainment of a good 'fit' between what the employee is seeking from his work—his job needs, expectations and aspirations—and what he is required to do in his job—the organizational job requirements which mould his experience

For our purpose we can summarize all these needs as aspirational, in that they relate to outcomes which the user aspires to achieve, and define them as:

> The requirement of an information system to support the medium- to long-term personal goals of the user.

2.4.3   Physical needs

The third category of user needs is derived from physical requirements. Users will vary in their own personal ability and disability to use computer equipment. At one extreme visually impaired and even blind users are unable to use visual display terminals and normal keyboards. Speech output systems are required to access screen-based textual information, and braille readers can be used for input. At a more common level, as we have seen, all users need appropriately ergonomically designed workstations. Individuals will also vary in their inherent adaptability to IT equipment. We define physical needs to be:

> *The requirement of the information system to perform the tasks in a manner which is well-suited to the physical characteristics of the user.*

2.5   User studies: developing a user specification

2.5.1   The purpose of user studies

Information systems developers have always needed to undertake user studies. Even without a user-centred or participative approach, by providing requirements some users have always played a vital role in the early stages of the systems development life cycle. Requirements should not just be supplied by the first-line client (the sponsor in Lodge's classification) but should be grounded in information about a wide range of real, individual people and the real tasks which they perform. It is now often standard practice to involve users in the modelling of data and activities. In the USE methodology Wasserman *et al.* (1985) add the analysis of user characteristics and usage characteristics to the analysis of data and activities. If we are to fully address all user needs (functional, physical and aspirational) there is much to do.

A user study which is likely to lead to a fully user-centred and usable product will include the following objectives:

- Identification of the activities which the users are performing.
- Specification of how, and how often, such user activities are performed.
- Description of the data on which these activities interact.
- Evaluation of the performance levels of user activities (e.g. times to perform certain tasks, error rates, etc.).
- Elicitation of user views (e.g. strengths and weaknesses in the current social and technical system) and determination of user satisfaction levels (e.g. of current and potential computerized systems).

User studies can be performed at a variety of stages within the life cycle. Within the analysis (requirements definition) stage a variety of techniques are employed to investigate and specify the tasks which users are undertaking. We will see in Chapter 6 how formal techniques such as hierarchical task analysis and GOMS-like approaches can assist in the detailed capture of user tasks. Often, in order to design systems which improve organizational efficiency it is necessary to undertake a deeper analysis of user views. The soft systems approach allows us to do this and will be reviewed in Chapter 4.

User studies are also carried out in the later stages of the systems development life cycle where the focus shifts towards an evaluation of the proposed software solution. Users will be involved in the evaluation of prototype software to determine whether required performance and satisfaction levels will be achieved. A variety of user study methods exist such as observations, interviews, document collection, questionnaires, participative methods and experiments. These differ in their ability to meet the objectives of user studying identified above. Table 2.4 provides a mapping between the objectives and each of the six methods quoted.

2.5.2 Ways of studying the user

Observation

Perhaps the most obvious method by which the user can be analysed is to observe him or her performing the job in a natural operational situation. Although observational techniques can capture the details

TABLE 2.4   *User studies: relating methods and objectives*

Study method	Objectives					
	Identification of activities/requirements	Specification of activities	Description of data	Determine user needs	Evaluation of performance	Elicitation of views and satisfaction
Observation	Yes	Yes	No	No	Not formally	No
Interview	Yes	Yes	Partly	Yes	No	Yes
Documents	Partly	Yes	Yes	No	No	No
Questionnaire	Yes	No	No	Yes	No	Yes
Participation	Yes	Yes	No	No	Yes	Yes
Experiments	No	No	No	No	Yes	No

of many individual tasks, they may not elicit the full picture of the work role. At the simplest level *passive observation*, where the person conducting the observation quietly observes and records the user activity, can be used to record some details of the processes which the user undertakes. Passive observation has the advantage that it minimizes the intrusion which the user experiences. It is, however, unlikely on it own to capture the richness of the situation.

One problem with passive observation is the practical difficulty in recording sufficient detail of the activity. This can be overcome through the *video recording* of user activity which, after transcription into textual form, can provide a highly detailed and finely grained analysis. Video recordings can be obtained of users performing their normal tasks. They also have an important role within the evaluation of software interfaces. In usability laboratories end users are asked to perform tasks using either prototype or commercially available software. Video recorders capture both a visual recording of the user's activities (keyboard operations, pauses for thought, etc.) together with a recording of VDU output as the user performs the required task. However, this can be a costly exercise; not just in terms of the physical equipment that is necessary, but also in the time it takes to analyse the recordings produced. A second drawback with the use of video is the relatively high level of intrusion that the process incurs. The higher the intrusion level the less sure we can be that the user is performing the tasks in a natural way.

One method which can augment passive observation without the financial costs of video work is that of concurrent verbal accounts. Here the user is asked to 'think aloud' and describe the activities he or she is performing as they are undertaken. While this may make transcription easier, it is probably even more intrusive than video recording.

Interviews

A discussion, or interview, with the user will provide a deeper understanding of the requirements for the new system and of the user tasks involved. It can also assist in finding out more about individual user perceptions. Manager users are able to describe the major system requirements during an interview, while end users can explain how the current system operates. A considerable amount of preliminary work is necessary if the effectiveness of an interview is to be maximized. First it is necessary to select the specific users for interview. It is unlikely to be possible to interview all users. Some will have key positions within the system under investigation while others may be chosen at random to represent the full user population.

Having determined whom to interview it is necessary to produce an interview plan for each session. Interviews can be structured, with well-defined questions, or unstructured in which case the interview is much more free-flowing in nature. Normally, if the interview is to elicit the required information in a specified time, it will be necessary to provide some structure to the interview. Newman and Lamming (1995) describe a number of elements of a successful interview:

- Determine some basic domain knowledge before the interview so that time is efficiently utilized during the interview
- Clearly state to the interviewee the purpose of the interview at the outset
- Enumerate all user activities with general and follow-up specific questions
- Find out how user activities are performed
- Trace interconnections with other users and other parts of the organization
- Uncover issues which determine and affect the performance of the user tasks
- Follow up on *exceptions,* the unusual activities which are unlikely to occur during observation

Document collection

The collection of all documents encountered during both observations and interviews will be necessary to provide a detailed picture of the way in which the user interacts with the information system. Documents are an important source for the identification of individual data items. Many structured design techniques adopt a technique called relational data analysis, or normalization, through which individual data items are placed into well-formed relational tables. Source and output documents are also important for the interface designer who will have the task of designing dialogue sequences and screen layouts.

Questionnaires

Questionnaires allow for a much larger spread within the user study. A well-designed questionnaire, or survey instrument as the document itself is often referred, can be sent out to the whole current, or potential user population in order to elicit user views and satisfaction levels. Designing a questionnaire is a much more complex task than it might at first appear. It is important to make the questionnaire easy for the user to complete. There are two quite obvious reasons for this. First in order for the analysis to be statistically significant it is necessary to generate a high return rate. If users find difficulty in completing the questionnaire they might not complete it, and only a relatively small proportion will be returned. The second reason why we should make it easy for the user relates to the accuracy in the answers given. It is important to avoid ambiguity in the questions which are posed. Ambiguous questions generate unreliable answers. For both these reasons, and for others as well, it is usual to trial the survey instrument with a small proportion of the intended population so that any design problems can be addressed before the main survey is carried out.

Before completing the design of the survey instrument it is worth considering how the data will be analysed. General comments are useful but if there is a large sample a lot of time will be required for analysis. It is also difficult to summarize a lot of general views. For these reasons it is usual to provide the user with a variety of responses When determining user perception it is useful to use an *attitude scale*. When conducting a survey of systems designers (Chapter 3) the author employed both of these approaches. Examples are provided in Fig. 2.10.

Question Type 1

Please circle the one statement which is most applicable:

- Project design and implementation was led by the user department
- Project design and implementation was led through a partnership between user department and central MIS/DP/consultants
- Project design and implementation was led by central MIS/DP/consultants

Question Type 2

How relevant were the following within the domain of user requirements?

Design of individual employee jobs and work structures

marginally relevant   1   2   3   4   5   highly relevant

FIGURE 2.10   *Survey instruments: two approaches*

Participative methods

A further way in which the designer can study the user is to get actively involved (to participate) in either real-life or simulated group activities. Participation itself is a central part of many user-centred design methods. The ETHICS method is perhaps the most well known of such techniques. Participation in the real-life activity would involve someone from the design team actually performing the user role within the organization. This could be achieved either with or without the knowledge of the other, permanent, users. This form of user studying is not a normal occurrence. Apart from needing approval from senior management it is likely to be both time consuming and costly, and would only be worth while if major difficulties in the identification of needs were evident.

Focus groups   A potential weakness of methods such as interviews, questionnaires, and think-aloud methods is that they are based on the activities and views of individuals on their own rather than as part of a wider socio-technical situation. According to O'Donnell *et al.* (1991):

> such methods rely in the subjective introspections of the user... psychological theories would suggest that any reliance on such methods should come with a health warning ...their usefulness is greatly affected by the empirical context in which they occur.

Individual user study techniques sometimes rely on recollections over a long period of time and can be affected by the ability of the users to communicative effectively their views. Group techniques on the other hand have the advantages that they allow subjects to remind each other of events, and encourage subjects to reconstruct processes. They also explore gaps in the subject's thinking, overcome the 'not worth mentioning' problem and importantly for HCI, through discussion, allow new solutions to emerge.

A focus group is one example of a participative user study technique. Focus groups have a long history in market research and consist typically of 8–12 representative subjects (users in our context). Within the group there is a leader, skilled in this activity, who has an agenda which he or she implements at a pace acceptable to the group. A number of current affairs television programmes in the UK have recently used focus groups as a way of determining the reasons why voters may be making their electoral choices. In our domain of information systems focus groups may be of use in understanding political and social issues affecting the system and in the design and evaluation of possible design solutions.

Scenarios and storyboarding   Scenarios are specific examples of individual user interactions with information systems. They are used within a participative study technique to structure and communicate information about how a design might be used in the real world. A scenario describes what a user has to do and the method by which he or she would perform specific tasks. The difference between a scenario and a task is that a scenario is design specific whereas a task is design independent (Lewis and Rieman, 1993). One task (for example adding a stock record to a file) might have two scenarios depending on different potential solutions (for example using a graphical user interface or conventional conversational menu). Clarke (1991) states that scenarios tend to be used where there is a large amount of task and domain information being discussed and that they have the advantage of being concrete and specific to the domain and problem at hand whereas design principles are abstract and generic. Through the use of scenarios, software developers are able to investigate various design options. Users are able to participate within a scenario in order for the developers to elicit user responses and to refine their proposed design.

Often scenarios can be represented by storyboards which are sequences of sketches showing what each of the screens would show, and what actions the user would take at key points within each task. Lewis and Rieman explain the advantage to them of a storyboard-based scenario technique:

> (it) allowed us to tell the uses what they really wanted to know about our proposed design, which was what it would be like to use it to do real work....a traditional design....is pretty meaningless to users as they can't provide any useful reaction to it

We are moving the shift from the analysis of current systems and tasks to the evaluation of proposed new solutions.

Experiments

Storyboarding-based scenario techniques can be considered as one example of experimental user studies. User-based experiments also play an important part in interface evaluation. Here real potential users of a system are selected and provided with a typical task scenario to perform with either a prototype or final software product. As part of the user study evaluators record details of the interaction between the user and the system. From the data that is collected usability metrics (such as the number of errors made) can be calculated, and levels of performance (such as the time to complete the task) recorded. These values can be used in a systematic evaluation of the interface.

For those embarking on detailed experiments in the arena of human–computer factors it will be helpful to emphasize the importance of well-founded experimental design to the successful collection and analysis of data. The competent application of sound statistical techniques is also crucial. Clearly this text does not have time to cover these details but the interested reader is referred to Greene and D'Oliveira (1982). We will return to experiments in usability evaluation in much greater detail later.

2.5.3   Acadmin: user studies

In Chapter 1 we outlined the Acadmin system: a commercial academic administration system for use in UK further and higher education institutions. When the Acadmin system was being developed for use in one particular institution it was necessary to identify a number of user groups together with their main interaction with the Acadmin system. These together with *some* of the possible user study techniques are presented in Table 2.5.

2.5.4   Developing the user specification

The results of a comprehensive user study are necessary input to two major reports: the requirements definition and the user specification. In our study we are particularly interested in the latter. Although there is no single standard method for recording the results of user

TABLE 2.5   *Acadmin user studies*

User group	Group by function	Access	Task(s)	Study method	Objective of study method
Computer staff	Professional	Direct	System maintenance	Interview	Elicitation of views
Lecturer	End user	Direct— read only	Look up student profile	Interview, question-naire	Determine user needs, elicitation of views
Course manager	End user	Direct— read/write	Receive course summary reports	Interview	Determine user needs, elicitation of views
Manager	Manager user	Indirect	Analysing trends, etc.	Interview	Determine user needs, elicitation of views
Dept. Admin.	End user	Direct— read/write	Input grades, produce reports	Observation, document collection	Identification and specification of current activities
Students	Customer	Indirect— printed output only	Receive individual profile output	Interview	Elicitation of views

studies, documentation is an essential part of any successful analysis and design project. Without appropriate documentation it is impossible to communicate and debate findings both within the design team and with the user community. Some system development methods (such as SSADM) provide a framework for documentation. Within the Plumbest exercises at the end of the chapter we provide two simple forms on which the results from a variety of user studies can be captured and which can form part of a full user specification.

2.6   Plumbest plc: finding out more about the users

2.6.1   Tasks

Plumbest Task 2.1

Having undertaken some initial interviews with the staff at Plumbest you have an initial understanding of the current system in operation, the role of each of the user groups and some of the user issues. The user groups who are likely to be involved are listed below:

- Mobile operatives (MOs)
- Foremen
- Service administrators
- Radio operators
- Service centre co-ordinator
- Operations manager
- Directors

Assuming that the 'minimum solution' job allocation system is implemented show how each of the user groups would map to Lodge's user classifications.

Plumbest Task 2.2

You have decided to ask Sunila, one of your project managers, to undertake a detailed user analysis. Prepare a briefing document which will advise her on the methods you think will be appropriate for a full user and system study at Plumbest. You may like to present your proposal in tabular form using the headings:

- User group involved
- Method of user study
- Objective/outcome of study

Plumbest Task 2.3

Design a questionnaire which will be distributed to mobile operatives. It will be used to elicit their perceptions about problems in the current system and to determine their individual needs. (No solution provided.)

Plumbest Task 2.4

You have decided to conduct an interview with one of the service administrators so that you have a better understanding of the detailed user and system needs. Plan a structure for the interview. What questions will you ask? (No solution provided.)

Plumbest Task 2.5

From the information which you already have try to place each of the named users/user groups on Eason's user taxonomy (refer to Table 2.1).

2.6.2   Solutions

Plumbest Solution 2.1

Table 2.6 provides a possible mapping:

Plumbest Solution 2.2

At the early systems investigation stage the user study methods will focus on observation, interviewing and document collection. The only user group of any significant size is the mobile operatives and a questionnaire may be an efficient way of capturing their views and needs. The main objectives at this stage will be to:

TABLE 2.6   *User group mapping*

Lodge classification	User groups
Governing body	Directors
Sponsor	Operations manager
User specifier	Service centre co-ordinator, operations manager
End user	Service administrators
Input generator	Service administrators, MOs
Output receiver	Radio operators, foremen

- Clarify system requirements
- Identify and specify all current activities
- Describe all data within the system
- Examine user perception of problems in the current system
- Determine individual user group needs

Table 2.7 provides some background to some of the user study methods which will be needed.

Plumbest Solution 2.5

Table 2.8 is only ONE possible mapping. A full user study of the individuals concerned may reveal a different picture.

TABLE 2.7   *User study methods*

User group	Study method	Objective/outcome
Mobile operative	Passive observation	Specification of activities: job processing
Mobile operative	Interview	Elicitation of views: problems in system
Mobile operative	Questionnaire	Elicitation of views: problems in system Determination of user needs
Foremen	Interview	Elicitation of views: problems in system Determination of user needs
Service administrators	Passive observation	Specification of activities: job allocation
Service administrators	Document collection	Description of data Specification of activities
Service administrators	Interview	Determination of user needs
Radio operators	Passive observation	Specification of activities: communications
Radio operators	Interview	Elicitation of views: problems in system Determination of user needs
Service centre co-ordinator	Interview	Elicitation of views: problems in system Determination of user needs
Operations manager	Interview	Elicitation of views: problems in system Identification: activities, system requirements
Directors	Interview	Elicitation of views: problems in system Identification: activities, system requirements

TABLE 2.8   *Plumbet's users by Eason's taxonomy*

User type	Individual
Professional	None
Enthusiast	Frances Dunckley, service centre co-ordinator
Servant	Jackie Lukes, service administrator
	Osei Allum, mobile operative
Malleable user	Ian Davies, foreman
Needful user	Paula Monaco, operations director
Demanding user	None
Habitual user	None
Forgetful user	None

2.6.3   Further information

The organizational level and user group level documentation sheets, capture the results from a full user analysis. The information within the documents will be used at later stages in the design process.

User Analysis—Organizational Level

Organization | Plumbest

System | Job Allocation

User group	No.	Reports to	Supervises	Location	Main functions
Mobile operative	51	Foreman	None	On the road in 3 regions	job completion associated admin.
Foreman	4	Operations manager	Mobile operatives	Based at one of 3 depots	job completion in region, job allocation (non-emergency)
Service admin.	11	Service centre co-ordinator	None	Service centre in Bedford	job processing office admin.
Radio operator	8	Service centre co-ordinator	None	Service centre in Bedford	communication with shift MOs
Service centre co-ordinator	1	Operations manager	Service admin. Radio operators	Service centre in Bedford	job allocation and associated admin.
Operations manager	1	Operations director	Service centre co-ordinator Foremen	Service centre in Bedford	job allocation, completion and admin. in all regions
Directors	3	Managing director	Middle managers	Head office in London	tactical and strategic management

Notes

1	All information relates to current system
2	Number of post holders likely to increase with UK Gas contract
3	Refer to separate User Group level sheets for further information on most user groups
4	

User Analysis— User Group Level

Organization [Plumbest]   System [Job Allocation]

User group [Mobile operative]

Number of personnel [51]

Section A   User Tasks

	Task/Process	Frequency	Documents involved	Location	Performance Criteria
1	receiving jobs via JIF from foreman	4 per day	JIF	received from foreman	
2	receiving jobs via telephone call from service centre	4 per day	None	received on the road	available to receive calls
3	actual job processing	4 per day	None	on the road	cust. satisfaction productivity monitored by foreman
4	JCF completion and return	4 per day	JCF	return to foreman at depot	all JCFs given to foreman at end of shift
5	JIF completion and return (non-emergency only)	4 per day	JIF	return to foreman at depot	all JIFs returned to foreman at end of shift
6					

Section B   User Role and Needs

1	The 'pet plan' system would imply direct user role, 'minimal solution' would imply input generator and output receiver roles
2	All MOs have little IT literacy and no previous computer experience – novice (perhaps casual) users – training important
3	*Physiological*: Mobile nature of job: access to standard VDT impossible for this end user role – consider H+S legislation
4	*Physiological*: Nature of the MO job implies largely non adaptable user role: possibly demanding user for 'pet plan' solution.

Section C   User Views

1	Basically satisfied with current system – needs to be persuaded of any need for change
2	Concern over the controlling aspect of a computerised allocation system, particularly 'pet plan' solution
3	Concern over potential change in reporting lines if pet plan system was implemented
4	

User Analysis— User Group Level

Organization | Plumbest | System | Job Allocation |

User group | Foreman |

Number of personnel | 4 |

Section A   User Tasks

	Task/Process	Frequency	Documents involved	Location	Performance criteria
1	Job scheduling and allocation (non-emergency)	daily	JIF	Depot	Appointment made within service target, Service Centre notified
2	Raising materials from warehouse	daily	JIF	Depot: Warehouse	Necessary parts available for repairs
3	Check/completion of JCF return to service centre	daily	JIF JCF	Depot	Return to service centre within 2 days of job completion
4	Monitoring performance of MOs	on-going	JCF	Region	monthly report to identifying 'exceptions'
5					
6					

Section B   User Role and Needs

1	'Minimum solution' would imply input generator and output receiver roles. Role unclear for 'pet plan' solution.
2	Range of skills: some foremen are IT literate with experience of computer systems, others less so.
3	*Aspirational*: maintenance of job function
4	

Section C   User Views

1	Considerable concerne about the implication for the foreman role: will they be made redundant as a result?
2	Problems with the current system considered to lie within the manual clerical system at Bedford
3	
4	

User Analysis— User Group Level

Organization [Plumbest]   System [Job Allocation]

User group   [Service Administrator]

Number of personnel   [11]

Section A   User Tasks

	Task/Process	Frequency	Documents involved	Location	Performance criteria
1	Processing customer job requests	average of 12 / hour	JIF	Service centre	JIF raised for appropriate jobs in target time
2	Administrative support (outside scope of JAS)	-	-	-	-
3					
4					
5					
6					

Section B   User Role and Needs

1	Both 'pet plan' and 'minimum solution' would imply data input end user role - relationship to radio operator unclear
2	Majority of have some prior IT experience (e.g. word processing, simple database work) - transferring users?
3	*Aspirational:* Experienced users of either JAS will be Servants - need to consider motivational aspects.
4	*Functional:* Safety critical nature of system has implications for how this user group will access new system.

Section C   User Views

1	General satisfaction with proposals for computerized JAS
2	Desire for rewards if role is enhanced
3	
4	

User Analysis—User Group Level

Organization [Plumbest]   System [Job Allocation]

User Group [Radio operator]

Number of personnel [8]

Section A   User Tasks

	Task/Process	Frequency	Documents involved	Location	Performance criteria
1	Manual allocation of emergency jobs to MOs	6 per hour	JIF	Service centre	Jobs allocated to MOs able to comply within target time
2	Communication with MOs	on-going	–	Service centre	–
3					
4					
5					
6					

Section B   User Role and Needs

1	Minimum solution would imply output receiver role.
2	*Functional:* majority have very little IT knowledge: potential novice user
3	*Aspirational:* maintenance/enhancement of job role
4	

Section C   User Views

1	Very concerned about implications for 'pet plan' on job role
2	
3	
4	

User Analysis—User Group Level

Organization | Plumbest | System | Job Allocation |

User group | Service centre co-ord. |

Number of personnel | 1 |

Section A   User Tasks

	Task/Process	Frequency	Documents involved	Location	Performance criteria
1	Managing operation of service centre	on-going	variety	Service centre	effective and efficient job allocation
2					
3					
4					
5					
6					

Section B   User Role and Needs

1	Mainly indirect user
2	Occasional direct use: experienced IT user, potential malleable and expert user
3	*Aspirational:* career and unit enhancement
4	*Functional:* efficient job allocation

Section C   User Views

1	Feels the MOs 'get away with murder' while 'on the job'.
2	She feels an opportunity exits for enhancing the role of the CSU. It could lead to more staff, perhaps with higher grades
3	
4	

Summary

In this chapter we have focused on the user and his or her role within an information system. In particular we have seen:

- The complexities inherent within the user role within an information system
- How a variety of methods can be used to classify users
- The way in which user needs vary between individuals and user groups
- That user needs can be grouped under the categories of functional needs, physical needs and aspirational needs
- The importance of human memory capabilities for interface design
- How a range of methods can be employed for user study
- One way in which the results of a user study can be documented

Questions

2.1 Consider the situation where a new patient administration system is being designed for a large hospital. In terms of Lodge's user classification what job roles would be involved?

2.2 Figure 2.4 provides a checklist for analysing compliance with health and safety legislation. Accepting that you do not have all the data necessary for a detailed analysis (e.g. the specification for required lighting levels) perform a brief survey of computer systems in operation within your working environment.

2.3 In Fig. 2.11 you will find a number of names randomly scattered across the page. In order to investigate Miller's magic number (7 plus or minus 2) show them to a number of colleagues for, say, 20 seconds. After this time ask them to write down as many names as they can remember. Find the average for, say, 5 people. Is the average score more or less than 7 and by how much? If your score is more than 9 (the upper bound of 7 plus or minus 2) why do you think this is? How might long-term memory be affecting the results?

Wallis		Ursula		Jeremy		Frederick	
	Timothy		Lionel		Alexis		
Vera		Fatima		Jerimiah		Gertrude	Humphrey
	Jean					Xerces	
		Bertrand		Anne-Marie		Eric	Hilary
Jervais			Martha		Sebastian	Pamela	Richard
	Yolanta			William		Betty	
		Georgina			Elizabeth		

FIGURE 2.11

2.4 Evaluate the relative importance of functional, physical and aspirational needs to each of the following usage situations (give practical reasons for your assessments):
 (i)   stock control clerk using an inventory program
 (ii) musician composing a score
 (iii) general public using the Internet for information searching
 (iv) doctor using an expert system for medical diagnosis
 (v)   airline pilot using a flight simulator
 (vi) research scientist using computer-controlled experiments
 (vii) marketing manager using a decision support system
2.5 A university is planning to introduce a new computerized system for the management of the library book stock (loans, returns, new stock identification and ordering, etc.). Identify the key user groups. What methods would you employ within a full user study to determine system and user needs?
2.6 How might user aspirational needs be related to the images within Beach's image theory?

References

Allport, G. W. (1969), 'The historical background of modern social psychology', in G. Lindzey and E. Aronson (eds), *The Handbook of Social Psychology*, Addison-Wesley, Reading, MA.

Atkinson, R. C. and Shiffrin, R. M. (1971), 'The control of short term Memory', *Scientific American*, 225, 82–90.

Bariff, M. L. and Lusk, E. J. (1977), 'Cognitive and personality tests for the design of management information systems', *Management Science*, 23, 820–829.

Beach, L. R. (1990), *Image Theory: Decision Making in Personal and Organizational Context*, Wiley, Chichester.

Carey, T. (1982), 'User differences in interface design', *Computer*, 18, 14–20.

Card, S. K., Moran, T. P. and Newell, A. (1983), *The Psychology of Human–Computer Interaction*, Lawrence Erlbaum, New Jersey.

Carver, M. K. (1988), 'Practical experiences of specifying the human-computer interface using JSD', in *Contemporary Ergonomics, Proceedings of the Ergonomics Society's 1988 Annual Conference*, Taylor and Francis, London.

Clarke, L. (1991), 'The use of scenarios by user interface designers', in D. Diaper and N. Hammond (eds), *People and Computers VI, Proceedings of HCI 91*, Cambridge University Press, Cambridge.

Dul, J. and Weerdmeester, B. (1993), *Ergonomics for Beginners*, Taylor and Francis, London.

Eason, K. (1988), *Information Technology and Organisational Change*, Taylor and Francis, London.

Eberts, R. E. (1994), *User Interface Design*, Prentice-Hall, Englewood Cliffs, New Jersey.

Greene, J. and d'Oliveira, M. (1982), *Learning to Use Statistical Tests in Psychology: a Student's Guide*, Open University Press, UK.

Lewis, C. and Rieman, J. (1993), 'Task-centred user interface design, a practical introduction', published on the Internet.

Lodge, L. (1989), 'A user led model of systems development', in K. Knight (ed.), *Participation in Systems Development: UNICOM Applied IT Reports*, Kogan Page, London.

Maslow, A. (1943), 'A theory of human motivation', *Psychological Review*, 50, 380–396.

Miller. G. (1956), 'The magic number seven, plus or minus two: some limits on our capacity for processing information', *Psychological Review*, 63, 81–97.

Mumford, E. and Weir, M. (1979), *Computer Systems in Work Design: the ETHICS Method*, Associated Business Press, London.

Newman, W. M. and Lamming, M. G. (1995), *Interactive Systems Design*, Addison-Wesley.

O'Donnell, P. J. *et al.* (1991), 'The use of focus groups as an evaluation technique in HCI', in D. Diaper and N. Hammond (eds), *People and Computers VI, Proceedings of HCI 91*, Cambridge University Press.

Singleton, W. T. (1974), *Man-Machine Systems*, Penguin, Harmondsworth.

Vaske, J. J. and Grantham, C. E. (1990), *Socialising the Human-Computer Environment*, Ablex, Norwood, New Jersey.

Wasserman, A., Pincher, P. A., Shewmake, D. T. and Kersten, M. L. (1985), 'Developing interactive information systems with the user software engineering methodology', *IEEE Transactions on Software Engineering*, 12(2), 326–345.

Woods, V. (1993), 'A suitable and sufficient display screen assessment', *Occupational Health*, June 1993, 196–200.

Further reading

Preece, J., Rogers, Y., Sharp, H., Benyon, D., Hillard, S. and Carey, T. (1994), *Human–Computer Interaction*, Prentice-Hall, London.

Shneiderman, B. (1992), *Designing the User Interface*, Addison-Wesley, Reading, MA.

Sutcliffe, A. (1988), *Human–Computer Interface Design*, Macmillan, Basingstoke.

Chapter 3

USER-CENTRED DESIGN

User needs:		Usability:
Functional Physical Aspirational	User-centred design	Effectiveness Efficiency Satisfaction

Chapter aims

The overall aims of this chapter are twofold. First it establishes a generic framework for further analysis and secondly it enables discussion on the specific role of the user within the design of a new information system. Specifically through study of this chapter the reader should be able to:

- Appreciate the importance of users to successful systems design
- Advise on the involvement of users in systems design
- Recognize the essential elements of user-centred design
- Relate theory of user-centred design to current commercial practice
- Propose design teams
- Evaluate the user-centredness of software projects

3.1 Overview

Having accomplished quite a detailed review of the essential qualities, characterisics and needs of the users of informations systems we are now able to move towards the central theme of our study: *the development of information systems which fully address such qualities, characterisics and needs*. In many ways this part of our analysis is a crucial one as we will refer back to many of the models introduced here. Effectively this chapter sets a structure on which we can build and eventually complete our study of users and information systems.

The last decade has seen important developments in the way in which information systems are designed. There has been a massive explosion in the number of design methodologies and a range of methods and tools have been proposed which claim to help the designer integrate the user within the design process. The development of a human-factor approach to the whole IT arena has also made a significant contribution and the discipline of human–computer interaction has enjoyed a rapid growth, in terms of content and importance, in recent years. Specifically in this chapter we will focus on the user role within the information systems design process. We will look at how users can be integrated within design itself, how support can be provided to enable them to make an effective contribution and how the procedures can be adapted to address user needs. The mechanisms by which users can effectively be involved in information systems development is what we will refer to as *user-centred design*.

3.2   Aims of a user-centred design process

3.2.1   The rationale for a user-centred approach: criteria for IS success

We have already seen the relatively low success rates for the introduction of new information systems. We noted that success or failure is often determined not just by technical matters but is often affected by user and organizational acceptance. Overall it is possible to identify three broad criteria for usability and IS success:

1. Effectiveness
2. Efficiency
3. Satisfaction

It is because of the growth in interactive systems and the resultant increase in the range and number of users that usability and acceptability issues are now much more important. During the 1970s when the majority of systems operated in batch mode with paper-based input (e.g. punched cards, optical recognition) the only real requirement was that of utility. A comparison of the two definitions provided in earlier chapters will show that the concepts of utility and effectiveness are closely related. Nowadays the two other usability criteria (efficiency and satisfaction) are equally important. User-centred design methods aim to ensure that all three criteria are met.

3.2.2   The user role in software development: an historical perspective

There is evidence that today systems designers are attempting to pay attention to the needs of the user, and thereby designing usable and acceptable software solutions. This can be seen from any number of trade journals. Simpson (1992), for example, states that:

> the key to success for IT departments is to get closer and to be more responsive to their customers, the users.

Historically, however, systems developers have often considered user involvement as a *necessary evil*; an activity which, albeit essential, is something that developers do not relish.

In traditional systems development methods (those that have their roots in the 1970s and before) the end user has little or no role to play in the design process. Some users, particularly managers or user specifiers, would, of course, be involved in the requirements gathering stage, but the user role would begin with requirements specification and end with product acceptance with little input in-between. Historically the vast majority of end users would have no involvement in the project until some training was provided prior to operation.

In more recent years, however, there has been documented evidence, for example as described by Raynor and Speckman (1983) over a decade ago, of the successful maintenance of effective genuine user participation in IT projects. In addition participative design methods, for example as described by Mumford (1983) have been established; particularly within the academic community.

3.2.3 Involvement, engagement, participation and user-centredness

The ideas behind user-centred design are now well established within the academic community. There is, however, a lack of clarity within the commercial software development community concerning approaches to user-centred design. Indeed a number of IS projects have recently come to attention and have demonstrated the fact that information systems would still appear to be failing because of a lack of effective user engagement. The question we need to address now is how far, and in which ways, have system developers moved away from considering user involvement as a necessary evil and begun to embrace it as a vital and positive ingredient in successful systems design and implementation.

Before attempting to address an answer to this question it is necessary to identify possible problems which may inhibit a shared understanding within the IT community (academics and practitioners) concerning the user role in systems development. The role of the user has been characterized in a number of ways and with a number of terms. We often see, or hear, reference to the terms user *involvement*, user *participation* and user *engagement*. As Kappelman *et al.* (1994) say:

> the choice of any of these terms is fraught with peril and the potential for misunderstanding

It is, therefore, not just a problem of semantics which has led us to focus, in this chapter, on the issue of *user-centred design* as opposed to mere user involvement. It could be argued by some practitioners that they do involve users. The involvement might just relate to requirements capture and product acceptance. A positive attempt has also been made to avoid central reference to the term *user participation* as this might imply the rather more specific ETHICS methodology which we will study in Chapter 4. For completeness sake it might be useful to look at some, more formal, definitions provided by Kappelman *et al.* (1994) for each term:

User engagement

A general term for the total set of user relationships towards information systems and their development, implementation and use.

User participation

The observable behaviour of system users in the information systems development process.

User involvement

The psychological or mental state of system users (i.e. their subjective attitude towards the process and its product).

Engagement, involvement and participation are related to each other and all are required for a user-centred approach. It is now necessary to attempt a definition, or at least an exploration, of what is meant by user-centred information systems design.

3.3   Defining user-centredness in software development

3.3.1   Towards a definition of user-centred design

Later we will look at a way in which user-centredness in software development can be evaluated. In many respects this approach can be used to provide a definition of user-centred design. However, the following statement may stand as a loose definition of user-centred design (UCD):

A fully user-centred information systems development approach is one where all potential users of the proposed information system have the opportunity of being actively involved, either directly or indirectly, in the whole analysis, design and implementation process. Instead of acting as passive, albeit more engaged, providers of requirements for functionally correct systems, users are able to contribute the development of systems which, in addition, demonstrate a high level of usability to both users and the organisation in which they operate.

Following on from this definition it is possible to identify a number of qualities which a fully user-centred design process will demonstrate:

User engagement (participation and involvement) in the design process
- Users having real decision-making powers
- Users having appropriate mechanisms for communication with, and negotiation between, developers

A socio-technical design process
- Containing iterative and evolutionary approach
- Where consideration is given to job satisfaction

Appropriate user-centred tools implemented
- Including elements of prototyping
- Where priority is given to user interface design

The ability to react to changing needs
- Functional
- Physical
- Aspirational

3.3.2   Three levels of user-centredness

If we adopt the approach outlined above we have some idea of what constitutes a fully user-centred approach. However, user-centredness in design is not a binary variate: it is not the case that it is either there or not there. Indeed user-centredness is a continuous quantity. Some IT projects will demonstrate a very high level of user-centredness while others will show very little evidence, with many somewhere in-between. Eason has developed a framework, which has been slightly modified (Fig. 3.1) to provide a comparison between three levels of user-centredness.

At level 1, with minimum user-centredness, we have *technical-centred design*. In this level, which might be characterized by traditional systems analysis design methods and many implementations of structured methods, users are largely tangential to the design process itself. All the design work is done by technical specialists (analysts, programmers, etc.) and the users are merely

Level	Design option	Contribution made by:	
		Technical specialists	Users
1	Technical-centred	Analyse, design and deliver	Commission and accept Are informed, consulted and trained
2	Joint user-specialist	Analyse, design and deliver Co-designers	Are represented in all stages of design Informed decision makers
3	User-led	Provide a technical service to users	All contribute to design

FIGURE 3.1   *Three levels of user-centredness (*source: Eason, K. (1988), *Information Technology and Organisational Change,* Taylor and Francis, London)

recipients of their work. They will, of course, be involved to a certain degree; they must provide functional requirements, approve various stages of the development process and be trained in its use. Their role, however, is a passive one.

The level with greatest user-centredness (level 3) has been identified as *user-led design.* Here the users take charge and are in full control of the development project and all (or as many as possible) potential users are actively involved in the design and development process. The technical specialist provides a service to the users. Implementations of user-led design might be seen in organizational information systems (where specific participative methods (e.g. ETHICS) have been adopted) or in end-user systems.

The 'half-way house' approach to user-centred design (level 2) is described as *joint user-specialist design.* Here users and designers enter into a genuine partnership in design. Recognizing that it is often impossible to involve all users, a range of users is elected or selected for the role. The primary responsibility for design rests with the technical specialist but there is sufficient user representation and involvement for active user involvement.

3.4   Three categories of UCD

The author has developed a method (Smith, 1993) in which approaches to user-centredness within information systems design can be analysed so that techniques adopted in organizations can be evaluated. The method is based upon the premise that user-centredness is constituted from three underpinning elements. These three elements are described as broad concepts, or categories, of *structures, processes,* and *scope.*

Structures are mechanisms that either support or inhibit the way in which the user is able to contribute to the design process. Structures include approaches to project management, the way in which teams of users and designers work together (design team structures), and other mechanisms that support involvement and communication between the design team and the user community.

Processes for design include any activity in which users might be involved and focus around the design methodology adopted and include issues relating to:

- Choice (or lack of choice) of design methodology
- Methods used to elicit requirements
- Task analysis methods
- Communication and specification methods
- Interface design methods
- Approaches to prototyping
- Systems implementation methods

The **scope** of the design process relates to how far the analysis reflects a socio-technical, as opposed to just a technical, solution. More specifically an IT project with only a narrow scope will focus on technical and functional requirements whereas one with a wider scope will address issues such as the allocation of function between man and machine, the design of work structures and individual jobs and ways of enhancing job satisfaction within the organization.

A diagrammatic representation of a user-centred design process is shown in Fig. 3.2. Within the IS development process users are engaged through membership of appropriate participative *structures.* The development itself contains a range of *processes* and will address a particular *scope* in design. If all three concepts are appropriate to the problem at hand it is likely that the product will demonstrate high levels of usability. We can take this approach to propose a second definition of user-centred design:

> *A user-centred information systems development approach is one in which all types of user needs (functional, physical and aspirational) are addressed so that usability (effectiveness, efficiency and satisfaction) is maximized in the end product*

We will now look at each of the categories of UCD in more detail.

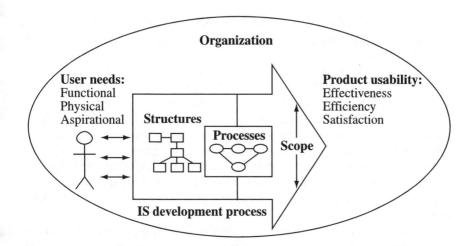

FIGURE 3.2   *The process of user-centred design*

3.5   Structures

Structures are mechanisms that either support or inhibit the way in which the user is able to contribute to the design process. Structures include approaches to project management, the way in which teams of users and designers work together (design team structures), and other mechanisms that support involvement and communication between the design team and the user community.

The structures category includes any mechanism that exerts some form of control over the contribution that the user might make to the design. The largest factor here is likely to be the way users are involved within design teams. Various design team structures are possible offering a variety of levels of user involvement. A secondary, yet significant, issue is that of project management. Effective project management is essential to the successful management of a software project but, as we will see, it can also affect the effectiveness of user involvement.

3.5.1   Design team structures

Successful IS development is not achieved solely through the work of individuals. It is often wrongly assumed by the general public that the software developer (especially the programmer) works largely on his or her own sitting at a VDU screen. The opposite is in fact the case. Software developers work in teams and spend much of their time interacting with other people. In a study McCue (1978) established that 50 per cent of a software engineer's time was spent in interaction with other team members and only 30 per cent of time was spent working alone.

As this book is not a study in software engineering we are not concerned here with the details of software management structures. It will be sufficient to state that, particularly in large software development organizations or departments, considerable emphasis needs to be given to the management of software development personnel, particularly in relation to the establishment of quality procedures. Here we are concerned with how *users* are involved in design teams. We need to note that the policies of the software development department or organization may be crucial to user engagement.

In many ways the user contribution to design teams will be determined by the level of user-centredness attempted. Technical-centred design (level 1 of the three levels of user-centredness) implies very little user involvement in the first place. While the software director of the development department or external organization will still place importance on the internal management of the design team, the user's interaction will only be at the requirements gathering stage and at formal approval or 'signing-off' stages. User-led design implies a much more flexible approach where the technical service provided by the specialists, to the users, often lies outside of a formal design team structure.

It is within joint user-specialist design (level 2) that user involvement in design teams becomes a major issue. As we will see later the vast majority of software developers support (or at least think they support) such approaches and so we may assume that these issues are important for the development of most information systems. Figure 3.3 provides an overview framework for the establishment of a structure for design teams within fairly large projects. It identifies four types of teams of personnel involved in systems design.

Normal management procedures

All organizations will have normal management procedures. Commercial organizations will have a board of directors and public sector organizations will have equivalent structures. A UK university will, for example, have a board of governors. In addition senior managers will meet with each other on a regular basis in order to successfully run the concern. There may well be other fixed structures such as trades union negotiating bodies. All these structures will be involved to some extent in the development of large and/or strategic information systems. While senior managers and directors may need

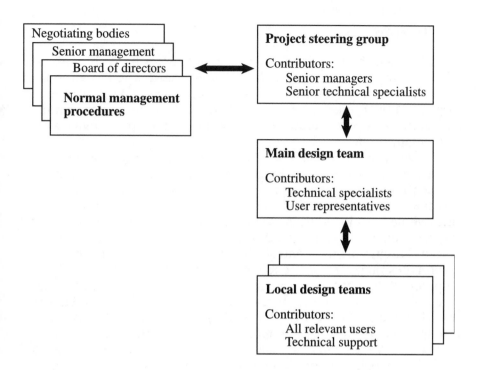

FIGURE 3.3   *A framework for structuring design teams (*source: Eason, K. (1988), *Information Technology and Organisational Change,* Taylor and Francis, London)

to give approval for the release of funds for large scale projects, the overall management of the project itself will often be delegated to a project steering group (PSG).

Project steering groups

The PSG should meet regularly to co-ordinate the project. Although reporting to senior normal management structures the PSG would be charged with the successful management of the project. The detailed work, however, will be undertaken by others. We are now moving to the domain of design itself. The framework provides for two types of design team. It includes a two-tier structure with the main design team delegating an amount of work to local design teams which should focus on specific aspects of the design. The amount of delegation will vary from one project to another and will be determined by specific issues such as the amount of time the organization is willing to devote to user participation.

Design teams

It is through these design structures that users will be able to make their contribution to design. In a highly user-centred environment there will be a range of local design teams each looking at different aspects of the project, each being determined by the specific nature of the activity to be computerized or by location of the activity within the organization.

As we have stated the main design team will aim to delegate much of the work to the local design teams. The main design team can concentrate on policy issues which are common across the organization (overall socio-technical strategy) and on co-ordination of the whole development process. Local design teams can manage aspects related to specific activities. As such they will be able to specify requirements, control the development and evaluation of prototypes, make recommendations for job design and training and support. Note that these local design teams are user-led. The technical specialist provides support to the users. We do not, however, have full user-led design (level 3 of the model) as the work of local design groups is constrained by the main design team which is in itself under the control of the PSG. A design team structure such as this enables effective involvement of a wide variety of users from senior managers (on the PSG) to end users (involved in local design teams) within a constrained environment.

User roles

The role of the user will vary greatly between the various elements of the structure. Representatives on the PSG may be required to attend a weekly two-hour meeting while those involved in the main design team may be required to spend at least half their time working with the designers. In many cases their contribution may require a full-time secondment to the project. Clearly such people will need to be carefully selected and trained for their new role. There is evidence to suggest that a significant proportion of such users never return to their original job, preferring, or being persuaded, to stay on in a support capacity within the IT/IS department.

3.5.2   Acadmin: establishing design teams

We will now explore the user involvement in design teams by looking again at the Acadmin system. When the system was initially being developed it was necessary to decide how best to involve users across the institution in the design process. As we are aware the first step was to perform a user analysis from which the user groups shown in Table 3.1 were identified.

A proposal for the establishment of a design team structure for the Acadmin system is presented in Fig. 3.4.

The following points are of note:

- A variety of permanent structures exist (governing body, academic board, etc.)
- The project steering group has fairly wide representation
- The design team itself has only two user representatives
- Representative members of the design team will need careful selection and training
- The main design team is balanced by the local design teams which focus on the needs of the various stakeholders in the system

3.5.3 Project management

A crisis in the management of software was identified at a NATO conference as far back as 1968. In many ways the problem is still with us and the industry is still trying to grapple with problems such as the failure to meet delivery times and exceeding budget. There remains, in the late 1990s, as there was in the late 1960s, a pressing need for the industry to continue to improve the productivity, quality and delivery of its products. Since the 1960s the management of software development has, however, matured considerably, boosted by the many developments within the discipline of software engineering. A detailed coverage of the management of software engineering projects is outside the remit of this book. Those interested will find plenty of information on the following topics in a range of software engineering texts:

TABLE 3.1 *Acadmin user groups*

User	Role within the system
Professional user	Running the computerized system. Includes computer manager and systems administrative staff
Manager user	Directorate, heads of department, registrar and similar personnel requiring to use the system for statistical information
Lecturer	Teaching on, or running a course and needing access to student results, etc.
Student	Attending a module and needing to register, obtain grades, etc.

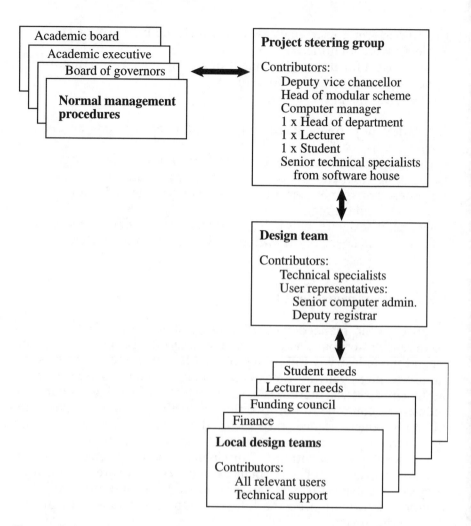

FIGURE 3.4   *Acadmin—a framework for structuring design teams*

- Project planning
- Project scheduling
- Project cost estimation
- Project risk management

While project teams who make use of these techniques are better able to control projects, with a greater degree of predictability and reliability, their use may well affect the potential for user involvement. Rigorous adherence to previously determined project scheduling decisions (for example as specified in PERT charts) may negate against effective evolutionary design in general, and prototype evaluation and modification in particular.

3.6   Processes

Processes for design include any activity in which users might be involved and focus around the design methodology adopted and include issues relating to:

- Choice (or lack of choice) of design methodology
- Methods used to elicit requirements
- Task analysis methods
- Communication and specification methods
- Human–computer interaction
- Approaches to prototyping
- Systems implementation methods

There is now an extremely large number of design methodologies available to the systems designer. Design methods are, however, not the only processes which go on during the analysis, design and implementation of information systems. In addition a range of human-factor tools and methods are available to *top-up* the design method at various stages in the life cycle. Some of these methods, such as task analysis will be discussed in detail in the later chapters. Strategies for systems implementation are also important.

There is therefore an enormous number of processes which the information systems designer can adopt. Some of these are technically-oriented while some are user-oriented. The choice of processes adopted will affect how the users are able to contribute to the design process; to overall user-centredness. We will now introduce some of these processes in more detail while remembering that a number are also addressed elsewhere in this book.

3.6.1   Choice (or lack of choice) of design methodology

It was noted at a conference on software quality management during 1995 that over 2000 methods were available. An alphabetical list of some of the most widely known and/or adopted (not necessarily the same thing) methods would include:

- ETHICS
- Information engineering
- Jackson structured design

- MERISE
- Multiview
- Object oriented design
- Prototyping methods
- Rapid application development (RAD)
- Soft systems methodology (SSM)
- Structured systems analysis and design (SSADM)
- Yourdon

With over 2000 methods to chose from how can the systems designer be sure of choosing appropriately? Hornby *et al.* (1992) cite case study evidence to support the proposal that the following factors contribute to systems failure:

- Lack of guiding organizational and business strategies as opposed to technical strategies
- Lack of end-user participation and 'ownership' of systems
- Lack of organizational resources and support concerning 'soft' requirements
- Lack of attention to organizational issues such as organization design, organizational culture and management style
- Lack of attention to psychological issues such as the design of jobs, the allocation of systems tasks and the usability of the system

When reviewing the applicability of system design methods to a user-centred approach it will be useful, therefore, to address how far the methods are task/technical, business/organization or human/user oriented, and to identify whether, and in which ways, the processes within the methods address the following issues:

- Business strategy
- Elicitation and specification of user requirements
- Task analysis, design and allocation
- Organization and job design
- Applicability to prototyping
- User interface design

It is not our purpose here to undertake a detailed comparison of specific design methods. It is clear, however, that structured methods such as JSD and SSADM do not address all the issues above. Floyd (1986) when commenting on JSD states that

> ...development stages (are) strongly connected; results from one stage are taken over unchanged to the next stage and elaborated there

She further suggests that all such methods are:

> essentially based upon a linear view of software development; for an evolutionary approach we need new methods.

It is useful to make reference to a project involving researchers with a social science background and industrial partners in the computer industry. In the project Hornby *et al.* (1992) set out to describe how existing systems analysis and design methodologies address human and organizational issues by specifically looking at technical, usability, economic and behavioural issues in large office-based systems. Fifteen methods and tools were chosen including SSADM, Yourdon, ETHICS, and live prototyping. Some of the findings are listed below:

- Most analysts use some form of mainstream method—the choice is often influenced by the employing organization.
- Methodologies are applied flexibly— the approach is related to the experience of the analyst.
- Coverage of human/organizational issues are patchy in mainstream technical methods.
- Methods which explicitly cover human/organization issues are very much in the minority.
- No method covers the whole life cycle or both content (what to do) and process (how to do it) issues.
- Gaps in methods are mainly in early phases of the life cycle (concerning business strategy) and late phases (concerning implementation).
- End users have difficulty understanding the method unless specifically designed to be understood by them.

While the Hornby survey did not include Checkland's soft systems methodology (SSM) or Martin's information engineering approach, it is clear that both these approaches would appear to offer an improvement in relation to human/organizational issues. SSM, for example, being neither primarily technically oriented nor solely 'human factor' oriented, but being a means of treating the two together, is a candidate for enriching structured systems development.

Although there is some disagreement within the academic community about the compatibility of the 'hard' and 'soft' approaches, attempts to incorporate human-factor issues into systems design methods are being made by a number of researchers. Silcock *et al.* (1990), for example, describe a method called JSD* which is composed of two parallel design strands representing both human factors and software engineering: JSD* (HF) and JSD* (SE). The approach is to address human-factor concerns during software development.

Structured design methods can be described as a 'cook book' method where clear instructions are provided as a recipe for analysis and design. An alternative approach is that of the 'tool set' approach which allows the designer to 'dip in' and apply a variety of methods and tools as he or she deems appropriate to the problem. Such a tool kit, known as HUFIT PAS (Human Factors in IT— Planning and Specification) has been developed at the HUSAT Research Centre at Loughborough University of Technology (Galer *et al.*, 1989).

3.6.2   Methods used to elicit requirements

The user-centredness of methods that are used to elicit requirements will be determined by two factors: the *types(s) of approaches* used and the *range of users* involved. We have seen how user study methods can vary from very participative methods, such as focus groups, through to the highly 'hands off' approach of document collection. The extent to which all users (managers/end users, direct/indirect users, etc.) are consulted during the requirements definition stage of the life cycle needs to be considered.

The way in which all user views and needs (physical, aspirational as well as functional) are ascertained will be a major factor in determining the user-centredness of the development process, and the quality (effectiveness, efficiency and satisfaction) within the end product.

3.6.3   Task analysis methods

Task analysis methods can be used within the arena of human–computer interaction for evaluating human activity systems and for producing detailed requirement specifications. Task analysis methods are used to attempt to gather and/or describe what the human user is required to do and how he or she processes information to achieve goals. Although such methods are not new, there is to date not much evidence of their take up in commercial environments. Specialists in task analysis tend to be found in academia. A good user-centred design process will, it is suggested, make some attempt at task analysis.

3.6.4   Communication and specification methods

The choice to adopt a design methodology will have a considerable effect on the way in which the design team communicate and specify its design options, both within the design team (hopefully with user representation) and to the wider user community. Readers who have studied systems and analysis methods will know of a variety of techniques:

- Data flow diagrams (DFD)
- Flow diagrams
- Entity–relationship diagrams
- Entity life histories
- Formal methods (state based)
- Natural language

In our study we are particularly concerned with user communication and need to address the issues of accessibility: can the user understand the technique being presented and make an effective contribution? Clearly the methods will vary in their inherent user-centredness. Not many lay users when presented with a mathematical schema written in the Formal Method Z will make much of it. Even more simple approaches, such as DFDs will involve considerable user training. As Floyd (1986) states:

> viewing the world in terms of actions and entities is artificial ..... lay users have serious problems coping with this abstract way of thinking.

3.6.5 Interface design methods

In recent years there has been a massive change in the style of human–computer interfaces. With the reduction in price of high capacity processing power, and the spread of high resolution graphics display terminals, the graphical user interface (GUI) is becoming a standard. While it is likely that a GUI will result in a more usable product (easy to learn, intuitive, etc.) this is in no way guaranteed. It is just as easy (possibly even easier) to design a poor GUI as a bad character-based interface. The skill is in the design. We will see in Chapters 6 and 7 how a range of processes such as usability engineering, the adoption of design rules and guidelines, the use of design rationale techniques and the systematic evaluation of the developing product can enhance usability.

3.6.6 Approaches to prototyping

The introduction of 4GL and rapid prototyping environments has promoted a great increase in the use of prototyping as a tool for the systems designer. Prototyping has been defined (Crinnon, 1989) as:

> building a physical working model of all or part of the proposed system, and using it to identify weaknesses in the understanding of the real requirements

It is necessary to consider what it is that is being prototyped. Computer-based tools make the prototyping of screens and dialogues relatively simple, while evolutionary prototypes might involve prototyping the full functionality. It is not only possible to prototype the technical (computer) system but also the social (organizational) system.

Various attempts have been made to produce a mechanism for integrating prototyping within a structured design method. Eason (1988) proposes an evolutionary design model to support a socio-technical implementation of prototyping. The use of prototyping in itself does not imply a user-centred approach. Lim *et al.* (1992) cite a case study where considerable effort was spent in developing a detailed prototype during which there was little user involvement. They also state that reports indicate that prototype evaluation and modification are often undertaken exclusively by experts. Furthermore prototyping can be an actual hindrance to user-centredness. Computer-based tools can, for example, introduce design constraints from project inception and can tend to defer human-factor considerations.

User-centred prototyping will involve both social and technical system prototyping, hands-on experience by end users as subjects in appropriate task scenarios, and an evaluation methodology the results of which can lead to prototype modification.

3.6.7   Systems implementation strategies

Implementation strategies are the methods by which systems changeover is managed. The new system is introduced into the organization and the previous system is replaced. These are further examples of processes which affect the user. A variety of methods exists. Eason (1988) provides a list of strategies in which the user adaptation necessary to complement the strategy decreases from the first method to the last:

- Greenfield site
- Big bang
- Parallel run
- Phased introduction
- Trails and dissemination
- Incremental evolution

A variety of criteria can be identified which can help the design team decide on the most appropriate strategy. The degree in which the new system involves major organizational change is the criterion which will have greatest effect on the user. Implementation strategies which involve trials/dissemination and evolution are likely to minimize user concerns. In many systems, however, other criteria may outweigh user needs in terms of implementation and require other strategies to be adopted. An example of such a situation is that of *critical mass* systems in which the nature of the problem requires an 'all or nothing' approach. It was because of this that the London stock-market system was implemented using a big bang approach even though other factors would have implied other methods.

3.7   Scope

We will now briefly remind ourselves of the third category of user-centred design which will be covered in Chapter 5 which addresses the social system and design for organizational acceptibility.

The *scope* of the design process relates to how far the analysis reflects a socio-technical, as opposed to just a technical, solution. More specifically an IT project with only a narrow scope will focus on technical and functional requirements whereas one with a wider scope will address issues such as the allocation of function between man and machine, the design of work structures and individual jobs and ways of enhancing job satisfaction within the organization.

3.8   The three concepts of UCD revisited

The three categories of *structures, processes and scope* have been used to explore approaches to user-centredness. To be fully user-centred a development process would need to exhibit a positive approach under each category. It is not sensible, for example, to set up well-designed team structures with extensive user representation if the users are unable to contribute to the processes which are adopted. It is also not possible to aim for a wide scope in design without establishing effective structures for representation, or without adopting processes

TABLE 3.2   *Categories of UCD*

Structures	Processes	Scope
Design team structures	Design methodology	Organization design
Project management	Prototyping	Job design
	Task analysis	Task allocation
	HCI methods	Job satisfaction
	User communication	
	System specification	
	Implementation strategies	

which will address social issues. Table 3.2 provides a summary of the three categories and their constituent elements.

3.9   Current practice in the UK

A number of IS projects have recently come to national UK attention supporting the assertion that some information systems would still appear to be failing because of a lack of effective user engagement. Classe (1995), on the other hand, writing in the weekly UK *Computing* magazine says that:

> companies are slowly beginning to recognise that early and sustained input by end users typically delivers better systems

The question we need to answer therefore is to what extent, and in which ways, genuine *user-centred design* principles have been integrated into mainstream commercial IS design. We will now look at what current evidence there is of the adoption of user-centred design techniques by IS practitioners and within user organizations. We will start by looking at two specific case studies and then move to more general survey evidence.

3.9.1   Case study in a UK bank

Hornby and Clegg (1992) describe a case study looking at the processes of participation during the design and implementation of a new computer-based information system at a large UK bank. The essential finding was that although user project managers claimed they were committed to the goal of effective user participation, the end-user's view was rather different. Hornby and Clegg tried to relate the results to two previous areas of research relating to participation and organizations.

1. Wall and Lischeron's (1977) framework for participation which consists of three interrelated elements:

   - The type and level of *interaction*
   - The flows of *information* that takes place between the participants
   - The nature and extent of the *influence* of one party over the other

2. Gowler and Legge's (1978, 1979) proposals on organizational context which places organizations within a two-dimensional matrix. One axis relates to organizational structure (mechanistic vs. organic) and the other to organizational process (stable vs. unstable)

Hornby and Clegg were able to substantiate the bank's approach to participation within the above framework. They conclude that it is possible to develop a much more sophisticated and differentiated view of participation compared to that achieved by the majority of information systems developers.

3.9.2 A further case study

Wroe (1995) describes how a user-centred team, called the Usability Services Group, has been set up within another UK bank in order to support the user-centred development of applications and systems. The group's aims are:

> ensure that customers and staff are able to work efficiently and effectively and with a high degree of satisfaction with the technology on which the bank depends

In pursuit of this goal the team works closely with the bank's central group IT department:

> and the rest of the business throughout the life of a project to raise the profile of usability issues, and to encourage users to be at the centre of the design process

The support provided by bank's Usability Services Group includes:

- Consultancy on user interface design and ergonomics to ensure that usability is a design driver
- Focus groups to generate views on design issues and get feedback on developments
- Workshops for context meetings and focus groups
- User interface evaluations to assess usability during design and development
- Evaluation of work patterns
- Post-implementation user questionnaires

Wroe states that by adopting this approach project teams can:

> deliver systems and applications which have been developed in a totally user-centred way and hence deliver real business benefit in the future.

We can try to analyse the approach adopted by Usability Services Group under the three categories of structures, processes and scope. Even without a detailed examination and just from the information provided above, Table 3.3 provides plenty of evidence supporting a user-centred design approach.

TABLE 3.3   *A user-centred design approach*

Structures	Processes	Scope
User focus groups	Interface evaluations	Work pattern evaluation
Usability services group	Usability engineering	
Group IT	Post-implementation questionnaires	

It seems likely that the establishment of a human-factors unit with a specific group of personnel possessing human-factor expertise and having the remit to promote UCD within the organization will result in positive developments. Not all organizations will have the resources to be able to do this. What generic evidence do we have of UCD throughout the profession?

3.9.3   Butler Cox Productivity Enhancement Programme

An interesting piece of work can be found in the Butler Cox Foundation (now CSC Index) Productivity Enhancement Programme (PEP). Butler Cox conduct regular surveys of sponsoring organizations in a range of IT topics. While the details of this are only available to sponsors of the foundation, two sources of information are within the public domain.

Lodge (1989) describes the result of telephone survey of 20 PEP subscribers to elicit their views on user-led design. Only 25 per cent believed that user involvement led to more cost-effective *development* and 20 per cent believed that it led to more cost-effective *use* of systems. While all informants saw it as a means of ensuring a close fit between business requirements and the end product, Lodge suggests that user-centred design will not be fully accepted until financial cost-effective benefits are established within the minds of systems designers.

As part of the Productivity Enhancement Programme Butler Cox have undertaken research to ascertain how organizations successfully involve users in systems development projects. Green (1992) reveals that 98 per cent of organizations 'consider the *involvement* of users to be an important aspect of their development practice' and that over 70 per cent claim to 'use methods that support user involvement', but that under 20 per cent support 'active' involvement. It is not clear, from the public domain material, which criteria Butler Cox use to determine whether involvement is active, but it would seem that concerns are more oriented towards *structures* as opposed to *processes* supporting user involvement.

3.10   A survey of user-centred design

In order to find out more about the adoption of user-centred practices the author has conducted a major survey of UK commercial user organizations (Smith, 1993). Further work has been published (Smith and Dunckley, 1995). As a result it was possible to identify which particular aspects of UCD are being adopted at a faster rate than others and to ascertain a number of factors which influence the degree of user-centredness in both UK organizations and IT projects.

3.10.1   Survey method

Although it would be possible to approach a number of interested parties within the systems development arena (end users themselves, user department management, user organization IT managers, analysts/designers) it was decided to focus on the individual within commercial user organizations who has the overall responsibility for the introduction of information systems. In choosing just one group of personnel within the development process it was accepted that results may not produce a fully representative picture of what is actually happening on the ground. It is possible, for example as shown by Hornby, that their views may not accord with that of the end users themselves.

The survey itself was organized in two stages. First a postal survey was distributed to a sample of UK companies. One-fifth took part in telephone 'follow-ups' which were conducted both to validate individual postal questionnaires and to substantiate conclusions drawn. The postal survey instrument was organized under broad topics (design method, project management, user requirements, prototyping, organizational issues) with individual questions within categories mapping to the concepts of UCD (structures, processes and scope). By scoring answers to individual questions within concepts it was possible to undertake a detailed exploration of the current state of play of UCD within UK industry.

3.10.2   Results— structures, processes and scope

The overall results obtained for each of the three UCD concepts (structures, processes and scope) suggests that there is far more movement towards the use of user-centred structures than towards a wider organizational scope in design.

Structures

Most progress towards user-centredness is being made within the area of structures to support the overall process. A large majority of organizations make attempts to support and involve the user. Over three-quarters involve end users, saying that projects are led by a partnership between users and designers. Structures are far more extensive at the organizational and formal representative level, rather than at the detailed local design level. The problems associated with further developing the use of user-oriented structures relate to the difficulty in recruiting appropriate, interested and skilled personnel who have the time available for project secondment.

Processes

While there is considerable evidence that traditional design methods still dominate the design process, the survey has shown that a wide variety of other methods, providing a range of user engagement, are in use. Structured methods are in use in approximately one-third of projects with one-fifth adopting SSADM. While information engineering, and soft systems are used in a significant number of organizations, there is no evidence of the take up of specific participative methodologies. While the shift to structured methods has come about mainly for reasons of efficiency and effectiveness within the design process it has also led to a significant increase in user involvement.

Emphasis within user requirements is given to high level issues (e.g. business mission and strategy) and less so to low level ones (e.g. task execution). There is evidence of some importance given to organizational issues (e.g. job design/work structures). While there is evidence of methods for task analysis and for the use of scenarios or dramas/storyboarding (tending to be a subset of those using task analysis), the majority use no formal method for eliciting or specifying requirements, relying exclusively on verbal interviews and natural language recording mechanisms. Traditional methods for user *communication* dominate.

Prototyping was found to be the most well-supported potential UCD topic. While the main reason for prototyping was to ensure system functionality, it is interesting to note that 38 per cent used prototyping for interface design and that 24 per cent say that prototyping was extended to the non-technical issues of work structures and processes.

Scope

Organizational issues is the area where the least progress is being made towards a user-centred approach. Although over 70 per cent cite partnership between users and designers to be important, only one-fifth are specifically able to integrate social and technical issues. There is evidence that designers are aware of the need to widen the scope of design but feel that organizational priorities and senior management policies negate against them making progress.

3.10.3   Comparative analyses

Self-standing and externally led projects

The sample was split into two subsets; those where all the IT expertise was provided from within the user organization and those where the IT expertise was primarily provided by an external consultancy. By performing separate analyses for the two subsets the results indicate that the use of external consultants has a negative effect on user-centredness. A number of reasons could be postulated. The result is probably not surprising. Lewis and Rieman (1993), when looking at user interaction give a quote from one software developer:

> Fortunately I don't have to worry about all this (user involvement). I work on contract stuff and all the requirements have been spelled out to me before I start.

Lewis and Rieman emphasize that it is one thing to meet the requirements and another thing to build a good system.

Company size

Results show that small companies would appear to be as likely to be user-centred in all aspects as large multinationals with medium-sized organizations lagging behind. Perhaps large organizations have the resources to support UCD while small ones find it inherently much easier.

Further evidence

There are a number of other possible underlying factors such as organizational policy, the individual skills and policies of the designer, type and size of the organization/project, and user attitudes. While at this stage it has not been possible to address all these issues an attempt has been made to further investigate the effects of the nature of both the organization and project.

Each of the participants within the sample was placed within one of three groups for organization type (manufacturing/production, service/retail, other) and one of five groups for project type (payroll/personnel, stock control, sales/order processing, finance/MIS, other).

From the subsequent analysis it would appear that organizations primarily providing a customer service, as opposed to manufacturing a product, tend to be more user-centred. This would seem to be quite an interesting result: organizations with direct access to the public (the real end user) tend to adopt a more user-centred approach to design. Is this because of a direct influence or due to some underlying factor?

The type of project might give us some further evidence. The results indicate that finance/MIS systems are more user-centred than sales/order processing (other figures were too small to draw conclusions). We may have an answer to the issue of company size and UCD. We might expect some relation between the two—but perhaps the dominant feature is that of project type and particularly project size. Finance/MIS systems are likely to be more complex than some other systems.

It could be postulated that the two issues of organization type and project type constitute some indicator of interactiveness: a service/retail company and a large cross-organization MIS system are likely to be more interactive. While it would not be surprising to find that interactive systems are more user-centred it is certainly quite a pleasing finding. Clearly further evidence is required here to substantiate and further develop this area of the work.

3.10.4   UCD—where are we now?

Clearly not all of the UK IT industry is approaching UCD in the same way or at the same pace. The survey would indicate that the state of play of UCD in UK industry can be summarized as follows:

Systems design and implementation is becoming more user-centred. This is occurring in part indirectly as a result of a shift towards structured methods such as SSADM. Systems designers have a commitment to user involvement which goes further than requirement elicitation. Blocks to the further development of UCD include management policy and styles, user skills and priorities together with a lack of resources. User-centred principles are not being adopted uniformly across the IT industry. First there is a disparity in the speed and depth of the adoption of the different aspects or concepts within UCD. While structures are increasingly common, and processes are developing, organizational issues are largely ignored. The second consideration influencing the uniformity of introduction relate to factors inherent in the specific company and project. A large number of influences are present but in particular it would appear that companies providing a customer service are more user-centred. Cross-organization projects also lead to more user-centredness. It seems likely that there is a relation between the interactiveness of the project and the degree of user involvement. A medium-sized sales order processing system, developed by an external consultancy and used by a limited number of VDU operators in a manufacturing company is likely to be less user-centred than an in-house flight booking system for an international airline. Overall approximately one-fifth of organizations/projects demonstrate a genuine practical user-centred approach.

An interesting issue is how approaches to UCD vary across the world. A number of factors will come into play. First different countries adopt different methods. While SSADM may be prevalent in some parts of the UK industry it will not be found elsewhere. MERISE and METRICA, for example, will be widely used in France and Spain, respectively. A second factor is likely to relate to cultural differences between countries.

3.11   Plumbest plc: setting up a design team structure

3.11.1   Tasks

Plumbest Task 3.1

In Chapter 2 we conducted an analysis of the users within Plumbest. The task now is to determine what design team structures should be created so that a fully effective socio-technical solution can be implemented. The following questions will need to be answered:

Steering committee or project manager?
- Who makes policy decisions, assesses progress, 'owns' the project and promotes it within the organization?
- How should the project relate to the existing management process and the industrial relations machinery in the organization?
- Who will represent the users?

Main design team
- Who is going to be involved in the design?
- Who will represent the users?

- Should they be full- or part-time and what training will they require for this role?
- How will the design team consult other users?

Local design teams
- Will there be any?
- What activities will they relate to?
- Who will be involved?

3.11.2 Solutions

Plumbest Solution 3.1

It is proposed that there should be a 'joint user-specialist' project design structure. We need to be aware that there are permanent management structures which will need to be considered:

- Board of directors
- Senior management board
- Union liaison committees

Project team structure A project steering group will be established (Table 3.4) which will report to the senior management board and co-ordinate the work of the main design team and through this local design teams.

TABLE 3.4 *Project team structure*

Project team structure	Role/responsibility
Project steering group	Overall responsibility for project management. Reporting to senior management board (SMB) the PSG will be responsible for implementing SMB decisions and liaising with trades unions.
Main design team	Responsible for detailed implementation of project and reporting to PSG the MDT will also co-ordinate local design teams.

Local design teams	Reporting to MDT the LDTs will communicate with all potential stakeholders and make detailed recommendations on activities.
	Three LDTs: Customer communications
	                Clerical procedures
	                Job delivery

Project steering group   Personnel selected for involvement in the various levels of the project team structure should be chosen upon the basis of their roles within the organization and upon their own individual qualities and experiences. One crucial element in the successful implementation of any new organizational system is the clear, positive and high-profile explanation of, and support for, the systems by senior management. Often it is useful to identify a system *champion*; someone in authority who can vigorously support the initiative. It seems clear that Jenny Birch, the operations manager, who already has a pet-plan should fulfil this role. Other members of the PSG will include Craig Onley, personnel director, who will need to determine how any new system might affect the organization and Keith Mathieson the finance director.

Main design team   Most of the detailed design work will be done by technical specialists from Usersoft. User involvement at the detailed level is, however, advisable. Representation at this level requires careful selection if users are to make an effective contribution. There are two potential candidates: both the service centre co-ordinator (Frances Dunckley) and one of the foremen (Ian Davies) could well fulfil this role. Selection will be quite sensitive here as each individual has opposing views and choice of either will give out clear messages to the rest of the company. A sensible compromise might be to ask both of them to join the main design team; and to hope that there will not be too many sparks flying. In order to be effective both Frances and

TABLE 3.5   *Membership of the PSG and the MDT*

Design group	Membership from Plumbest	Membership from Usersoft	Membership from unions
Project steering group	Operations director— Paul Monaco (Chair) Finance director— Keith Mathieson Personnel director— Craig Onley Operations manager— Jenny Birch	Programme director— yourself Project manager— Sunila Blake	Union representative
Main design team	Service centre co-ordinator— Frances Dunckley Foreman—Ian Davies	Programme director— yourself (Chair and providing link to PSG) Project manager Sunila Blake Team members	None

Ian will need to receive support. Particular importance will need to be given to training in the design methodologies Usersoft adopt. It seems probable at this stage that we might be looking at half time secondment to the project for each of them. Table 3.5 shows the membership of the PSG and MDT.

Local design teams   It is proposed to establish three local design teams as shown in Table 3.6.

It might be useful to extend membership on the LDTs so that there is some link between the groups for Plumbest staff. As detailed above such linkage would be provided by Usersoft personnel and the project steering group.

TABLE 3.6

Design team	Role	Membership from Plumbest	Membership from Usersoft
Customer communi- cations	To advise on a suitable interface between the new computer systems and the customer requiring a service.	Service centre co-ordinator— Frances Dunckley Service administrator— Jackie Lukes Radio operator— Alison Laird	Appropriate team members
Clerical procedures	To advise on systems to record and process clerical information within the service centre	Service centre co-ordinator— Frances Dunckley Service administrator— A N Other	Appropriate team members
Job completion	To advise on a suitable interface between the new computer system and the MOs as they carry out their daily tasks	Mobile operatives	Appropriate team members

Summary

In this chapter we have seen:

- Two alternative definitions of user-centred design
- That we can define three levels of user-centredness:
  - technical-centred design
  - joint user-specialist design
  - user-led design

- How design team structures can be established to support and involve the user
- That user-centredness can be analysed by three categories:
  - structures
  - processes
  - scope
- How design methodologies can be assessed for user involvement
- Current practice relating to user-centred design in the UK

Questions

3.1 'Organizations and computers exist to serve human needs. Humans do not exist to serve organizational or computer needs' (Vaske and Grantham, 1990). How can a user-centred design process address these essential issues?

3.2 User-centred design can only be successful if a range of individuals are able to work in effective partnership. What possible obstacles might there be to such a partnership? Consider individual and organizational issues which may be significant.

The following **research tasks** can be undertaken individually or as a group project:

Identify an information system which has been recently been implemented and for which you are able to interview a number of participants to the process; both users and developers.

3.3 To what extent did the IS developers attempt a user-centred approach?

3.4 Do the users have the same view of the approach as the developers?

3.5 Is there agreement between users and developers that a user-centred approach produces more successful systems?

References

Classe, A. (1995), 'Sink or swim', *Computing*, 30 November 1995.

Crinnon, J. (1989), 'A role for prototyping in information systems design methodologies', *Design Studies*, 10(3), 144–150.

Eason, K. (1988), *Information Technology and Organisational Change*, Taylor and Francis, London.

Floyd, C. (1986), 'A comparative evaluation of system design methodologies', in T. W. Olle *et al.* (eds), *Information Systems Design Methodologies: Improving the Practice*, North-Holland, Amsterdam.

Galer, M., Taylor, B. *et al.* (1989), 'The HUFIT toolset. Human factors in IT', in *Contemporary Ergonomics, Proceedings of the Ergonomics Society's 1989 Annual Conference*, Taylor and Francis, London.

Gowler, D. and Legge, K. (1978), 'Participation in context: towards a synthesis of the theory and practice of organisational change, Part I', *Journal of Management Studies*, 15, 150–175.

Gowler, D. and Legge, K. (1979), 'Participation in context: towards a synthesis of the theory and practice of organisational change, Part II', *Journal of Management Studies*, 16, 139–170.

Green, P. (1992), 'Encouraging user involvement', *Software Management*, 29, 10–11.

Hornby, P. and Clegg, C. W. (1992), 'User participation in context: a case study in a UK bank', *Behaviour and IT*, 11(5), 293–307.

Hornby, P., Clegg C. W., Robson, J. I., Maclaren, C., Richardson, S. C. S. and O'Brien, P. (1992), 'Human and organisational issues in information systems development', *Behaviour and IT*, 11(3), 160–174.

Kappelman, L. *et al.* (1994), 'User engagement in the development, implementation and use of information technology', in *Proceedings of the 27th Annual Hawaii International Conference on Systems Science*.

Lewis, C. and Rieman, J. (1993), 'Task-centred user interface design, a practical introduction', published on the Internet.

Lim, K. Y. and Long, J. B. (1992), 'Pitfalls of rapid prototyping: observations on a commercial systems development project', in *Contemporary Ergonomics, Proceedings of the Ergonomics Society's 1992 Annual Conference*, Taylor and Francis, London.

Lodge, L. (1989), 'A user led model of systems development', in K. Knight (ed.) *Participation in Systems Development: UNICOM Applied IT Reports*, Kogan Page, London.

McCue, G. M. (1978), 'IBM's Santa Teresa Laboratory— architectural design for program development', *IBM Systems Journal*, 17(1), 4–25.

Mumford, E. (1983), 'Participative systems design: practice and theory', *Journal of Occupational Behaviour*, 4, 47–57.

Raynor, R. J. and Speckman, L. D. (1983), 'Maintaining user participation throughout the systems development cycle', in *Proceeding of AFIPS*, 1983 National Computer Conference, AFIPS Press, Arlington, Virginia, 173–180.

Silcock, N., Lim, K. Y. and Long, J. B. (1990), 'Requirements and suggestions for a structured analysis and design (human factors) method to support the integration of human factors with systems development', in *Contemporary Ergonomics, Proceedings of the Ergonomics Society's 1990 Annual Conference*, 425–430.

Simpson, I. (1992), 'Business and IT together', *Software Management*, 29, 16–17.

Smith, A. (1993), 'A Survey of User-Centred Design', M.Sc. Thesis, Interactive Computing Systems Design, Loughborough University of Technology.

Smith, A. and Dunckley, L. (1995), 'Human factors in software development', in K. Nordby *et al.* (eds), *Human–Computer interaction, Proceeding of INTERACT-95*, Chapman and Hall, London.

Vaske, J. J. and Grantham, C. E. (1990), *Socialising the Human Computer Environment*, Ablex, Norwood, New Jersey.

Wall, T. D. and Lischeron, J. A. (1977), *Worker Participation: a critique of the literature and some fresh evidence*, McGraw-Hill, London.

Wroe, B. (1995), *In Interfaces*, No 28, British HCI Group.

Further reading

Avison, D. E. and Fitzgerald, G. (1995*), Information Systems Development: methodologies, techniques and tools*, McGraw-Hill, London.

Eason, K. (1988), *Information Technology* and *Organisational Change*, Taylor and Francis, London.

Preece, J., Rogers, Y., Sharp, H., Benyon, D., Hillard, S. and Carey, T. (1994), *Human–Computer Interaction*, Prentice-Hall.

Chapter 4

	SSADM	SSM	RAD	ETHICS
Structures				
Processes				
Scope				

INFORMATION SYSTEMS DESIGN METHODS

with Lynne Dunckley

Chapter aims

This chapter attempts to review some of the key concepts and terms used to describe information systems design. Some of the most influential of today's design methodologies are then evaluated through their approach to the identification of user needs, to the attainment of usability in the end product. Specifically through study of this chapter the reader should be able to:

- Appreciate the inherent socio-technical requirements of information systems
- Identify the different approaches taken by methodologies
- Outline the activities involved in a number of methodologies
- Evaluate the role of the user in different design methods
- Compare methodologies in their approach to usability criteria
- Select a methodology to meet specific user and system needs

4.1 Socio-technical systems theory: the foundation for human–computer factor design

Although in this section of our study we will seek to review a wide range of approaches to information systems design there is one salient point that we must emphasize at the outset. It is an issue which the reader by now may see as obvious, but it is one that is too often ignored in practice: *human–computer systems are socio-technical systems*. We have examined Land's four classes of information systems (Chapter 1). Three of these involve systems where the interaction with the environment is sufficient to produce changing requirements needing flexibility and adaptability of response. In addition Ackoff and Emery (1972) have established that what particularly distinguishes socio-technical systems is not the different *proportions* of human and technical components, but the inherent *nature* of the human component: people have the ability to alter their own objectives to be purposeful and change requirements from within the system.

We have seen how many of the reasons why information systems fail to achieve the necessary improvements relate to the inherent socio-technical nature of the system in question and to the often only marginal importance given to this fact by systems designers. An effective socio-technical system (STS) is one in which the technical nature of the solution (hardware and software) is in balance with the social system (people and procedures) in which it operates. It is not possible to separate the technical nature of the IT system from the organization into which it is to be introduced, or from the users who are going to operate it. The socio-technical approach provides the foundation for our study in human–computer factors and we will therefore emphasize the nature of such systems before proceeding with a comprehensive generic review of approaches to information systems design.

4.1.1   Case studies in socio-technical systems theory

There are a number of well-known case studies that have supported the development of socio-technical systems theory. Perhaps the most well known is a study undertaken by Rice (1958) working from the Tavistock Institute in London. The Ahmedabad textile mills in India had introduced new semi-automatic looms into the weaving mill. Unfortunately, rather than achieving the predicted increase in efficiency, the new looms actually led to a reduction in both quality and output. Rice performed an organizational analysis and determined that the workers at the mill had a high degree of task specialization, with 12 different job roles, within a complicated reporting structure. As a result of Rice's work a new organizational structure was introduced which involved fewer job roles and a much greater emphasis on team working. Only after embedding the new social system was the mill able to meet required quality and output targets.

4.1.2   Principle of co-optimization

The lessons from the Ahmedabad textile mill should be learned by everyone who is attempting to introduce a new technical system into an organization: *without addressing the social system at the **same time**, required benefits may not be achieved.* In the case of information systems the technical system (hardware, software, etc.) may not deliver success unless the social system (organization hierarchy, job titles, job functions, etc.) is developed in parallel and operates in synergy with it. Emery and Trist (1969) refer to the principle of *co-optimization* between the social system and the technical system that both support the primary transformation from input to output within social-technical systems theory (Fig. 4.1).

One fundamental criterion that we should use for the selection of an overall approach to information systems design is the degree to which it addresses this basic foundation of design.

4.2   The need for methodologies

Design methodologies have been developed in order to address the weaknesses within traditional approaches. As a result of their introduction both the process of development, and the results from development, should be enhanced. By introducing a high degree of commonality, or standardization, the process of design can be streamlined. Communication is also easier: both within the design team (between systems analysts, business analysts and software developers) and between the design team and the user community. It has been claimed that information systems developed through the application of a variety of design methodologies, meet business objectives, are functionally correct, reliable, robust, usable, acceptable, easy to maintain and lead to increased job satisfaction for end users. Development will also take place at an acceptable rate and be delivered on time. Not all methods claim to generate all results. The trick is choosing the best method, or methods, for any particular problem.

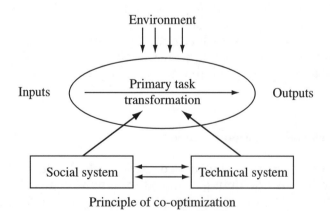

FIGURE 4.1   *Socio-technical systems theory*

In many cases a methodology has a series of *phases* that, taken together, cover all or part of the systems development life cycle. Often methodologies break each phase into a number of stages. During the method the systems analyst is expected to use a range of clearly specified tools and techniques, in a specified order, so that a degree of rigour is brought to what is much more of an engineering problem. Some researchers, taking an alternative view, say that rather than adopting a set method, a 'tool set' approach is more appropriate. Here the developer will select a number of tools and techniques from a variety of methods and apply them to the best advantage of the particular problem at hand.

4.2.1   Traditional systems design

Avison and Fitzgerald (1995) cite the following examples of the weakness of the traditional systems development life cycle approach that we introduced in Chapter 1:

- Failure to meet the full needs of management
- Unambitious systems design process
- Instability in the solution
- Inflexibility in the final product
- User dissatisfaction
- Problems with documentation
- Lack of control
- Incomplete systems
- The development of an applications backlog
- Maintenance workload

Having considered some basic human-factor elements, we can note that user dissatisfaction often arises from the failure systematically to address:

- User needs
- Usability criteria

One of the main problems of the early systems development approach was that it was largely *process*-based. The whole thrust was to replace one set of, often manually-based, business processes, such as payroll or stock control, by another computerized set. The focus on current processes yielded a number of problems. Information technology can offer much more than the computerization of *operational* processes. The strategic and tactical needs of management (e.g. for new and enhanced management information systems) will not emerge through an operational process-based approach.

Processes within an organization are subject to change, and therefore process-driven methods are likely to lead to unstable and inflexible solutions.

We have already been introduced to a number of design methodologies when investigating the *processes* implemented during user-centred design (Chapter 3). Here we will look at a number of these methods in more detail. Our focus, however, remains a human-factor one: a study in users and information systems. Our aim is not to analyse all the methods in detail. The interested reader will be able to locate elsewhere a vast array of texts supporting systems analysis and design. In this chapter we will attempt a human-factor review of a variety of methods and place particular emphasis on those methods that focus on the user's interaction with the information system.

4.2.2   Information systems design: concepts and terms

The literature on the subject of the development and practice of IS methodologies can often be very confusing and often does not even agree a definition of key terms. The reader of texts on information systems development will soon discover a confusing variety of use of the terms method, methodology and process model. In order to clarify the issues we will begin by setting out a series of definitions that are adapted from those put forward by Schach (1993) and by Wynekoop and Russo (1995) on which we will subsequently expand through examples and discussion.

- *Methodology*, which is *a collection of procedures, techniques, tools and documentation linked by a philosophical view of the system* and in which we can distinguish between:
    - *software methodology*, which is *a systematic approach to conducting at least one phase of software production* and is concerned with software, analysis, design and implementation and which is a subset of:
    - *system methodology*, which is *concerned with the system itself, the procedures, people and organizational structures as well as possibly including software development.*
- *Technique*, which is *a collection of specific steps for conducting a portion of a phase of software production or systems analysis* and includes examples such as task analysis and top-down design.
- *Tool*, which is *a means of supporting the design and development process*, for example CASE tools, data dictionaries and 4GLs.
- *Process model*, which is another key concept *providing a framework in which methodologies are defined through their use* and can be taken as representative of the sequence of stages through which a software product or information system evolves; the earliest process

model to be identified was the systems development life cycle or waterfall process model.

When the development process largely follows the waterfall model of software development each stage is completed before the subsequent stage is started. More recently several different process models have been proposed and some of these are briefly described later. Some methodologies prescribe, or imply, the adoption of a particular process model while others allow the developer considerable freedom of choice.

In this chapter when we use the term information system *design method* we mean to cover a development process that incorporates a methodology and a specified process model. To summarize, we suggest:

IS design method = Methodology + Process model

Prototyping is a term that is confusingly used in systems development texts to describe two different things. When used as part of an evolutionary development approach, with the prototype eventually becoming the working system, then by our definitions prototyping is a *process model*. However, if user interfaces are prototyped within a methodology then it can be considered to be a requirements or specification technique. To reduce this confusion we will use the term *prototyping process model* (PPM) for the former and *prototyping* alone for the latter.

4.3   Underpinning concepts

4.3.1   Philosophical approaches to methodology

Methodologies each have a different philosophical, or epistemological, basis underpinning their approach. This philosophical basis is normally rooted in the nature of the information system which the methodology attempts to address. Some place the emphasis on *strategic business planning* and attempt to ensure that strategic objectives of the organization are supported by the information systems that are implemented. Others focus more on the technical, or *hard*, nature of the problem, while others recognize the fundamental *soft* nature of many systems. In our study of users and information systems we will be particularly interested in design methods which attempt either a socio-technical (as opposed to merely technical) or a soft (in contrast to a hard) approach to design

Before we can consider the methodologies themselves in more detail we need to understand the underlying philosophy and in particular how changes in the philosophical approach has led to changes in the ways in which methodologies have been developed. The earliest methodologies were considered to follow the *scientific method* of investigation that can be summarized as consisting of six stages as shown in Fig. 4.2. This method has been described as a *reductionist* approach as there was a focus on splitting up the system during analysis by studying individual components in detail. Quantified techniques were extensively used to optimize the output. However, many systems designed prior to 1970 were sub-optimal in that the system approach was not adopted but rather independent systems were designed for interdependent activities.

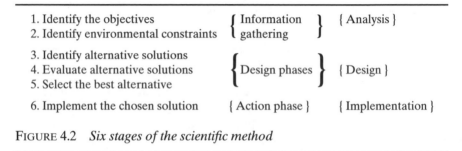

FIGURE 4.2   *Six stages of the scientific method*

From the 1970s onwards, following the development of the database concept, a systems approach was widely adopted which placed emphasis on the data in the system, as the structure of the data was considered to be much less likely to change than the processes which accessed it. The scientific paradigm as described above was still used, but there was an emphasis on the systems approach and synergy. The emphasis on quantified techniques continued and there were aspirations for analysts to be objective through techniques such as data analysis. This period is typified by the development of structured methodologies such as Yourdon and MERISE.

In the early 1980s Checkland intervened by proposing *soft systems thinking* and introduced the concepts of human activity systems and multi-perspectives. He considered that human activity systems needed a different approach to investigation than that used for the natural world or physical design systems. This is because human beings interpret and place meanings upon their sensations of the world that have to be included in both the investigation and analysis of the system. There followed a number of methodologies that focused on user participation and stakeholder concepts.

In the 1990s there have been attempts to develop methodologies that combine both philosophies, although to what extent these have been successful is still a matter of debate. From the outlines above it should be clear that the philosophy underpinning a methodology can have significant practical effects. We will therefore consider the nature of these different philosophical approaches in greater detail.

Lewis (1994) describes the intellectual framework in which the methodology operates in terms of three main concepts that he describes in technical terms as follows:

- *Ontological assumptions,* these are the beliefs about the nature of the objects in the real world.
- *Epistemological assumptions,* about the identification of knowledge and how the world can be investigated.
- *Ethical values,* which constrain the way the system can be investigated.

We will look at each of these in turn, but first we need to reconsider the scientific method and its significance for systems analysis. One of the problems is to agree what is meant by the scientific approach. Schrödinger, one of this century's most influential scientists, identified the scientific method (1954) as inherited from the Greeks, particularly Democritus, as being based on two general principles:

- *The principle of the understandability of nature,* linked to ideas of cause and effect.
- *The principle of objectivity,* the fact that science aims to make true and adequate statements about its objects and about hypothesis concerning the real world.

In order to be *objective* the scientific investigator is required to *become an onlooker who does not belong* to the world, which by this procedure becomes an objective world. A systems analyst adopting this philosophy would seek objectivity by adopting an onlooker approach to the investigation. However, Democritus' view of the scientific method has been undermined in two ways:

1. Since the second half of the nineteenth century scientists started to use the term *model* for conceptual constructs in recognition that they were not dealing with the real world itself.
2. All our scientific knowledge rests entirely on our sense perceptions: we cannot make an observation about an object without getting in touch with it, and the object will then be affected by our interaction or intervention in the system.

These views are important because there has been an attempt to classify methodologies under the headings *subjectivism* and *objectivism.* Klein and Hirschheim (1987) distinguish between two extreme ontologies (beliefs about objects) which they term *realism* and *nominalism.* Realism assumes that there exists a common external reality with predetermined nature and structure that exists independently of any observer. Nominalism considers that reality is complex because it is observed, and that it cannot exist separated from the observer. For this reason they class the scientific, or hard systems, approach as objectivism. However, we have noted that this is a simplification of the scientific approach. In the same analysis Klein and Hirschheim classify two epistemologies (beliefs about how knowledge can be investigated) as *positivism* and *interpretism*. Positivism is characterized by a belief in causal relationships and general laws that can be investigated through rational action. This leads to an objectivist paradigm that assumes that real-world data structures exist independent of the data analysis and can therefore be identified and investigated. Interpretivism allows for no individual account to be correct since these cannot be proved against objective knowledge of reality.

The subjectivist paradigm claims the real world can only be interpreted through socially created and transmitted perceptions of the observer. This view of the world is related to the post-modernist philosophy concept that there is no absolute knowledge, only cultural relativity. By the end of this chapter we should have an idea as to strengths and weaknesses of the objectivist and subjectivist approach in relation to user-centred design.

4.3.2   Hard vs. soft systems theory

We have seen that the philosophical basis of design methodologies affects the approach the designer would adopt and ideally should be compatible with the nature of information systems which the methodology attempts to address.

The objectivist approach requires the analyst to be able to stand outside the system and not affect the system greatly by the process of analysis. The designer of a flight simulator, for training airline pilots in the use of a new aircraft, is clearly dealing with such a system. While the user role is crucial, the underlying problem is solely technical in nature. Mathematical techniques can be applied by aeronautical and software engineers and modelled within the system to replicate the real-life operation of the aircraft. Many real-time and process control systems are essentially hard systems.

In contrast to the designer of the flight simulator the systems analyst attempting to implement a new computerized sales system within a large organization may well find many elements of a soft system where a subjectivist approach is more appropriate. The different user groups (sales, management, administrators) may well have different views about the issues that are affecting overall sales performance. As a result initially there may well be only a limited understanding about what the real problems are, and what the needs of any new system might be. There is likely to be a strong focus on analysis and investigation before any real design can be undertaken. Furthermore the different user groups may seek to involve or influence the analyst so that an objective approach is impossible to adopt.

According to the subjectivist view there is no absolute knowledge of reality so there is no way of knowing whether the hard or soft system approach is correct. However, the application of one view may be more appropriate for some information systems. We may summarize that an objectivist approach may be more appropriate for hard systems and a subjectivist approach to soft systems. Some of the differences between hard and soft systems are shown in Table 4.1.

4.3.3   Classifying methodologies

We will now investigate a number of well-known methods under the following headings:

- Software methodologies
    - structured systems methodologies
    - object oriented design
    - formal methods
- Systems methodologies
    - soft systems methodologies
    - socio-technical systems methodologies
    - rapid/prototyping methodologies

TABLE 4.1   *Hard vs. soft systems*

Hard systems	Soft systems
Well defined, and can easily be described by rational, quantitative descriptions	Ill defined as they are often affected by the complex and fuzzy nature of organizational life
Aims that are clear before the process of analysis starts	Aims that only emerge from the process of analysis
Primarily technical in nature	Inherently socio-technical in nature
Largely independent of the values and beliefs of individuals and the organization in which they operate	Strongly affected by the values and beliefs of individuals and the organization in which they operate
Easily investigated by an onlooker approach	Investigation of the system involves the analyst interacting with it

4.4   Software methodologies

4.4.1   Structured systems methodologies

Since the early 1970s structured approaches to software and IS design have evolved. Such methodologies provide sets of notations and guidelines about how to create a software system. Structured methodologies have much in common, and over the years have developed to include three separate views of a system. These three views are a time/control view (commonly represented by state transition diagrams or entity life history diagrams), a functional view (described by data flow diagrams) and a data view (often described by entity–relationship diagrams). Each of these views can be checked with each other for compatibility. Structured methodologies can be classed as objectivist, with the analyst taking an onlooker approach in order to model the real world.

It is assumed that the reader is familiar with the basic elements of structured analysis techniques. We will look in some detail at the structured systems analysis and design methodology (SSADM) and briefly mention three other structured methods; information engineering, MERISE and Jackson Structured Design (JSD).

SSADM

The single methodology that has arguably had the greatest impact on systems design within the UK is SSADM. The structured systems analysis and design methodology as initially developed by the Central Computing and Telecommunications Agency (CCTA), was to be the standard design methodology for UK government projects developing batch and on-line data processing applications within a centralized environment. Derivatives of SSADM can now, however, be found in use in a wide range of UK commercial organizations.

SSADM is a structured methodology for the development of logical and physical specifications for computer systems applications. It does not cover aspects of information systems strategy or implementation. In terms of the life cycle of computer applications SSADM is therefore *headless* and *tailless*. Over the years SSADM has undergone a number of modifications. At the time of writing SSADM V4 and V4+ are the most recent versions.

SSADM V4 is based on the structural model that consists of a set of modules each of which consists of one or two stages, which in turn are broken down into a number of steps (Fig. 4.3). Each module has a defined purpose and a set of products. There are no direct links between modules but the products of one module are used as input into the next module. SSADM V4 specifies a number of techniques and procedures that are incorporated into the modules. These are entity–relationship diagrams, entity life histories and data flow diagrams. Modules are defined independently to enable the method to be tailored to specific projects.

Module	Stage
Feasibility study	0 Feasibility
Requirements analysis	1 Investigation of current environment 2 Business system options
Requirements specification	3 Definition of requirements
Logical system	4 Technical system options 5 Logical design
Physical design	6 Physical design

FIGURE 4.3   *The stages of SSADM (version 4)*

Within SSADM V4 the requirements of the new system are identified by analysing the current system to gain an understanding of the business constraints within which the system must operate. This is combined with a statement of requirements given by the users to build an outline of the new system that is modelled in detail. The models are cross-checked with one another and some functions are prototyped to gain a clear picture of what is needed. Detailed logical design and dialogue aspects of the system are developed in parallel with the implementation platform of the system. The complete logical specification for the system is then converted into a design for a specific hardware/software configuration.

SSADM V4+ makes few significant changes to the technical content of SSADM but does deliver a number of changes in emphasis. The structural model is de-emphasized and a system development template including a three-schema specification architecture is provided on which all the products (outputs) of SSADM can be placed (Fig. 4.4). The structural model of previous versions could be criticized in that it focused on information systems solutions and implementation rather than on the business requirements: it tended to perpetuate existing systems design. Within the system development template the:

- *Investigation* element, through requirements analysis and business activity modelling, enables the analyst to decide what it is which needs to be done.

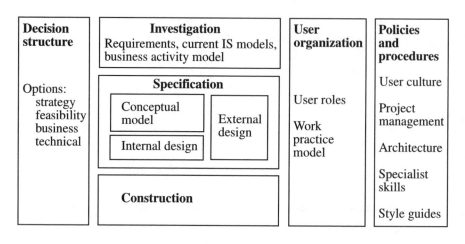

FIGURE 4.4   *SSADM V4+—three-scheme specification in the systems development template*

- *Specification* element enables conceptual services to be defined through the use of logical data modelling, relational data analysis, entity behaviour modelling, conceptual process modelling and database update and enquiry specifications.
- *External design* element maps to user organization and interface technology through the use of data flow modelling, function definitions, dialogue design, physical dialogue and I/O specifications and prototyping.
- *Internal design* element maps to data storage technology.
- *User organization* element allows the analyst to decide who is to use the system and how they will do so; the work practice model is important here.
- *Policies and procedure* element allows for interface design with technical policies and standards including user culture, project management and interface design style guides.

Over the years SSADM has shifted the emphasis on the user and his or her role in the development process. When SSADM was first introduced the way in which the various stages in the method were applied was far more rigid. Although newer versions are far more flexible, the early emphasis was supportive of a limited degree of user-centredness. By separating out the individual stages and steps and requiring the user/client to sign-off each stage, limited user engagement was promoted; at least at a level that was an improvement on traditional techniques. SSADM V4+ continues the trend in increasing the user role both in terms of meeting needs, and capacity for involvement, in the design process.

Specifically the strengths of SSADM V4+ in terms of the user-centredness can be listed:

- Clearer identification of user roles.
- Closer mapping between functions, dialogues and work practice—the work practice model is a mapping of the business activity model onto an organization (management structure, user roles) to specify which users carry out each business activity and where these are carried out).
- Guidance in dialogue design including considerations for graphical user interfaces.
- More emphasis on the use of style guides.
- Usability requirements added as part of requirements definition.
- Command structures link dialogues that support coherent tasks in the user's job description.
- Use of elements of the soft systems method.
- Broadening in the use of prototyping.

In our study we have identified (Chapter 2) the three types of user need (functional, physical and aspirational). Clearly even early versions of SSADM have been seen to be of use in addressing functional needs; although a weakness has been identified in that functional requirements may follow too closely from those embedded in any current system. More recent versions of SSADM are beginning to address a number of physical needs; specifically in terms of interface design. SSADM as currently defined would seem to provide little support for the user's aspirational needs.

Information engineering

During the 1980s information engineering (IE) introduced the concept that strategic management planning should be integrated with systems development in order to develop strategic information systems. A number of versions of IE are available based upon the works of James Martin and Clive Finkelstein (Martin and Finkelstein, 1981 and Finkelstein, 1992), working both together and independently. The aim of IE is to align hardware and software resources to the organization's corporate plan.

A major assumption about IE is that data is at the centre of the information system and that new systems should be developed based upon the structure of the underlying data. IE is clearly a data-driven methodology. Unlike, certainly early versions of SSADM, IE is philosophically rooted in business objectives. High-level business entities are identified from strategic plans and these are broken down in stages to generate the lower level entities that form the basis of detailed design.

As with SSADM, IE continues to evolve. Currently it does have a number of strengths in terms of user-centredness. It has been claimed (Avison and Fitzgerald, 1995) that the emphasis within IE on diagrammatic techniques is very appealing to end users and end-user management. It enables them to understand, participate and even construct for themselves the relevant IE diagrams thus ensuring that their requirements are truly understood and achieved.

While IE provides little support for the physical and aspirational needs of the user, it could be argued that its emphasis on strategic and corporate planning, as opposed to short-term specific objectives, will ensure that the users' functional needs are likely to be addressed within the organizational context for a longer period of time.

MERISE

MERISE is one of the most widely used international methodologies, originating in France in 1979 but with its influence subsequently spreading to Spain, Switzerland, and North America. Specifically MERISE has the following features:

- The method is quite wide in *scope* and addresses several aspects of systems development not addressed by other methods that tend to focus on technical and functional aspects and do not include business and organizational objectives.
- The method uses a number of *processes* that take account of both the static and dynamic aspects of an information system.
- It is often used in conjunction with CASE tools.
- It can be used to model concurrent systems in a way not readily achieved by SSADM.

MERISE is based on the philosophy that the business enterprise is a group of dynamically interacting elements organized according to an objective, and within an environment (Tardieu *et al.*, 1991). The enterprise is modelled as consisting of three interacting subsystems; an *operations* system, an *information* system and a *guidance* system, with each interacting information. There is also a recognition within this philosophy that there will be formal and informal information systems. The formal information system is identified by a set of codified rules of operation while the informal system is based upon relationships between individuals and work groups. It is clear, therefore, that although MERISE would be classed as an objectivist approach it offers much to a developer seeking a user-centred approach and wide *scope* within the design process.

MERISE consists of six stages: strategic planning, preliminary study, detailed study, development, implementation, maintenance.

Within the detailed study analysis is based on an abstraction cycle (Quang and Chartier-Kastler, 1991), which aims to design an information system by following a modelling logic consisting of three levels:

1. *Conceptual,* what are we trying to do?
2. *Logical/organizational,* who, when and how?
3. *Physical,* what means and constraints?

The purpose of the conceptual level is to capture the management rules that underlie the business. This conceptual level uses a *conceptual data model* (CDM) to represent all the data used by a firm and a *conceptual process model* (CPM) to describe the activities of the firm. The data models and the processing models are developed independently, even to the extent that different analysts may be involved. MERISE uses a data-modelling process that identifies the entities involved in the system, the relationship between these and the functional integrity constraints linked to each relationship. The conceptual process model, regards a process as a set of operations defined from the point of view of the management rules of the firm.

One of the strengths of MERISE is that during the initial stages it combines an examination of business objectives and critical success factors with a technical design process.

Jackson Structured Design

Jackson Structured Design (JSD) was developed in the late 1970s and early 1980s by Michael Jackson (1983) as a methodology encompassing both analysis and design. In contrast to other structured approaches JSD places an emphasis on modelling the actions of the system in terms of their effect on the input and output data streams, rather than on the direct functional tasks (Budgen, 1993). Whereas other structured methodologies can be said to be top-down, or *decompositional* (in that they break down a system from a high-level view of what is required), JSD can be described as *compositional* in that designs are built bottom-up from the identification of entities within the system. In this respect it has been claimed that JSD has much in common with object oriented methods that we will look at in the next section.

While JSD may have much to offer the user in terms of functional needs and requirements, particularly for large real-time systems, it offers little in terms of physical or aspirational needs. It is important to emphasize at this stage that the previous statement should not be considered a mere criticism of the method. As long as we note the strengths and weaknesses of the methods in terms of the user, we can adapt methods and integrate techniques to suit specific individual systems.

4.4.2   Object oriented design

In recent years a new approach to software development has emerged. Object oriented modelling and design approaches (OOD) have been developed to support the greatly increasing use of object oriented programming languages, of which currently the most prominent is C++. In object oriented design the developer is required to identify and model real-world *objects* within the application and then use these models to build a language independent design organized around these models. Proponents of OOD (e.g. Rumbaugh *et al.*, 1991) say that the use of such approaches, throughout the life cycle:

> provide a practical, productive way to develop software for most applications, regardless of the final implementation language

Object oriented techniques such as the object oriented modelling technique (OMT) of Rumbaugh *et al.* (1991) mean that software is organized as a collection of discrete objects which incorporate both data structure and behaviour. This is clearly different to other methods where the two are only loosely connected. Each of the objects within the system will belong to a class of objects and can inherit properties through a class hierarchy. Each object is related to a number of operations, or actions, that it performs or is subject to.

The OMT approach (Rumbaugh *et al.*, 1991) involves four stages as shown in Table 4.2.

In common with structured methodologies the OMT approach places a significant emphasis on diagrammatic techniques. As with structured methodologies three abstractions are modelled. Although there are some similarities, they are not the same abstractions. An object model describes the static structure of the object within the system showing both class hierarchy and object relationships. The dynamic model uses state transition diagrams (see Chapter 6) to describe aspects of the system that change over time. Finally the functional model adopts a data flow diagramming technique.

In our study of human–computer factors, object oriented techniques are important, because being strongly in support of the event driven approach, they provide an important basis for the development of software interfaces. However, object oriented design is not limited to the interface, and the use of such methods for the design of a wide range of applications is increasing. At present, however, the approach is by no means as mature as the structured method.

TABLE 4.2   *OMT approach*

Analysis	Given a clear statement of the problem, and using application domain objects in the real world, the analyst builds a concise, precise abstraction, or model, of what the desired system should do.
Systems design	High-level decisions are made about the overall architecture and the required system is organized into subsystems based upon the analysis structure and the proposed architecture.
Object design	A design model is built based upon the analysis but containing implementation details. The focus is on the data structures and algorithms needed to implement each class of object.
Implementation	The object classes and relationships developed during object design are finally translated into a particular programming language, database or hardware implementation.

In terms of user-centredness, object oriented techniques for design would appear to make a positive contribution. By focusing on real-life objects within the system and through the adoption of clear diagrammatic modelling techniques, the user is able to contribute actively to the design process.

4.4.3   Formal methods and methods integration

In a search for solutions to the problems associated with complex software systems there has been a call for an even more rigorous, or formal, approach to software design appropriate for an engineering discipline. The term *formal method* is used for a number of mathematical-based techniques for requirements specification and program design. However, these formal methods do not correspond to a full methodology or design method. Within such methods system requirements are specified using discrete mathematics, its design is expressed in the same mathematics and can be programmed using a programming language that has precise mathematical semantics. The application of mathematical formalism provides the possibility that software systems specifications can be proved or at least partially checked. The major application of formal methods to date has been in the program design stage of the systems development life cycle, particularly for safety critical systems.

Formal methods tend to divide into state-based models and process algebras. The Vienna Development Method (VDM) (Jones, 1986) was developed at the IBM Vienna Laboratories. The formal specification language Z (Spivey, 1992) was developed by the Programming Research Group at Oxford University. Specifications written in Z use a combination of natural language and mathematical descriptions or schemas. The state-based models, Z and VDM, describe the world in terms of data as typed sets and processes as operations and functions. In contrast process algebras model events and can be used for concurrent systems. The main methods developed in the UK are CSP (communicating sequential processes) and CCS (calculus of communicating systems).

Within an area of research known as *methods integration* a number of researchers have proposed the integration of formal methods with structured methodologies in order to enrich their application to large system specification (e.g. Polack and Whiston, 1991; Semmens and Allen, 1991). The vast majority of users are not at all well versed in a level of mathematics sufficient to generate even a basic understanding of formal methods and their application has largely remained as an internal mechanism for the software developer to enhance the rigour within requirements specification. Dunckley and Smith (1996), however, show how the integration of Z with MERISE can improve the access of both the user and the commercial software developer to formal methods. They describe the integrated approach as a *user-centred formal method*.

In terms of our definition of systems success and usability, we may summarize the main contribution of formal methods to be the enhancement of *effectiveness*.

4.5   System methodologies

4.5.1   Soft systems methods: SSM

Checkland's soft systems methodology (SSM) (Checkland, 1981) was initially developed in the 1970s at the University of Lancaster but has continued to evolve. SSM is an analysis method that can be used at the early stages of the life cycle and does not encompass systems design. SSM, as an example of the subjectivist approach, contrasts with 'hard' systems methods that tend to emphasize rational, quantitative descriptions of organizational processes. According to Eason (1988), SSM:

> is used in systems analysis which recognise the more complex and fuzzy nature of organisational life where a variety of goals are being pursued and there are many views of the reality with which staff have to deal

SSM has been developed over a number of years through action research and practical experience. Central to the SSM approach is the premise that a system is a device for thinking about some part of the world. This contrasts with the hard approach where it is assumed that the world is composed of clearly defined systems and subsystems.

The use of the term *system* to represent a tool for the expression of the real world allows us to capture multiple perspectives of the world as viewed by a variety of people involved in real-world activities. Checkland refers to these views as *holons*. A football match might, for example, generate a number of holons. It may be viewed by the club's marketing director as a means of providing entertainment, whereas a football fan may consider it as an opportunity for displaying tribal loyalty. The police chief may see it as a mechanism for testing out crowd control skills. SSM also allows for the inclusion of values and beliefs within the analysis (social and political analysis) and takes account of how the intervention, or analysis, itself may affect things. When initially developed SSM was described as a seven-stage process (see Fig. 4.5). More recent descriptions outline a more flexible and iterative approach based upon two parallel strands; cultural analysis and logic-based analysis.

Cultural analysis

Within the cultural analysis stream a *rich picture* is developed by the analyst primarily for his or her own use in further structuring the

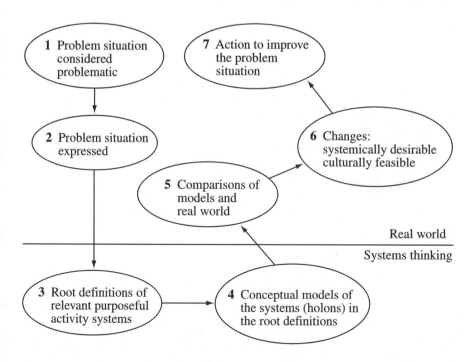

FIGURE 4.5   *The conventional seven-stage model of SSM*

investigation. There is no one formal way of drawing the rich picture that helps to identify different viewpoints (holons). Rich pictures *depict organizational structures* (that are slow to change), *processes* that occur, *issues* that are expressed and felt by people within the organization, and the overall *climate* within the system. Eyeballs, crossed swords and cartoon balloons are used to express outside scrutiny, conflict and internal issues.

Essential to the SSM approach is the study of a *problem situation* rather than a clearly defined problem. As we have noted an important aspect of SSM is the ability to capture multiple perspectives of the world as viewed by the variety of individuals involved in real-world activities that constitute the problem situation. Systems that are suited to the SSM approach may be complex human activity systems in which human components may react differently when examined singly as when they play their role within the whole system.

Within the cultural stream an attempt is made to identify *roles* that are either institutionally or behaviourally defined, *norms* that describe expected behaviour and values that are local to the situation and which define organizational performance. Political analysis is concerned with managing relations between different interests and identifying how power is expressed within the organization. SSM overtly aims to take account of the intervention by the analyst within the problem situation and can therefore be considered to be subjectivist in approach.

Logic-based analysis

From the rich picture different holons can be identified. In the logic-based stream these are then described by developing a *root definition*. Checkland provides a framework for specifying root definitions based upon the acronym CATWOE as shown in Table 4.3.

Conceptual models that detail the activities that must exist for the system to achieve the transformation, are then constructed. By comparing these conceptual models of what should occur (perception of real world not the real world itself) with the real world, changes

TABLE 4.3   *CATWOE*

C	Customer	Beneficiaries/victims of the system/transformation
A	Actor	Those who carry out the transformation
T	Transformation	Core process
W	Worldview	Beliefs/view of the world which makes transformation meaningful
O	Owner	Those with the power to modify/stop the transformation
E	Environment	Constraints

can be proposed. Changes will be *culturally feasible* in the light of views, background and experiences of people and *systemically desirable* to support the transformation. Methods for comparison include discussion/observation and formal questioning together with scenario-based techniques.

SSM and user-centred design

SSM has much to offer the system developer attempting to develop a user-centred system. Philosophically it is highly user-centred in that it places the individual and his or her values, beliefs and views at the centre of the process. It leads to the identifications of changes that are not just systemically desirable, i.e. technically possible, but feasible within the organizational culture. The modelling techniques used within the method are also highly accessible by users within the system. Although the rich picture may primarily be developed for the analyst's use, it will be readily understood by all those involved. The use of elements of the SSM approach could enable a large range of functional, physical and aspirational needs to be identified and addressed within a proposed solution.

4.5.2   A socio-technical systems method: ETHICS

ETHICS is an acronym for effective technical and human implementation of computer systems and has been developed by Mumford at the Manchester Business School. ETHICS is a highly *participative* design method that explores goals, values and sources of job satisfaction in addition to information flows and key tasks. It leads to the ranking of efficiency and job satisfaction needs and to the design of both a social and technical solution. While the detailed implementation of ETHICS has not spread widely within UK organizations, elements of the approach can be seen in a number of projects.

According to Mumford (1983, 1989) participative systems design means handling responsibility for the design of the new system to the people who will eventually have to use it. Participation should be seen as involving personnel at all levels within the organization. Such methods, she proposes, are growing in acceptance as an efficient and ethical approach. Arguments in support of this approach are that users have a moral right to control their own destinies, that activities are eventually controlled by those who perform them, that important knowledge for the successful operation of the system rests with user, and that the process itself acts as a motivator.

Mumford cites three forms of participative design. *Consultative* design leaves the bulk of design with traditional designers, but the design process includes issues such as job satisfaction and enrichment not normally found in other methods. *Representative* design is a process in which user representatives at all grades and functions within the organization are formed into a design group. The *consensus* approach, as embodied in ETHICS, attempts to involve all staff in the organization continuously throughout the design process.

The ETHICS method establishes two participative structures: a design group and a steering group. The design group follows an analytical procedure under the guidance of a *facilitator* who is an expert in such a method (Mumford herself in many of the case study publications). Essentially the procedure places importance on the analysis of the needs of business efficiency, effectiveness, job satisfaction and future change. These needs are then translated into objectives that are addressed by two components of design: technical and organizational. ETHICS is arguably the most user-centred full methodology met so far within our study, focusing as it does on aspirational, functional and perhaps to a lesser extent on physical needs.

4.6   Hybrid approaches

In recognition of the wide variety of needs inherent in different types of information systems a number of academics and practitioners have attempted to combine the subjectivist and objectivist approach in order to get the best of both worlds. The usual approach has been to embed SSM concepts within a structured methodology in order to ensure the requirements have been correctly identified with relatively little consideration given to the compatibility of the different philosophies. This has been attempted in Multiview and there is a proposal to use SSM in the feasibility study stage of SSADM. Miles (1988), however, has suggested that a more profitable approach would be the reverse in which structured approaches are embedded in an overall SSM-driven analysis. This could promise much for a user-centred approach but to date no examples have been reported.

4.6.1   Multiview: synthesizing a range of methods

Avison and Wood-Harper (1990) have attempted to synthesize (make into a coherent whole) in their *Multiview* methodology a variety of approaches to analysis and design. It is greatly influenced by the socio-technical approach and implements ideas found in both hard and soft methods such as soft systems and information engineering. Multiview provides a flexible approach to information systems development and, although it includes techniques found in a number of other methods, the authors' claim that it is more than a 'hotchpotch' of alternative methods. The five stages of Multiview are:

1. *Analysis of human activity*, in which, based upon SSM, the analysis focuses on how the information system will further the aims of the organization using it.
2. *Analysis of information*, which attempts to identify what information processing functions the system is to perform—from the root definitions and conceptual models developed in stage one functional and entity models are produced.
3. *Analysis and design of socio-technical aspects*, in which through the ranking of social and technical objectives (similar to the ETHICS approach) the focus is on how the information system can be fitted into the working lives of the people using it—the output from stage three is referred to as the *computer task requirement*, a *role-set*, the *people tasks* and the *social aspects*.
4. *Design of the human–computer interface*, which determines, in broad terms, how the individuals concerned best relate to the computer in terms of operating it and using the output from it.
5. *Design of technical aspects*, which specifies the technical system that will come close enough to meeting the identified requirements.

In common with ETHICS, Multiview can be considered to address socio-technical design, an issue that is central to the development of usable human–computer systems. Based upon the principle that there needs to be co-optimization between the social and technical elements, both approaches attempt to identify technical and social alternatives, rank these in terms of meeting the identified objectives, and having considered constraints select the best socio-technical solution as illustrated in Fig. 4.6.

We will adopt the socio-technical design framework in our further study of users and information systems, for example Chapter 5 (The social system: designing for organizational acceptability) and Chapter 7 (The technical system: designing for interface usability).

4.7   Process models

We introduced the concept of the process model as a framework in which methodologies are defined by the sequence of stages through which a software product or information system evolves. In traditional systems development dating from the 1970s, a number of distinct stages could be identified, as follows:

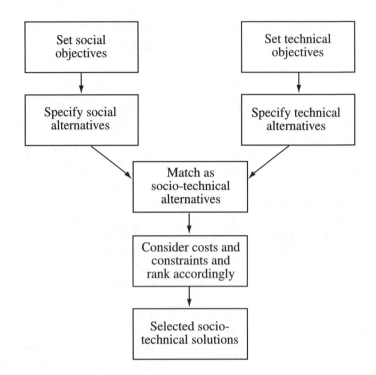

FIGURE 4.6   *Socio-technical design process*

- Feasibility study
- Systems investigation
- Systems analysis
- Systems design
- Implementation
- Review and maintenance

In the waterfall model each stage is completed before the next phase can begin and the outcomes of one stage become the inputs for the next phase. However, there are a number of problems with this development process model. For example organizational changes are often required by the introduction of new information systems and these need to be included at some stage. Although the waterfall concept looks straightforward, in practice it is difficult to manage and control because of the uncertainties at the beginning of the project. User requirements are difficult to specify completely at the start of the life cycle but are more likely to emerge during several stages. For these reasons alternative process models have been put forward.

4.7.1 Alternative process models

Spiral model

The spiral model has been proposed by Boehm (1988) to improve planning and control by including several iterations of requirements gathering, design and implementation. It also introduces the idea of prototyping to identify user requirements.

The V model

The V model (Fig. 4.7) is designed to show how phases of the life cycle can operate in parallel with information flowing to several stages at once. It is called the V model because its shape goes down through sequential levels. This means the study looks at the whole of the system before the development takes place. The early top-level initiatives are integrated with bottom-level coding and testing.

This process model includes testing at each stage thus reducing the need for iteration and involves the user throughout the specification and building phases. The disadvantages include the fact that it is still difficult to go back to rectify errors, and much time is spent investigating each phase.

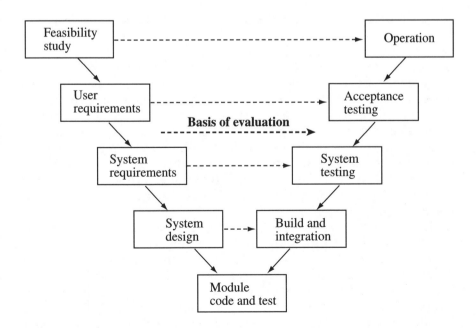

FIGURE 4.7   *The V model*

Prototyping process models

Many structured and post-structured development methodologies are still loosely based upon the standard waterfall model; albeit with enhanced iteration between stages. However, with such an approach problems can result if the designers of interactive systems do not find all requirements before they begin the design. Indeed not all requirements, such as aspirational and physical needs can be clearly specified. In addition it is difficult to ensure that discovery, during analysis and design reflects back on previous activities.

In order to meet the needs of interactive systems an evolutionary approach to development has been proposed where the emphasis is placed on the rapid building of prototype systems with which the user can quickly interact. Following an evaluation of such an interaction the designers can improve the solution making it more usable. In a *prototyping process model* based approach we have a purposeful design process that tries to overcome the inherent process of incomplete requirements specification by cycling through several designs, incrementally improving upon the final product with each pass. This approach is worthy of a more detailed analysis.

4.7.2   Rapid/prototyping methods

Rubenstein and Hersh (1984) make a comparison of information systems design methods with techniques used during the design of a new car. Specifically they identify two different approaches. First in the top-down, or functional approach the car buyer specifies the horsepower, braking power and fuel economy required, but does not see the car until completion. In the outside-in approach the car buyer specifies the external interface required, such as internal and external design and styling (from type of car, down to dashboard layout) and the car designers work with the purchasing community to define the functionality required to produce the car. In terms of information systems design the functional approach is well supported by a number of methodologies discussed so far, but the inside-out way of working does not, so far, appear to have support. In fact a number of development techniques have emerged in recent years that do, to some extent, embody this approach. They can be referred to as *evolutionary*, *prototyping* or *rapid* development methods. They place an emphasis on satisfying the user, through those parts of the system with which he or she interacts, even if this may be at some expense of detailed functionality and correctness. If the users are happy then so should the developers!

Types of prototyping

A prototype can be considered to be:

an artefact that simulates or animates some, but not all, of the features of an intended system.

Prototypes can be used for various purposes as a technique for requirements specification:

- Eliciting user functional requirements
- Testing a functional design
- Interface testing and evaluation

There are a number of different ways in which prototyping can be used as a process model within the overall development approach. While prototyping is the generic term, *rapid prototyping* is a specific attempt to produce a version of the software solution quickly, perhaps using a separate software system (e.g. Visual Basic or 4GL), thereby allowing quick user interaction and a faster final delivery of the product.

In *horizontal prototyping* (refer to Fig. 4.8) the whole, albeit limited version, of the required system is prototyped and at each iteration of the evolutionary process more and more detail of the system is added. This is in contrast to *vertical prototyping* where a full version of one part of the system is developed.

Evolutionary prototypes are those which will eventually mature to be the final used system and are therefore developed using the software that will implement the final solution. *Throw-away* prototypes, on the other hand, are developed separately from the final product, often with

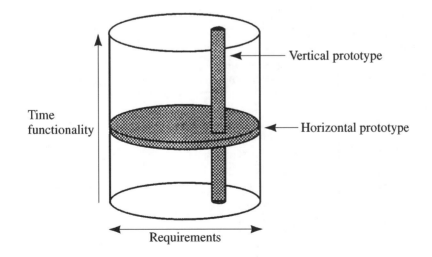

FIGURE 4.8 *Horizontal vs. vertical prototyping*

a different software development system, and are used *as experimental or exploratory prototypes* to test out particular aspects of the system.

Prototyping is often seen as a user-centred process model. The fact, however, that a software developer is developing a prototype is not, in itself, an indicator of user-centredness. Prototypes built by programmers to test out the functionality or correctness within part of the system and tested by themselves may enhance the quality of the product but will not engage the user in the development process. To contribute to the enhancement of user-centredness, and usability, prototyping needs a user-focused evaluation method.

Prototype evaluation

We will return to the evaluation of software interfaces in Chapter 7. For now it will be sufficient to emphasize that user-centred prototyping should be within an evolutionary, or iterative manner as depicted in Fig. 4.9. Having specified the requirements, a prototype version of the system is built. For each iteration of the development process a set of clear evaluation criteria are set. Although these may not change from one pass to the next, it is possible that actual hands-

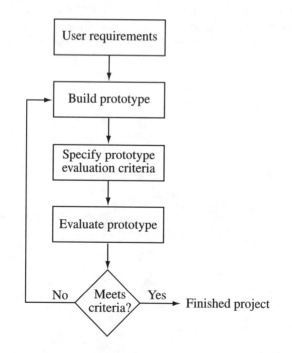

FIGURE 4.9   *The iterative nature of prototyping*

on use may elicit further requirements that will need to be evaluated. The evaluation criteria need to be clearly specified. It is not sufficient that the users are satisfied with the system, although a formal evaluation of user views, through satisfaction surveys such as those proposed by Shneiderman (1992), may form part of the process. In addition performance objectives may be set, such as the time to complete a task, or the amount of errors made by the user during the evaluation. In an evaluation of the prototype real potential users of the system are involved in implementing typical tasks that they are likely to encounter when the systems is in operational use. In a sales-ordering system, for example, a number of potential users may be asked to use the prototype to process a number of sales orders. Training in the use of the prototype may be needed and input documents may need to be designed so that a real-life evaluation can be conducted. The prototype is only acceptable if it meets both subjective user satisfaction levels and objective performance levels.

Rapid applications development (RAD)

While prototyping on its own is best described as a technique rather than a methodology, the general approach is now being implemented within more general methodologies. There are two main thrusts for the emergence of what are generally referred to as rapid applications development (RAD) methods.

First the requirements specification phase of the software life cycle has been recognized (e.g. Sidoran et al., 1995) as being critical for the development of large, complex software systems. Rapid prototyping techniques can be applied to develop executable models to help eliminate the ambiguity, inconsistency and incompleteness in requirements specification, which are often the source of errors and inefficiencies in subsequent life cycle stages.

The second thrust for the expansion in RAD is in response to the driving force for the adoption of IT systems. The business users of software systems, in order to respond to economic pressures and changing circumstances, are now demanding a faster development and implementation of new systems. In many ways recent years have seen a shift from IT being led by the central IT department to a far more business-led approach.

A number of RAD methods have been published, some of which are specific to a language, industry, or software development tool. One method that has received support is the dynamic systems development method (DSDM). In DSDM version 2:

- User involvement is imperative
- Development is iterative and incremental

- The focus is on frequent delivery of products rather than on how they are produced
- Every deliverable must meet its business purpose

One of the main problems with a prototyping process model is to identify when to stop each iteration stage. DSDM is based on strict timeboxing that means that the development stops even if all the planned functionality has not been achieved.

DSDM has been implemented in a number of UK organizations. Early adopters include British Airways which says (*Computing*, 20 November 1995) that:

> DSDM has improved the quality of systems development .... in *(traditional)* systems development, you typically articulate all requirements before development occurs, with airlines you often cannot do this, so this is where RAD comes in.

In DSDM, collaboration and co-operation between all project stakeholders is seen to be vital and as such it should offer much to the user-centred information systems developer.

4.8   Comparing methods and evaluating user implications

The vast array of methodologies, methods and techniques each address one or more aspects of systems development. Some give a business focus, others a technical one and a few provide a user focus. A variety of approaches are implemented including structured, object oriented, and formal. The process model to which the method relates can, for example, be based on the waterfall, evolutionary or iterative model. Some IS developers reject the methodology approach altogether on the basis that all systems are different and that each needs a unique approach. Rather than a cook-book or recipe approach, where the ingredients and procedures for development are specified, a tool-set approach is preferred. In this way of working the developer picks and mixes from an array of methods that he or she feels are the most appropriate.

While within the last decade a great amount of effort has been made by the IT industry and academia to devise new methodologies there has been relatively little evaluation of their use in practice. As Wynekoop and Russo argue (1995):

> although many systems development methodologies exist, there is no universal agreement that existing methodologies are useful today, nor is there general agreement that they have ever been useful

They identify four questions that need to be answered before methodologies for the next century are produced:

1. Are methodologies used?
2. How are methodologies selected?
3. Do methodologies work?
4. Are methodologies obsolete?

A recent survey (Smith and Dunckley, 1995) of UK commercial organizations was undertaken in order to elicit approaches to systems design and implementation. It showed that while there is considerable evidence that traditional (pre-structured) design methods still dominate the design process, there is a wide variety of other methodologies in use. Structured methods were shown to be in use in a large number of organizations and SSADM was the method most quoted. There was little evidence of the take-up of specific participative methodologies although there was evidence of the application of SSM and IE. The shift to structured methods was shown to have come about mainly for reasons of efficiency and effectiveness within the design process. The full figures are given in Table 4.4. The percentages do not add up to 100 as many organizations used more than one method during a project. Many of the respondents in the 'other' category used in-house methods that were variations on the structured theme. While it is clear (Nielsen, 1995) that the developers of off-the-shelf software products, such as Microsoft, pay considerable attention to the integration of human factor and HCI issues within their overall method, this is still not the case across mainstream commercial bespoke software development.

4.8.1 Ways of comparing methods

A number of authors have produced guidelines and checklists for comparing methodologies. Lantz (1989), for example, focused on quality issues. A useful approach for evaluating user-centredness is Bjorn-Andersen's (1984) checklist for methodologies:

- What research paradigms/perspective form the foundation for the methodology?
- What are the underlying value systems?

TABLE 4.4   *Choice of design methods*

Design methods	Percentage
Traditional	45
SSADM	18
SSM/IE	17
Jackson/Yourdon etc.	5
Object oriented	6
(Other/in-house	45)

- What is the context where the methodology is useful?
- To what extent is the modification enhanced or even possible?
- Does communication and documentation operate in the users' dialect either expert or not?
- Does transferability exist?
- Is the societal environment dealt with, including possible conflicts?
- Is the user participation really encouraged or supported?

In the following sections we will attempt a comparison of methodologies with regard to the user role. Overall we have identified six classifications of methodology (structured, object oriented, formal, soft, socio-technical, and rapid/prototyping). At present object oriented *design methods* (as opposed to programming techniques) have not matured sufficiently, and formal methods do not constitute a full methodology, these will be excluded from our analyses. We will attempt a comparison of four methodology approaches (structured, soft, rapid/prototyping and socio-technical) against four broad criteria:

1. User and organizational perspectives
2. User needs
3. User-centred design
4. System success

Note that the tables that follow should not be considered as a comprehensive comparison of each method. Rather the aim is to identify a few comments that describe a strength or weakness of each method in relation to the criteria.

4.8.2 By user and organizational perspectives

In Chapter 3, from the work of Hornby *et al.* (1992), we identified that it was necessary to identify whether, and in which ways, the processes adopted within various methodologies address a number of issues such as business strategy and the elicitation and specification of user requirements. All of these issues are included in Table 4.5 where we attempt a summary comparison. Note that the second row of the table (elicitation and specification of user requirements) is the user need category which is dealt with in more detail in Sec. 4.8.3.

4.8.3 By user needs

We have seen that to ensure fully usable systems a range of user needs should be identified. Table 4.6 provides a comparison of the four methods by the way in which they elicit user needs.

TABLE 4.5   *Comparing methodologies: by organizational perspective*

	Structured	Soft	RAD	Socio-technical
Business strategy	No general support	Support for identifying underlying issues	Emphasis on meeting specific business needs	Supports organizational change
Elicitation and specification of user requirements	Emphasis on specification of functional needs	Range of functional, physical and aspirational needs identified	Functional and physical needs emphasized	Functional and aspirational needs addressed
Task analysis and design	No general support	No specific methods	Should include task analysis	Support for task analysis in socio-technical design
Allocation of function between user tasks and device tasks	No general support, although SSADM 4+ is an improvement	Not a design or implementation method	Should include allocation of function	The focus of the socio-technical process
Organization and job design	No general support	Needs should be identified	No general support	A major focus
Applicability to prototyping	No general support, although SSADM 4+ is an improvement	Not a design or implementation method	The major focus	Process supports protyping
User interface design	No general support, although SSADM 4+ is an improvement	Not a design or implementation method	Should include detailed HCI design	Process should support effective HCI design

4.8.4   By user-centred design

User needs are met in a usable information system through the adoption of a user-centred design process. We have seen how user-centred design can be categorized by structures, processes and scope. In Table 4.7 we compare the methods with respect to how they cope with a user-centred approach to design.

TABLE 4.6   *Comparing methodologies: by user need*

	Structured	Soft	RAD	Socio-technical
Functional	Structured analysis techniques enable effective requirements specification	SSM conceptual modelling enables desirable and feasible changes to be identified	RAD approach ensures that business needs are met quickly	Functional needs addresses in parallel to organizational needs
Physical	Little emphasis, although more recent versions of SSADM address HCI	Some issues may be identified, but SSM is not a design/ implementation method	Iterative process should ensure usability needs are met	Overall process supports identification of needs
Aspirational	No support	Rich pictures and social systems analysis provide significant support	No specific support	Social systems design in parallel with technical design

4.8.5   By system success criteria

We have related systems success to usability criteria (effectiveness, efficiency and satisfaction). The degree to which each of the methods, on their own, are likely to meet such criteria are explored in Table 4.8.

4.8.6   Comparing methodologies: a summary

The choice, or indeed lack of choice, of an information systems design methodology can have major implications for how human-factor issues are identified and catered for. In the majority of cases, however, it is not these human-factor issues that determine the choice of method. Many other factors such as the skills and experiences of the analysts and developers, and the nature of the application itself take precedence. Indeed while in our study we are firmly supporting a user-centred development approach on the basis that this is likely to lead to more usable products, we strongly recognize that functionality issues are paramount. While we would not wish to see systems which although technically correct, generate significant usability problems, we recognize that a product with a well-designed interface, clearly

TABLE 4.7   *Comparing methodologies: by user-centred design*

	Structured	Soft	RAD	Socio-technical
Structures	Users will need considerable training to be effective participants	Process designed to involve all stakeholders	End users fully able to contribute to output focused development	Designed to integrate users in design process
Process	Many techniques difficult for majority of end users	Majority of processes are accessible to end users	Focus on output, rather than process assists end users	Emphasis on making design accessible to users
Scope	Emphasis on technical issues only	Wide in scope, soft/fuzzy analysis	Probably limited and technically focused	Wide in scope, socio-technical design

TABLE 4.8   *Comparing methodologies: by system success criteria*

	Structured	Soft	RAD	Socio-technical
Effectiveness	Claimed to produce well-engineered solution	Logic-based analysis should identify feasible solutions	Emphasis on speed of delivery may be at the expense of rigour	Technical design addresses utility
Efficiency	Some recent versions (SSADM V4+) address HCI	Not a design/ implementation method	Iterative approach should ensure that an efficient interface is provided	Socio-technical design addresses usability
Satisfaction	Do not necessarily lead to acceptable solutions	Social and political analysis should identify needs	Iterative approach could enable some issues to be addressed	Social design addresses acceptability and satisfaction

meeting aspirational and physical needs but failing to correctly perform the task, is plainly useless.

We should not attempt to determine the 'best' method for the development of user-centred systems: it would be a meaningless exercise. However, the developer of information systems seeking to address human factors should ensure that if a methodology is adopted then the way in which human issues are dealt with is evaluated and appropriate modifications are made if necessary. If the tool-set approach is used then the pot from which techniques are selected should include those developed by human-factor specialists.

4.9   Plumbest plc: systems analysis

4.9.1   Tasks

Note: it is recognized that this chapter has not provided sufficient detail of each design method for the reader to complete a detailed systems analysis and design. Indeed this is not required for our study of human–computer factors. However, in order for us to further investigate a human-centred solution for Plumbest we will need to undertake aspects of this stage in the life cycle. The reader has two alternatives:

- To access details of the methods from other sources (see References and Further reading sections).
- To study the solutions where provided.

General tasks

Plumbest Task 4.1

What are the strengths and weaknesses of the following systems design methods for analysing and designing a new job allocation system (JAS) at Plumbest? (No solution provided.)

- Soft systems methodology
- SSADM V4+
- Formal methods
- ETHICS

Soft systems tasks

Plumbest Task 4.2

Draw a rich picture of the current problem situation at Plumbest as represented by the information currently available.

Plumbest Task 4.3

Use the CATWOE mnemonic to define a system that allocates jobs to mobile operatives.

Plumbest Task 4.4

Draw a conceptual model to define the activities involved in the job allocation system. What changes will be necessary to support the conceptual model?

Structured analysis tasks

Plumbest Task 4.5

Identify the major entities that are relevant to the JAS. Associate attributes to these elements, thereby describing their relational tables. Draw an entity–relationship diagram for this part of the JAS.

4.9.2 Solutions

Plumbest Solution 4.2

The rich picture, shown in Fig. 4.10 identifies four major processes or activities within the Plumbest service centre operation:

1. Allocation of jobs from customer to mobile operative or foreman by service administrators.
2. Allocation of non-emergency jobs by foreman.
3. Completion of job by mobile operatives and *subsequent* completion and return of job completion form to foreman.
4. Pricing of job by foreman (prior to de-programming which is outside our overall system).

It is therefore possible to identify at least four different transformations and derive root definitions and conceptual models for them. In our study it will be sufficient for us to look in detail at the first of these (allocation of jobs from customer to mobile operatives or foreman by service administrators).

Note also from the rich picture that there are a number of concerns about both the social and technical elements of the system that can be looked at.

Plumbest Solution 4.3

Note that the transformation, shown in Table 4.9, defines the other elements within the CATWOE. The customer of the transformation is the direct one; in this case the mobile operative.

From the CATWOE it is possible to derive a root definition for job allocation:

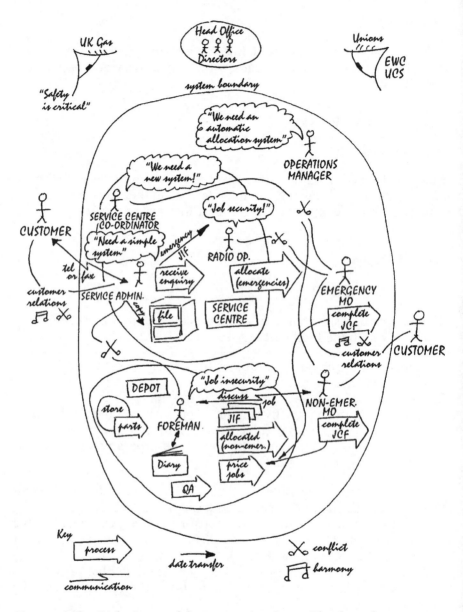

FIGURE 4.10   *Rich picture of the current situation at Plumbest plc*

A system operated by a service administrator whereby requests for jobs (from customers) are determined to be either emergency or non-emergency and thereby allocated to either a mobile operative or foreman. The allocation can be modified by the service centre co-ordinator and assumes that the number, location and diaries of mobile operatives are appropriate to accept jobs.

TABLE 4.9   *Plumbest CATWOE*

C	Customer	Mobile operatives
A	Actor	Service administrators
T	Transformation	Job allocated: an unallocated job is allocated to a mobile operative or alternatively passed to correct foreman
W	Worldview	That there are sufficient mobile operatives available to accept job
O	Owner	Service centre co-ordinator
E	Environment	Number, location and diaries of mobile operatives are appropriate to accept jobs

Plumbest Solution 4.4

Refer to Fig. 4.11 for the conceptual model of the JAS. SSM conceptual models describe what should happen to support the transformation rather that what is happening. Checkland suggests an analysis of each activity, and also each link between each activity (which we will not cover), within the model. This is provided in Table 4.10.

Plumbest Solution 4.5

The three major entities are customer, mobile operative and job and are shown in Table 4.11.

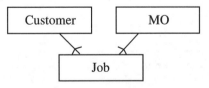

Entity–relationship diagram

It should already be clear that the SSM process has enabled us to identify a number of actions that can be incorporated into the new JAS. From the rich picture/social systems analysis we can identify the following issues:

1. Concerns over job security: redundancies or redeployments will be needed.
2. Variety of conflicts which will need resolving in social systems design.

FIGURE 4.11   *SSM conceptual model of the job allocation system at Plumbest plc*

TABLE 4.10

Activity	Exist or not in real situation?	How is it done?	How is it judged?	Comments
1 Receive job	Yes	Post fax tel.		
2 Decide on criteria for jobs	Yes	By service centre	MO feedback	Outside JAS
3 Decide on nature of job	Yes	By service admin.	MO feedback	Remain human task
4 Obtain territory	Sometimes	Informally	Delays, etc.	Needs rigour
5 Obtain location of MOs	Sometimes	Informally	Delays, etc.	Needs rigour
6 Allocate job	Yes	By service admin.	Delays, etc.	Support needed

TABLE 4.11

Customer table		MO table		Job table	
Customer name	char(20)	MO name	char(20)	**Job number**	**num(7)**
Customer number	**num(8)**	**MO number**	**num(6)**	Date entered	num(6)
Customer address 1	char(20)	Depot	num	Date finished	num(6)
Customer address 2	char(20)			Time finished	num(4)
Customer address 3	char(20)			*Customer number*	*num(7)*
Customer type	num			*MO number*	*num(6)*
Customer account	num				

3. Need for usable (simple) interface to JAS: HCI issues will be important.
4. Need for suitable training programmes.

From the logic-based/conceptual modelling we can add the following issues:

5. Need to specify required performance criteria (mean, max. delays, etc.) of JAS.
6. Need to derive a method of monitoring the real-time performance of JAS against the criteria and to report results to the service centre co-ordinator.
7. Need to derive an algorithm for job allocation based upon MO and foreman location and MO availability.

Items 1 and 2 will be covered in Chapter 5 whereas item 3 will be addressed in Chapters 6 and 7. Chapter 8 covering training and user support will provide the solution to item 4. The degree in which the interface can affect performance (item 5) will be addressed in Chapter 7. Other aspects of item 5, and items 6 and 7, although crucial to the success of the project, are solely functional issues and are therefore outside the remit of our study.

Summary

In this chapter we have seen:

- An overview of a wide range of software and systems design methodologies.
- How the underpinning philosophical approach to methodologies can determine appropriateness to specific systems.
- That the methods vary in the manner in which they address:
  - user and organizational perspectives

     – user needs
     – user-centred design
     – system success criteria
- That information systems design methods should be chosen carefully to meet specific project requirements.

Questions

4.1 What do we mean by objectivism as opposed to subjectivism in the design of an information system? To what extent are the following methodologies essentially subjective or objective in approach:

    SSM
    MERISE
    ETHICS
    SSADM
    Object oriented design

4.2 What are the strengths and weaknesses of the subjectivist and objectivist approach to an information systems developer seeking a user-centred method?

4.3 Compare the following design approaches in terms of the ease in which they allow for user participation:

    JSD
    Multiview
    RAD
    Formal methods

4.4 Three well-known process models are the evolutionary, the waterfall and the V model. What are the strengths and weaknesses of each in terms of the identification and effective attainment of a wide range of user needs?

4.5 Compare the following methodologies by using Bjorn-Andersen's criteria:

    SSADM
    SSM

4.6 Choose an organization to which you have access and which has recently been active in introducing information systems through the implementation of a well-known methodology. Try to compare both user and developer perceptions of the approaches to the design adopted. You will need to design your own methods for research but should consider:

    Nature and success of the process model adopted
    How user needs were identified
    How users were able to participate in the process
    The degree to which the method led to systems success

References

Avison, D. E. and Fitzgerald, G. (1995), *Information Systems Development*, McGraw-Hill, London.

Avison, D. E. and Wood-Harper, A. T. (1990), *Multiview: An Exploration in Information Systems development*, Alfred Waller, London.

Ackoff, R. L. and Emery, F. E. (1972), *On Purposeful Systems*, Tavistock Institute, London.

Boehm, B. W. (1988), 'A spiral model of software development and enhancement', *IEEE Computer*, 21(5), 61–72.

Bjorn-Anderson, N. (1984), 'Challenge to certainty', in T. M. A. Bemelmans (ed.), *Beyond Productivity: Information Systems Productivity for Organizational Effectiveness*, North-Holland, Amsterdam.

Budgen, D. (1993), *Software Design*, Addison-Wesley, Wokingham.

Checkland, P. (1981), *Systems Thinking, Systems Practice*, Wiley, Chchester.

Computing (1995), 'DSDM group refine method', *Computing*, 20 November.

Dunckley, L. and Smith, A. (1996), 'Improving access of the commercial software developer to formal methods: integrating Z with MERISE, *Methods Integration 1996 (Leeds)*, Springer-Verlag.

Eason, K. (1988), *Information Technology and Organisational Change*, Taylor and Francis, London.

Emery, F. E. and Trist, E. L. (1969), 'Socio-technical systems', in F. E. Emery (ed.), *Systems Thinking*, Penguin, Harmondsworth.

Finkelstein, C. (1992), *Information Engineering: Strategic Systems Development*, Addison-Wesley, Sydney.

Hornby, P. and Clegg, C. W. (1992), 'User participation in context: a case study in a UK Bank', *Behaviour and IT*, 11(5), 293–307.

Jackson, M. A. (1983), *Systems Development*, Prentice-Hall, London.

Jones, C. B. (1986), *Systematic Software Development Using VDM*, Prentice-Hall, London.

Klein, H. K. and Hirschheim R. (1987), 'A comparison of data modelling paradigms and approaches', *Computer Journal*, 30(1).

Lantz, K. E. (1989), *The Prototyping Methodology*, Prentice-Hall.

Lewis, P. (1994), *Informations Systems Development*, Pitman, London.

Martin, J. and Finkelstein, C. (1981), *Information Engineering, Vols 1 and 2*, Prentice-Hall, Englewood Cliffs, New Jersey .

Mumford, E. (1983), 'Participative systems design: practice and theory', *Journal of Occupational Behaviour*, 4, 47–57.

Mumford, E. (1989), 'User participation in a changing environment—why we need it', in K. Knight (ed.), *Participation in Systems Development: UNICOM Applied IT Reports*, Kogan Page, London.

Nielsen, J. (1995), 'Getting usability used', in K. Nordby *et al.* (eds), *Human–computer Interaction. Proceedings of INTERACT-95*, Chapman and Hall.

Polack, F. and Whiston, M. (1991), 'Formal methods and systems analysis—Z and SSADM', Methods Integration Conference, KBSL/Leeds Polytechnic.

Quang, P. T. and Chartier-Kastler, C. (1991), *MERISE in Practice*, Macmillan.

Rice, K. (1958), *Productivity and Social Organization: The Ahmedabad Experiment*, Tavistock Institute, London.

Rubenstein, R. and Hersh, H. (1984), *The Human Factor, Computer Systems for People*, Digital Press.

Rumbaugh, J. *et al.* (1991), *Object Oriented Modelling and Design*, Prentice-Hall, Englewood Cliffs, New Jersey.

Schach, S. R. (1993), *Software Engineering*, 2nd edition, Irwin.

Semmens, L. and Allen, P. (1991), 'Formalising Yourdon', Methods Integration Conference, KBSL/Leeds Polytechnic.

Shneiderman, B. (1992), *Designing the User Interface*, Addison-Wesley, Reading, Mass.

Schrodinger, E. (1954), *What is Life?*, Cambridge University Press, Cambridge.

Sidoran, J. L. *et al.* (1995), 'A case study on rapid systems prototyping and its impact on system evolution', in *Proceedings of Sixth IEEE International Workshop on Rapid Systems Prototyping: shortening the path from specification to prototype*, IEEE Computer Society Press.

Smith, A. and Dunckley, L. (1995), 'Human factors in software development', in K. Nordby *et al.* (eds), *Human Computer Interaction. Proceedings of INTERACT-95*. Chapman and Hall.

Spivey, J. M. (1992), *The Z Notation: A Reference Manual*, 2nd edition, Prentice-Hall, London.

Tardieu, A. *et al.* (1991), *Methode MERISE: principles et outils*, 4th edition, Editions d'Organization, Paris.

Wynekoop, J. and Russo, N. (1995), 'Systems development methods: unanswered questions', *Journal of Information Technology*, 10, 65–73.

Furthur reading

Avison, D. E. and Fitzgerald, G. (1995), *Information Systems Development*, McGraw-Hill, London.

Budgen, D. (1993), *Software Design*, Addison-Wesley, Wokingham.

Lewis, P. (1994), *Informations Systems Development*, Pitman, London.

Chapter 5

User needs:

Functional and aspirational → Human-centred social systems design → **Organizational** acceptability

THE SOCIAL SYSTEM: DESIGNING FOR ORGANIZATIONAL ACCEPTABILITY

with Ken Eason

Chapter aims

We have emphasized that a wide *scope* should be adopted for the design of successful and usable information systems. This requires the analyst to follow the socio-technical principle. In this chapter we focus on how we can ensure, or at least enhance organizational acceptability. Specifically through study of this chapter the reader should be able to:

- Appreciate the relationship between information systems and organizational change
- Define organizational acceptability and rejection
- Evaluate the user and organizational effects of proposed information systems solutions
- Propose social systems which result in organizational acceptability
- Recognize the ingredients of successful change management
- Evaluate the user implications of different implementation strategies

5.1 Acceptability: attitude, resistance and rejection

We have adopted the ISO definition of usability as being 'the effectiveness, efficiency and satisfaction with which specified users can achieve specified goals' and noted that satisfaction is defined as 'the comfort and *acceptability* of the system'. In our study of users and information systems we have recognized that we need to take a wide view of acceptability (Chapter 1) and map it to both the user and the organization. Satisfaction relates to individual user *attitude* within an organizational context. Through inappropriate individual attitudes an information system may experience user *resistance* and even positive strategies of rejection. In this chapter we will review the theories underpinning user resistance and analyse strategies to maximize individual and organizational acceptance of information systems.

5.1.1   Resistance and rejection

Hirschheim and Newman (1988) provide an extensive review of the theory and practice of user resistance. They state that:

> User resistance to the development and implementation of computer-based information systems is legendary and can take many forms. It can range from the physical sabotaging of a new system, as was the case of the US postal workers pouring honey and inserting paper clips into their data entry devices, to the simple non-use of a system, to the more subtle and covert political manoeuvring which accompanies a system which is perceived to redistribute organizational power.

Marcus (1983) describes three broad theories explaining why information systems may come up against resistance:

1. A people determined theory
2. A system determined theory
3. An interaction theory

In the *people determined theory*, resistance occurs because of factors internal to the person or group using the system. Within this theory two possible underpinning explanations of resistance exist. First it could be that *all* people tend to resist change brought about by the introduction of new information systems and technology. An alternative suggestion is that whereas *some* people (particularly those possessing analytic cognitive styles) tend to accept such systems, *others* (specifically those with high levels of intuitive thinking) are more likely to resist them (Chapter 2).

The *system determined theory* is founded on the assumption that resistance occurs because of factors inherent in the application or information system itself. Within this category we can include all aspects of systems and interface usability.

In the *interaction theory* resistance is brought about by an interaction between characteristics related to the people and characteristics related to the system. Within this category Marcus identifies two variants:

1. *A socio-technical variant*, in which the interaction is between the system and the division of labour within the organization (organization design).
2. A *political variant*, in which the interaction is between the system and the distribution of organizational power within the organization.

Strategies to overcome, or at least minimize, the effects of the people determined theory include the principle of user-centred design (Chapter 3) and effective strategies for the management of change. The system determined theory of resistance is addressed by designing for technical, and particularly interface, usability (Chapter 7). Here we will look at strategies to mitigate the effects of interaction theory and primarily focus on the socio-technical variant. Before doing so it may be useful to refer back to the work of social psychologists as it could provide additional insight as to why individuals develop particular attitudes to computers.

5.1.2   Attitude and behaviour

Within what is referred to as *attitude theory*, social psychologists define an attitude as:

> a learned and organised collection of beliefs towards an individual, object or situation predisposing the individual to respond in some preferential manner
>
> (Bentler and Speckart, 1979)

In our context of users and information systems we are interested in the users' predisposed attitude to their workplace object: the computer. While effective user interface and social systems design will, through the production of usable systems, mitigate against inappropriate predisposed attitudes, systems success cannot be ensured without addressing attitudinal issues prior to implementation. Luckily as attitudes are learned they can be changed.

Although a large body of research within social psychology has shown that the relationship between attitude and behaviour is not as strong as one might expect, a knowledge of individual attitudes is one ingredient in predicting user behaviour. Other aspects that determine behaviour relate to the specific nature of the situation, the type of individuals concerned, and to normative influences on individual behaviour. In our terms user behaviour can range from full systems acceptance, through marginal resistance to total rejection. Hirschheim and Newman (1988) expand on the types of behaviour associated with resistance and distinguish between:

- *Aggression,* a behaviour that represents an attack (either physically or non-physically) with the intent of injuring or causing harm to the object presenting the problem.
- *Projection,* a behaviour exhibited when the person blames the system for causing difficulties.
- *Avoidance,* which occurs when a person defends himself from the system by avoiding or withholding from it.

Individuals who hold negative attitudes are unlikely to make effective and efficient use of information systems. Attitudes to, and behaviours resulting from, the introduction of computer systems are often very complex. However, through an understanding of the factors that determine attitude and behaviour we can improve the way in which we design the interaction between human and computer. Mechanisms that involve the user within the design process and which train and support them in the implementation stage are likely to promote more positive attitudes and lead to greater success.

We have already seen (Chapter 2) how *image theory* can help to explain how individual users can generate particular perceptions of information systems and can make initial decisions on whether to accept or reject such systems. In summary image theory, Beach (1990) proposes that decisions are based upon a *framing* process whereby elements of an individual's *value, trajectory* and *strategic* image are identified and used as a basis for both *adoption* and *progress* decisions. Image theory provides us with a framework for decisions made (in our case attitudes formed) at particular instances in time. However, as we have stated, attitudes can be changed and it is a particular focus of this book that a user-centred design process can modify and maximize user responses.

A second foundation for the analysis of user attitude can be found in the work of Bentler and Speckart (1979) who describe a generic *attitude behaviour model* which, based upon prior behaviour, individual social and personal norms, and individual attitude to specific behaviours, attempts to describe how individuals might decide to take up particular behavioural positions. In an attempt to propose a specific *behaviour model for users of information systems,* Fig. 5.1 extends Bentler and Speckart's behaviour model, applies it specifically to the users of computerized information systems and integrates aspects of image theory. In addition to generic determinants of behaviour, the model adds both system and implementation issues and attempts a more detailed exploration of Marcus's interaction theory of resistance.

The model proposes that individual behaviour in response to computerized information systems can be described by image theory in relation to the value, trajectory and strategic images held by the user but that the framing and decision-making process can be influenced by five factors:

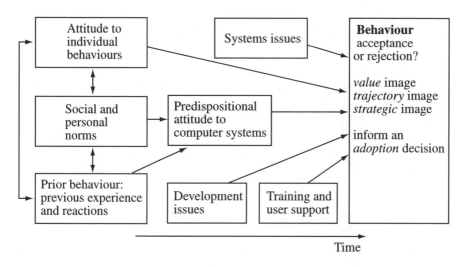

FIGURE 5.1   *A behaviour model for users of information systems*

1. *Attitude to individual behaviours,* all individuals differ in their likely behaviour patterns, some workers are inherently less likely to react in negative ways.
2. *Predispositional attitude,* based upon prior behavioural patterns (such as reactions to earlier computer implementations), and social and personal norms of behaviour (which are themselves affected by attitude to individual behaviours), individuals will form a predispositional attitude to the use of computer systems.
3. *System issues,* the major elements within the socio-technical system are also important, those systems that clearly demonstrate high levels of usability and functionality will tend to mitigate against the effects of predispositional attitude.
4. *Development issues,* the actual process of user participation in development (Chapter 3) can also minimize the negative effects of predispositional attitude.
5. *Training and user support,* which, as we will see in Chapter 8, can mitigate against negative attitudes.

5.2   Information systems and organizational change

It is widely acknowledged that the introduction of information technology can revolutionize organizational life (Eason, 1988). As the pace of technological developments continues to increase the relationship between information systems and organizational change will become even more crucial to both organizational and information systems success. Broadly speaking we might identify two possible relationships between information systems and organizational change. In the first situation, of *remedial social systems design*, it is only after the introduction of new computerized systems that the organization appreciates the need to adapt and to revise its social system. The alternative of *planned social systems design* represents the situation where, as a consequence of organizational strategy, both the organization (the social system) and the information system (the technical system) are designed in parallel. We have already referred to this as socio-technical systems design (Chapter 3). Within an effective socio-technical system the social system and the technical system are in synergy under the principle of co-optimization.

When managing the successful expansion of a range of information systems within an organization we need to strike an effective balance between allowing information systems to inform organizational change and ensuring that organizational strategy defines information systems design. In many ways, therefore, social systems design can be seen as both a top-down and a bottom-up process.

5.2.1   Organizational strategy defining information system design

In the top-down approach to development both social and technical systems design should be rooted in organizational strategy. Although there is no academically agreed definition of strategy we will quote Porter (1980):

FIGURE 5.2   *A hierarchy of social and technical strategies*

Strategy is a broad based formula for how business is going to compete, what its goals should be, and what policies will be needed to carry out those goals.

Strategy encompasses long-term objectives, plans of action and the allocation of resources. The detailed specification and implementation of organizational strategy should be dependant upon organizational structure. By taking one example of an organizational structure, Fig. 5.2 describes a hierarchy of social and technical implementation decisions based upon organizational, divisional and departmental/functional strategies. The model itself has been developed from one proposed by Robson (1994). The information systems strategy should support the other functional aspects of the organization such as marketing, production and particularly personnel. Ward, Griffiths and Whitmore (1990), in a model of a planning process, suggest that an IS strategy plan should contain three elements:

1. *Business information strategy*, showing how information will be used to support the business.
2. *Information systems functional strategy*, demonstrating how resources (physical and personnel) will be developed.
3. *Information systems/technology strategy*, defining the hardware and software policies and the IT/IS department's role.

We have noted that for *planned social systems design* the organization (the social system) and the information system (the technical system) are designed in parallel. In order to achieve this, large organizations need to ensure an effective relationship between IT/IS and human resource (personnel) strategies. Many organizations establish standing (semi-permanent) IT or IS steering committees through which such relationships can be fostered. Effective representation from users throughout the organization, together with appropriate support from a range of managerial, personnel and IT specialists, is required. If an organization does not set up standing IT/IS committees it is crucial to ensure extensive representation on project specific steering groups (Chapter 3).

5.2.2 Information systems informing organizational change

One particular example of how the introduction of an information system can lead to the revision in the organization's social system is provided by Collinson (1993) in a discussion of the effects of the replacement of batch processing by on-line information processing (OLP) systems within the UK insurance industry. The following is an edited and restructured extract:

OLP eliminated the need for a great deal of clerical discretion, knowledge and experience in the processing of insurance policies. Corporate personnel recognised the paradoxes and dangers of introducing a highly expensive OLP system which deskilled and de-motivated the very employees on whom the company relied (and as a result) a (job) regrading scheme was devised and agreed with workers. The transition to OLP was accompanied by widespread organizational restructuring (with) dramatic reductions in the size of branch networks.

Huczynski and Buchanan (1991) in an analysis of how a range of new technologies can affect the organization and the people who work in them, show how technology can, to a lesser or greater extent, make determinant demands on its users. Specifically they identify six main issues:

1. *Tasks*, the kind of work which needs to be done
2. *Job design*, the horizontal division of labour
3. *Organization of work*, the grouping of jobs together
4. *Organizational structure*, the hierarchy through which work is planned and organized, alternatively referred to as the vertical division of labour
5. *Knowledge and skills*, needed to perform the tasks
6. *Values, attitudes and behaviour*, of those performing the tasks

A variety of studies (e.g. Eason, 1988) have shown that the list identified above is equally relevant to users of human–computer systems. The order of items within the list is significant as it represents a chronological ordering of the processes and effects within social systems design and implementation. Systems and task analysis will specify the tasks within the overall social-technical system. After a process of allocating tasks between the human and computer elements of the whole system the manual user *tasks* can be specified, and these can determine *job design*. Individual job designs then inform the *organization of work* and the *organizational structure*. In order to operate the new system users require *knowledge and skills* and after implementation their *values, attitudes and behaviour* may be modified.

5.3   Human and organizational requirements for information systems

The information systems developer who is committed to the human-factor approach will need to communicate, and work effectively, with organizational and human resource specialists in the implementation of a socio-technical solution. Although the information systems developer will not need to be a specialist in these areas, it is clear that before he or she would be able to participate in a well-founded social systems design it would be necessary to appreciate the essential human and organizational requirements of information systems. For our study an elementary coverage of organization and job design will also be informative.

5.3.1   Organization design

In the long history of organizational and administrative theory two concepts have been especially important to understanding how people co-operate in performing large tasks: the *division of labour* and the *distribution of power* (Eason, 1996). The seminal work of Weber (1947), for example, showed that a large organizational task such as building a motor car can be undertaken by a team of people if the overall task was subdivided into subtasks and these allocated to members of the team. *Task specialization* is thus a pervasive characteristic of large organizations. Once the large organizational task has been divided and allocated there is then the question of co-ordination and control and the traditional approach has been to create a *hierarchy* in which managers have responsibility for these control tasks. As a result there is often an uneven distribution of power in organizations although the modern movement towards team working and flatter organizations is to some extent both reducing the emphasis on task specialization and increasing the distribution of power.

Organizational theories

Vaske and Grantham (1990) discuss three major *social organizational theories* which, taken together, provide a philosophical basis for the development of organizations, for the type of information system that they need, and for the most appropriate methods of design (Chapter 4). The three theories can be summarized as:

- *A structural approach,* in which, through organizational hierarchies, emphasis is given to formal roles and responsibilities within the organization.
- *The human relations school,* through which emphasis is given to informal patterns of communication within an organization on the assumption that individual output is strongly affected by the attitude of employees both to each other and to the organization itself.

- *Open systems theory,* in which the emphasis switches from assigning priority to internal organizational issues evidenced in both the structural and human relations approach to the wider interaction between the organization and its environment.

Within the structural approach Hunt (1986) helps us to understand how and why such organizational hierarchies have evolved. The traditionalist approach to hierarchies was developed from practising managers in the late 19th and early 20th century and led to a number of well-known organizational design concepts such as the need to maintain clear lines of authority, that authority should be delegated to as minimum a number of levels as possible, and that the span of control (the number of posts co-ordinated by a single manager) should be limited.

The human relations school places importance on a wide range of human needs, such as those documented by Maslow (Chapter 2), as these have been shown to be important in the analysis of motivation. Central to the human relations school are the concepts *of participative management* and *job enrichment.* Job enrichment involves redefining narrow, fragmented job roles into positions that encourage thinking and promote personal growth opportunities (Vaske and Grantham, 1990). In terms of information systems design, participative management is embodied in user-centred design which in turn through job design should lead to job enrichment. Both the structural and human relations approaches are examples of *closed* systems theory. Socio-technical systems theory (Chapter 4), on the other hand, is one example of an *open* systems approach.

Organizational structures

There are a number of ways in which an organization can be hierarchically structured in order to fulfil its objectives. Structures are created through policies designed to co-ordinate organizational activities and assign responsibilities to particular management hierarchies (Vaske and Grantham, 1990). The three most common forms of organizational hierarchy are the *bureaucratic,* the *centralized functional* and the *divisional* structure. A variety of alternative modes of operation, collectively known as *dual hierarchy* structures, are essentially variants of a centralized structure, and often operate at departmental levels. Examples of such dual hierarchy structures include organization by *project teams,* and the *matrix structure.* An extension to the project team structure is the concept of autonomous work groups that typically comprises four to seven multi-skilled individuals charged with common primary tasks and operating within a self-governing and regulatory framework. A summary of these five types of organizational hierarchy, together with implications for information systems design is presented in Table 5.1.

The process of organizational design

A simplified description of the basic process of organizational design could be described by the following steps:

- *Establish the business purpose*
- *Set the business objectives*, the future desired states of the business
- *Establish goals and tactics*, the intermediate steps to the achievement of goals

TABLE 5.1   *Organizational hierarchies*

Hierarchical structure	Description	Implications for information systems
Bureaucratic	A highly centralized and task-oriented managerial style, sometimes found in the public sector, in which all tasks are distinct subsets of the primary task.	Computerized information systems are increasingly important in modifying or controlling behaviour within such structures.
Centralized functional	A structure based upon the functions of the organization (e.g. finance, marketing), providing a high degree of centralized decision making yet affording increased flexibility.	Individual functions can readily be supported by information systems. Cross-organizational management information systems are increasingly important.
Divisional	A structure that reduces the size of individual units. Division is often based upon the product with each division having separate internal structures.	Divisions usually have their own information systems.
Project teams	Based upon a number of task-oriented groups, each member of the team works to a common goal in fulfilment of a specific project.	Project teams need to have autonomy: information systems should not restrict this.
Matrix	Individual employees are responsible jointly to two authorities representing two arms of a matrix structure.	Effective cross-organizational management information systems are very important

- *Specify the broad tasks*, which support the achievement of goals
- *Group the tasks into meaningful groupings*
- *Organize tasks into jobs*
- *Refine the tasks*, at individual worker level

Having specified the broad tasks that are required as shown above it is necessary to arrange the tasks into meaningful groupings and derive appropriate ways of working. The most frequently used alternative forms of work organization have been shown to be grouping by:

- *Function,* leading to single function jobs
- *Product,* generating multi-function jobs
- *Customer,* requiring multi-function jobs serving specific customers

We can investigate the three approaches with reference to the Acadmin student administration system. A college or university organized by *function* would have central administrative facilities with individual employees specializing in particular aspects of student administration generic to all students (e.g. grants, examinations, etc.). The second alternative of arrangement by *product* would require personnel to be proficient in all aspects of student administration for certain students on particular courses (e.g. undergraduate, postgraduate, research). The third approach implies that employees would provide all services related to a specific set of *customers* (e.g. full-time, part-time, industry).

Clearly identified criteria are necessary in order to select the most appropriate form of task grouping. Eason (1988) identifies six criteria for evaluating and selecting the most suitable form of work organization. They are presented below in *decreasing* order of priority as usually evidenced in practice:

1. *Cost,* the initial outlay to establish the work organization
2. *Productivity,* resulting from the re-organization
3. *Tradition* within the organization, which is often difficult to overcome
4. *Organizational effectiveness,* which may affect, but is not the only determinant of productivity
5. *Health and welfare,* of employees within the organization
6. *Satisfaction and motivation,* of the workforce

When selecting the form of work organization to match a new information system the fact that satisfaction and motivation are usually far less significant than initial outlay is further evidence both of the lack of emphasis given to social systems design and of the reasons for information systems failure.

5.3.2   The ORDIT method for analysing organizational implications

The HUSAT Research Institute has developed the Organizational Requirements Definition for Information Technology (ORDIT) method for analysing the most appropriate form of work organization. ORDIT is a set of methods for the articulation of organizational requirements by modelling future socio-technical systems and exploring the implications of the different possibilities (Eason, 1996). At the heart of ORDIT is a modelling language that uses responsibility analysis as a method of exploring the way in which the social and technical systems combine to achieve the primary task. The underlying concept is that large tasks are achieved by assigning responsibility for different subtasks to members of the social system and, in order that they can execute their responsibilities, they need access to the tools, resources, information, and so on, appropriate to their role. The responsibilities are assigned to work roles and then the pivot upon which an effective socio-technical system must rest; the responsibilities define the role relations between members of the social system and the necessary distribution of technical resources.

We will apply aspects of the ORDIT method at the end of this chapter within the Plumbest case study.

5.3.3   Job design

Within our study job design is a central aspect of organization design. The work of individual employees should be planned so that it is equal to the abilities of the worker without asking too little, or too much, of him or her. There are three elements that underpin successful job design:

1. Task complexity
2. Job efficiency
3. Job satisfaction

Although studies have shown that, for an individual worker, there is an optimum level of task complexity (Fig. 5.3) for which both job satisfaction and job efficiency are maximized, the specific level of optimum task complexity will vary from one worker to another and for each, levels of job satisfaction and efficiency will change. Job satisfaction is a crucial determinant of individual acceptability of information systems. Within the organizational context of a number of user groups, overall levels of job satisfaction can make or break an IS project. Job design should therefore be based upon well-founded rules from the theories of organizational design, and should overtly aim to maintain and, if possible enhance job satisfaction. Job

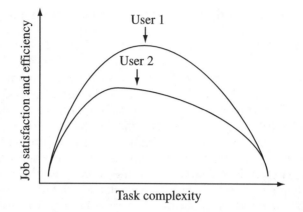

FIGURE 5.3   *Effects of task complexity on job satisfaction and efficiency*

satisfaction is closely related to two conflicting concepts: occupational stress and levels of boredom.

Stress and boredom

The term *stress* was first introduced after the Second World War in the field of medicine and was defined as *the 'reaction of the organism to a threatening situation'*. Stress is a physical condition and can be quantitatively measured through the identification of a particular type of hormone found in urine samples. It can lead to a number of stress reactions including a rise in heart rate and blood pressure, an increase in sugar released by the liver and an increased metabolism. Although long lasting stressful situations can lead to serious gastro-intestinal and cardio-vascular conditions, a limited amount of stress is present in all aspects of our everyday lives. Grandjean (1987) defines occupational stress as *'the emotional state (or mood) which results from a discrepancy between the level of demand and the person's ability to cope'*.

A major cause of boredom at work is the existence of a poor match between the employee's level of education, knowledge and ability and the specific content of the job being undertaken. Lack of motivation, whether by cause or effect, is a significant contributory factor. According to Grandjean (1987) *'a monotonous environment is one that is lacking in stimuli, and the individual's reaction to monotony is boredom'*. In terms of our study although prolonged repetitive VDU work has been shown to lead to increased boredom levels, information systems in general can either increase or reduce boredom. The workload requirements of some systems has been shown to enlarge, thereby reducing boredom whereas others have demonstrated how the routine and repetitive nature can increase it.

Determinants of job satisfaction: criteria for good job design

From surveys and theoretical considerations (e.g. Tynan, 1980) we can identify a number of conditions within the development and implementation of information systems that will affect job satisfaction within the work environment. They have been grouped together in four classifications as illustrated in Fig. 5.4. Through appropriate job control mechanisms, particularly user-centred design, the user is able to influence the other classes. We shall now further investigate each of these determinants of job satisfaction.

Job control: human-centred job design   Throughout our study we have emphasized the importance of user-centred design of information systems. From our standpoint it follows that the job design process itself should involve the individuals who will perform the jobs: it should be human-centred. By increasing the level of participation

FIGURE 5.4   *Determinants of job satisfaction*

workers have far greater *control* over their working situation and can influence the other determinants of job satisfaction. It has been shown that a lack of employee input to work practices can produce emotional and psychological strain. Development projects that are not user-centred are associated with low levels of job control and their users are therefore unable to achieve other aspects of job satisfaction.

Franklin *et al.* (1992) explore the advantages of employee participation in job design and describe a case study in *human-centred job design*. They show that the analysis of tasks, and an emphasis on socio-technical design and human–computer interaction, on their own are insufficient for fully effective job design. Individual working environments are far richer than any task analysis technique can capture. Central here are the ideas of *tacit knowledge and skill* which are discussed by Franklin but previously identified. Those who ascribe to the tacit nature of knowledge and skill argue that such knowledge and skill can never be adequately described by formal methods. It is necessary for those who possess such qualities to input them directly through a human-centred job design process.

Job content   The aims of job design should be to reduce stress and boredom by making work both worth while and meaningful. Human resource personnel often refer to the process of job enrichment through which employees are given increased information and responsibility. Dissatisfaction with job content can lead to stress and lack of job satisfaction. There are a number of specific issues:

- *Task variety*, a mix of tasks and a variety of method tends to enhance satisfaction.
- *Task complexity*, we need to strike the appropriate level (Fig. 5.3) and take account of the effects on boredom and stress.
- *Work pace and load*, the quantity of work required and how it matches the employee's capacity.
- *Task identification*, the degree to which the job makes a coherent whole and through which employees are able to make a visible contribution to the organization and identify with an end product of their efforts.

Organizational issues   A number of determinants of job satisfaction have been found to relate to interpersonal communication and contacts within the organization:

- *Discretion, autonomy and privacy*, the extent to which employees are able to execute their tasks independently from others, and carry responsibility for their own actions.
- *Standardization/formality*, the extent to which the technical system affects the flexibility in which the task can be achieved.

- *Feedback mechanisms,* the way in which the organization informs individuals about their performance.
- *Social support*, a lack of personal, face-to-face, support from colleagues and supervisory staff increases stress: information technology and communication systems tends to reduce social support.

Personal issues   The single most important personal aspect of job satisfaction is that of *job security* or the threat of unemployment. Information technology is often perceived as such a threat. In addition the following issues are relevant:

- *Career prospects*, which can represent a positive aspect if new opportunities are opened up thorough job design.
- *Individual status*, how the proposal may affect the user's status within the organization.
- *Pay and rewards*, performance should be linked to rewards, non-pay issues include the provision of opportunities to learn and develop.
- *Physical environment*, ergonomic issues relating to workstation design, issues such as system response time and computer breakdown can cause stress.

5.4   Evaluating the effect of technical solutions

Evaluation plays an important part in the user-centred design of information systems and can occur at a number of stages in the systems development life cycle. User-based evaluations are central to ensuring usability within the technical system (Chapter 7), and may take place at a variety of stages in the development of the software interface. However, at a relatively early stage within the life cycle, such as during the feasibility study, or at early stages in analysis, it is possible to evaluate how a proposed technical solution will affect the organization and the individual users in which, and through whom, it will operate. This evaluation process is crucial to a socio-technical design process and deserves a detailed coverage within our study.

5.4.1   Evaluation studies: the process of impact analysis

Eason (1988) describes a method by which the impact of a proposed technical system on a target organization can be judged. The process as depicted in Fig. 5.5 has been modified from the version proposed by Eason. Having developed an outline technical system for proposed implementation within a user organization the process of impact assessment can include four stages:

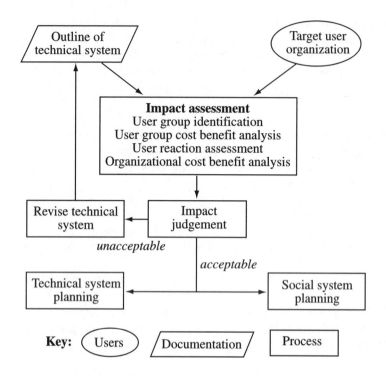

FIGURE 5.5   *Assessing the impact of proposed technical solutions* (source: Eason, K. (1988), *Information Technology and Organisational Change,* Taylor and Francis, London)

1. *User group identification*, through which the individual user groups that could possibly be affected by the proposed technical system are identified.
2. *User group cost benefit analysis*, in which the potential effects of the proposal on each user group are analysed.
3. *User reaction assessment*, through which the probable responses of both winners and losers in the organization are identified.
4. *Organizational cost benefit analysis*, in which the global effect on the organization and user groups is summarized.

As a result of impact assessment an overall judgement can be made as to whether the proposal is acceptable or not. If the judgement is positive then the technical system can be further specified, and any changes necessary in the social systems can be identified and undertaken. If the judgement is negative then a revised technical solution should be proposed.

The whole process of impact assessment is clearly one crying out for user participation: to be integrated within a user-centred design process. In terms of the participative *structures* category of user-centred design (Chapter 3), the process of impact assessment should be managed by the main design team with appropriate communication and representation from local design teams.

5.4.2   Cost benefit analyses: the mechanism for impact analysis

Well-founded criteria are essential to the accurate assessment of the impact of systems on organizations and user groups. The criteria should be based upon the specific ways in which the system may affect individuals within each user group and the organization as a whole. In terms of individual users Eason (1988) identifies a number of generic criteria grouped under the categories of job security, job content, organizational procedures, and personnel policies and shows how it is possible to add a number of systems specific criteria relating to the functionality provided by the technical solution.

Figure 5.6 provides a User Cost Benefit Assessment sheet developed from the one provided by Eason. It includes five sections each of which can be analysed under a number of issues. The way in which the proposal affects each issue is noted in the *change* column. For a quantitative analysis an average grade, say 0 to 5, for each of the five sections can be placed in either the *cost* or *benefit* column. By summing up the columns an overall assessment for each user group can be made. A cross-organization analysis can be undertaken by analysing all user group data. We will look at each section of the assessment sheet.

System facilities   This part of the assessment process allows us to focus on specific aspects of the functionality afforded by the technical proposal and how it will affect the user group. By using the same facilities for all user groups a comparison between groups can be made.

Job security   For individual users this is clearly the most significant issue affecting job satisfaction. Although it has not been subdivided on the assessment sheet, it is of equal weighting to each other section.

The remaining three sections analyse the other aspects (job content, organizational issues and personal issues) of job satisfaction as categorized and described in pages 171–173.

5.5   Implementation

Implementation is the fifth of six stages within the systems development life cycle. Far too often implementation is simply equated with technical changeover whereby one technical system is replaced, either in one go, or over a period of time, by another. However, if we are implementing a socio-technical solution then the

User Cost Benefit Assessment Sheet

Organization [＿＿＿＿＿]　　　System [＿＿＿＿＿]

User group [＿＿＿＿＿＿＿＿]

Number of personnel [＿＿＿]

	Issue	Change	Benefits	Costs
1	System facilities 1.1 .... 1.2 .... 1.3 .... 1.4			
2	Job security			
3	Job content 3.1 Task variety 3.2 Task complexity 3.3 Work pace and load 3.4 Task identification			
4	Organizational issues 4.1 Discretion/autonomy 4.2 Standardization/formality 4.3 Feedback 4.4 Social support			
5	Personal issues 5.1 Career issues 5.2 Individual status 5.3 Pay/rewards 5.4 Physical environment			
	Totals			

FIGURE 5.6　*User Cost Benefit Assessment sheet* (source: Eason, K. (1988), *Information Technology and Organisational Change,* Taylor and Francis, London)

implementation process involves the management of both *technical changeover* and *organizational change.*

5.5.1 Managing organizational change

We can make the assumptions that all organizations are socio-technical in nature: they have both people and technology. All socio-technical systems experience continual change and the implementation of all new systems will involve some form of organizational change. Organizational change cannot be totally predicted but its inherent unpredictability can be mitigated by effective strategic management, including a commitment within such a strategy to employee (in our case user) participation.

Successful organizational change management involves high-level planning and management skills. In order to implement a change identified from the process of organization design, the manager or managers responsible for the change need to *unfreeze* the organization from its present position and then *refreeze* it again following implementation. Those responsible also need to understand the internal and external pressures, or driving/restraining forces (Fig. 5.7), within an organization, that are likely to exist, both for and against the change.

Driving forces can relate to:

- *The nature of the project itself,* some projects have an inherently greater momentum than others (project management methods are important here as are issues relating to finance, such as incentives or penalties that may result from early or late delivery).
- *Corporate management issues,* active support and determination to succeed within the management group can be important.
- *Personnel responsible for implementation,* the personality and mode of operation of those responsible for implementation is often significant.

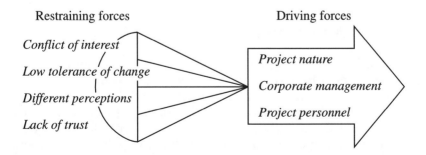

FIGURE 5.7   *IS implementation—driving and restraining forces*

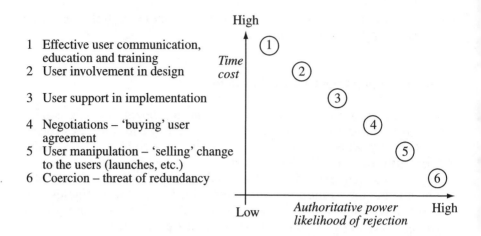

1 Effective user communication, education and training
2 User involvement in design

3 User support in implementation

4 Negotiations – 'buying' user agreement
5 User manipulation – 'selling' change to the users (launches, etc.)
6 Coercion – threat of redundancy

FIGURE 5.8   *Overcoming forces restraining organizational change*

Restraining forces may occur as a result of:

- *A conflict of interest,* between those requiring change and those affected by it.
- *A low tolerance of change,* of employees who consider that they have experienced too much change.
- *Different perceptions*, concerning the need for change between those requiring change and those affected by it.
- *A lack of trust,* or misunderstanding, between users and those implementing change.

A number of approaches to overcoming restraining forces have been identified. Six of these are listed and presented in Fig. 5.8 from which it is unfortunate to see that those which are less costly and quicker to implement tend not only to represent a higher degree of authority but also lead to lower levels of acceptance.

5.5.2   Managing technical changeover

Several different strategies for technical systems implementation have been identified (e.g. Eason, 1988) and were introduced in Chapter 3. In the greenfield site and big bang approach implementation is immediate, in the first case as there is no previous system to replace, and in the latter through 'overnight' replacement. Alternative methods include parallel running, phased introduction, trails and disseminations and incremental evolution. As we have seen the degree to which the changeover method involves organizational change is the criterion that will have the greatest effect on the user.

5.6   The process of social systems design

The process of social systems design is not essentially one that should be rigorously specified. Rather it should be flexibly applied in each individual situation. Accepting this, in order to place some of the theories of organization, and human resource management within a coherent context of information systems design two approaches to the specification of social systems design will be explored:

1. **Hierarchical checklist**. In Fig. 5.9 we set out some rules that can be applied in chronological order under each of the categories of user-centred design (structures, processes and scope). It is suggested that the IS developer can reference these rules as a checklist to evaluate the approach that he or she is adopting within a specific project. The list will be complemented by a similar one for interface design that will be presented in Chapter 7.
2. **Outline activity model**. A model of the typical activities that may be involved in social systems design is presented in Fig. 5.10 that provides a pictorial representation of the main stages.

Because both social and technical design should be undertaken in parallel both the checklist and the activity model provide one abstraction, or view, of the whole development process. The essential elements within this *social system abstraction* are set out below:

- As with other aspects of information systems design, social systems design should be participative, with a range of technical specialists and employees working together within an effective design team structure. A human-centred job design process will maximize job control and enhance job satisfaction and efficiency.
- The social systems design process should be underpinned by two main inputs: a *user specification* (Chapter 2), and a *requirements definition* (Chapter 1). These are both required for exploratory design and the assessment of impact leading to the selection of an outline technical solution.
- The requirements definition is also a vital ingredient in the determination, through task analysis techniques (Chapter 6), of a specification of all tasks whether they will be part of a computerized system or part of a remaining human activity system.
- Given the nature of the proposed outline technical solution, the socio-technical task specification can be separated, through the process of human–computer allocation, into a technical task

1 Establish participative **structures** that will enable effective user participation:

  1.1   Establish project steering and/or standing IT groups:

          1.1.1   Ensure wide representation from all functional areas

  1.2   Establish main design team:

          1.2.1   Select *users as designers* as members of main design team

          1.2.2   Select specialists in human resource management as well as other technical specialists

  1.3   Establish local design teams:

          1.3.1   Select *users as designers* as members of local design teams

2 Adopt **processes** that lead to acceptable solutions:

  2.1   Perform comprehensive user analyses:

          2.1.1   Determine user aspirational needs

          2.1.2   Determine user functional needs

  2.2   Perform task analysis, derive a socio-technical task specification

  2.3   Evaluate the social implications of outline technical solutions

  2.4   Perform human–computer allocation:

          2.4.1   Derive a technical system task specification

          2.4.2   Derive a social system task specification

  2.5   Consider organization and job design:

          2.5.1   Consider alternative forms of work organization (function, product, customer)

          2.5.2   Organize tasks into groups

          2.5.3   Refine tasks at individual employee level

  2.6   Plan for technical and organizational implementation

3 Ensure that wide **scope** is achieved:

  3.1   Base design on organizational strategy

  3.2   Relate IS and personnel strategic plans

  3.3   Strike a balance between IS informing organizational change and organizational strategy defining IS design

  3.4   Aim for job satisfaction

  3.5   Aim for job enrichment

FIGURE 5.9   *Hierarchial checklist for social systems design*

specification and a social systems task specification.

- The technical task specification will include all tasks that will be performed by the computer element of the total information system. As such it may be used to inform both functional design and interface design.
- The social systems task specification will be required for both organization and job design.

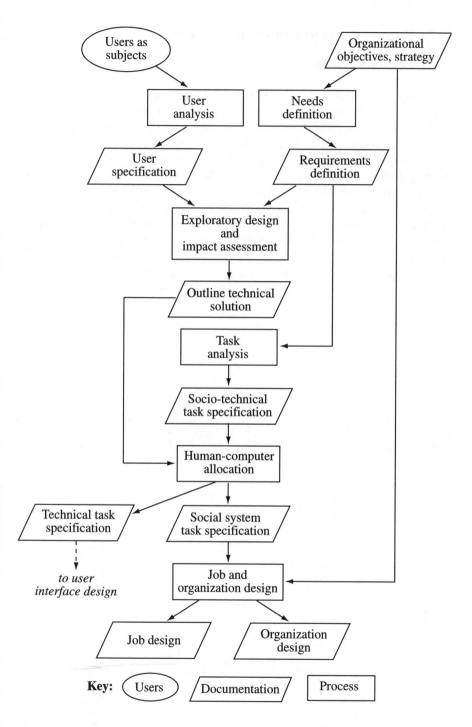

FIGURE 5.10 *An activity model of social systems design*

5.7   Plumbest plc: designing the social system

5.7.1   Further information

The project steering group has decided to adopt the ORDIT approach to the definition of work roles and responsibilities and has produced a simplified ORDIT model for the current allocation system as shown in Fig. 5.11. It should be noted that each of the responsibilities contains not only the major operational requirements that a task analysis would identify, but also the less operationally defined responsibilities upon which organizational success may depend, for example taking care of customer relations. Figure 5.11 also specifies the major relationships between roles and distinguishes between functional relations where responsibilities for work are passed from one role to another to enable the next function to be undertaken, and structural relations such as supervision which imply a power relationship enabling one role holder to exercise co-

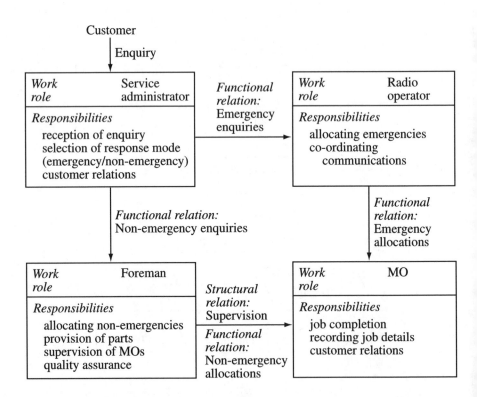

FIGURE 5.11   *ORDIT responsibility analysis*

ordination and control over another. We should note that a full ORDIT model would also list all the technical resources allocated to each role.

Within the project steering group Jenny Birch, operations manager, has been strongly supporting the idea of her 'pet plan' whereby a semi, or fully automatic, job allocation system and mobile communications system would, according to her, eliminate all the current inefficiencies in the service centre. Other members of the PSG remain to be convinced of the merits of the proposal and have supported the 'minimum solution' approach. Craig Onley, personnel director, who has some previous experience in another company of the introduction of new technology, has been emphasizing the relationship between information technology and organizational change and is keen to see how any new system might affect the organization. An outline of the requirements definition for the 'pet-plan' solution has been derived and is provided in Fig. 5.12.

In response to questions in the PSG from Craig Onley you have advised that an impact assessment of each of the alternative proposals should be made. Given the undoubted support for the 'pet plan' you have decided to approach the analysis from this point of view to start with. If however, as a result of impact judgement, revisions are necessary then they will be recommended.

5.7.2 Tasks

Plumbest Task 5.1

You have decided to use the user cost benefit assessment sheets to investigate the potential effects of the pet-plan solution on each of the user groups.

Identify the major aspects of the system facilities that will affect the user groups and which will be implemented in Section 1 of the assessment sheets.

Complete an assessment sheet for each of the following groups:

• Mobile operatives
• Foremen
• Service administrators
• Radio operators

Summarize the main effects by providing an impact judgement. Is the proposal acceptable?

General requirements
- Faster response to emergency jobs
- Prompter responses to non-emergency jobs
- Capable of coping with increased work load of UK gas contract
- Improved customer service

Technical system requirements
- Semi-automatic allocation system in service centre:
  - system allocates jobs to MO, but service centre staff can override allocation
  - job deletion facility
  - clear specification of emergency and non-emergency jobs
  - well-defined algorithm for job allocation based upon MO location and availability
- On-line access at service centre to database of jobs by a variety of access methods:
  - by MO number
  - by customer name or number
  - by time
- Direct data transfer from service centre to terminals in each van
- On-line access by MOs in their vans:
  - to individual job schedules
  - for recording of jobs on completion
- Performance monitoring facilities
  - Facility for mobile interrogation of database— job control mechanisms
- Well-designed user interface
- Safety critical implementation

Social system requirements
- More efficient overall utilization of staff
- Maintain effective supervision of MOs
- Maintain limited radio back-up facilities
- Overall expansion in organization to enable retraining where possible so as to minimize redundancy
- Enhance job satisfaction

FIGURE 5.12   *An outline requirement for pet-plan solution*

Plumbest Task 5.2

Although detailed job design can only be finished after complete social systems task analysis and specification, it is possible at this stage to undertake some preliminary work.

Having considered the cost benefit analyses and given the desire, within the situation of expansion, to retrain and redeploy where possible, together with any other issues that you see as relevant, propose a revised organization design:

1. Evaluate alternative forms of work organization by considering appropriate criteria.
2. Specify a new organizational structure.
3. Provide outline job designs including an ORDIT responsibility analysis for the proposed allocation system.

5.7.3   Solutions

Plumbest Solution 5.1

Although there are a wide number of issues that could be considered, four major aspects of the system facilities provided by the pet-plan solution are:

1. *Automatic allocation*—the way in which the computer would allocate MOs to individual jobs.
2. *Data communications*—the fact that there would be direct computer communication between the service centre and vans.
3. *Job recording*—the manner in which the system records details of individual jobs for future processing.
4. *Job control*—how appropriate supervision and monitoring of job would be undertaken.

In the following user cost benefit assessment sheets the probable effects of the pet plan on each of the user groups is specified. At this stage in the analysis it is clear that the role of the radio operator is effectively removed, except for a limited radio back-up facility, and that the role of the foreman is reduced to that of supervision only.

A summary of the overall individual user group cost benefit assessment (CBA) scores for each user group, an average of all groups, and a weighted average, having taken account of the number of employees in each group is provided Table 5.2.

From the table it can be seen that while both the foremen and the

TABLE 5.2   *Summary of CBAs*

User group	CBA score (S)	Number of employees (N)	S x N
Mobile operatives	0	52	0
Foremen	−13	4	−52
Service administrators	+12	11	132
Radio operators	−12	8	−96
Average	**−3.25**	**Weighted av.**	**−0.25**

service administrator roles are significantly negatively affected by the pet-plan solution, the overall effect, certainly taking account of the weighting factor of user group numbers, is only marginally negative. Assuming that the pet-plan solution can be developed to be functionally sound, the cost benefit analysis is not sufficiently negative in itself to cause it to be rejected by the PSG. Plumbest is in an enviable situation as it is in a period of potential growth. Although the radio operator and foreman roles will, in their current form disappear, it is likely that the individual employees will have the opportunity of redeployment within a growing workforce. In order to minimize resistance careful organization and job design will be necessary but overall, assuming technical practicality, the pet-plan solution would appear to have the potential for organizational acceptability.

User Cost Benefit Assessment Sheet

Organization | Plumbest | System | JAS—pet plan |

User group | Mobile operative |

Number of personnel | 51 |

	Issue	Change	Benefits	Costs
1	System facilities 1.1 auto. allocation 1.2 data comms. 1.3 job recording 1.4 job control	✓clearer job specification ✓faster response ✓on-line access x greater control exercised	+2	
2	Job security	No significant overall effect from JAS on security for this role, except those unwilling/unable to train. Expansion secures employment	0	
3	Job content 3.1 Task variety 3.2 Task complexity 3.3 Work pace and load 3.4 Task identification	✓enhanced by computer – increased, but OK x probable slight increase – no change	+2	
4	Organizational issues 4.1 Discretion/autonomy 4.2 Standardization/formality 4.3 Feedback 4.4 Social support	x reduced x increased – depends on supervision x reduced		–4
5	Personal issues 5.1 Career prospects 5.2 Individual status 5.3 Pay/rewards 5.4 Physical environment	– no significant change – no significant change ✓ possible increase x computer access in van may be a negative issue	0	
		0 **Totals**	**+4**	**–4**

User Cost Benefit Assessment Sheet

Organization | Plumbest | System | JAS—pet plan |

User group | Foremen |

Number of personnel | 4 |

	Issue	Change	Benefits	Costs
1	System facilities 1.1 auto. allocation 1.2 data comms. 1.3 job recording 1.4 job control	x non-emergency role removed x reduces supervisory role x eliminates role x reduces personal control exercised by foreman		−4
2	Job security	x The removal of non- emergency job allocation and the job control provided by the JAS are both negative determinants of security		−3
3	Job content 3.1 Task variety 3.2 Task complexity 3.3 Work pace and load 3.4 Task identification	x reduced to supervision x probable reduction − depends on security x no identification with full task		−2
4	Organizational issues 4.1 Discretion/autonomy 4.2 Standardization/formality 4.3 Feedback 4.4 Social support	x reduced x increased − no effect x reduced − limited MO contact		−3
5	Personal issues 5.1 Career prospects 5.2 Individual status 5.3 Pay/rewards 5.4 Physical environment	− limited x reduced − limited − access to JAS required		−1
		−13 Totals		−13

User Cost Benefit Assessment Sheet

Organization `Plumbest`   System `JAS-pet plan`

User group `Service administrators`

Number of personnel `11`

	Issue	Change	Benefits	Costs
1	System facilities 1.1 auto. allocation 1.2 data comms. 1.3 job recording 1.4 job control	✓increased responsibility - no effect ✓data access provided ✓increased role	+3	
2	Job security	✓The JAS will lead to an increase in the importance of this role. Job security overall will be enhanced, but some may be concerned	+5	
3	Job content 3.1 Task variety 3.2 Task complexity 3.3 Work pace and load 3.4 Task identification	✓increased - increased, but OK x probable increase ✓increase	+3	
4	Organizational issues 4.1 Discretion/autonomy 4.2 Standardization/formality 4.3 Feedback 4.4 Social support	✓increased x increased - no effect x reduced		-2
5	Personal issues 5.1 Career prospects 5.2 Individual status 5.3 Pay/rewards 5.4 Physical environment	✓enhanced role ✓increased ✓potential for increase x servant IT role	+3	
		+12	Totals	+14	-2

User Cost Benefit Assessment Sheet

Organization [Plumbest]   System [JAS—pet plan]

User group   [Radio operators]

Number of personnel   [8]

	Issue	Change	Benefits	Costs
1	System facilities 1.1 auto. allocation 1.2 data comms. 1.3 job recording 1.4 job control	x main role removed x main role removed - no effect - no effect		−3
2	Job security	x removal of role to that of a back-up facility is a major threat to job security for this role		−5
3	Job content 3.1 Task variety 3.2 Task complexity 3.3 Work pace and load 3.4 Task identification	for the back-up facility: - no change - no change - unpredictable - no change	0	
4	Organizational issues 4.1 Discretion/autonomy 4.2 Standardization/formality 4.3 Feedback 4.4 Social support	for the back-up facility - no change - no change - no change - no change	0	
5	Personal issues 5.1 Career prospects 5.2 Individual status 5.3 Pay/rewards 5.4 Physical environment	for the whole group: x greatly reduced x reduced x limited - no change		−4
	−12	Totals		−12

Plumbest Solution 5.2

Forms of work organization   Currently the service centre operates on *functional* lines: the service administrator takes the phone calls (or processes the faxed/posted requests), the radio operator processes emergency jobs, and the foremen process non-emergency jobs. The MOs are organized by *customer*, on a regional (depot) basis.

For practical reasons of geography and flexibility it seems sensible to retain the regional basis of MOs operating from the four depots. Three alternative basic forms of work organization for the service centre can be considered and these are evaluated as shown in Table 5.3. From the table it can be seen that, as in the majority of real-life cases, the overriding issues are those of cost and effectiveness. The service centre should continue to be organized on functional lines.

New organizational structure   It is unlikely that any computer system of itself will be sufficiently expert to act totally independently in the allocation of jobs to MOs. The current radio operators and service administrators are unable to exert supervisory control over the job execution process and such expertise needs to be supplied by staff proficient in the task domain. A supervisory role with on-line data access will still be required. It is proposed therefore to retain the majority of the foremen in the role of local area co-ordinators. These personnel will be depot-based but with a mobile van facility and will:

- Have knowledge of the local area and associated potential problems
- Know the strengths and weaknesses of individual MOs
- Through on-line access (in van or depot) be able to mediate automatic allocation where necessary
- Be expert in the MO role and provide support as required

A second organizational issue stems from the introduction of the computer systems. Computer systems staff will be required to provide both systems management and maintenance facilities and user support mechanisms. We will return to the latter in Chapter 8.

The revised organizational chart, provided in Fig. 5.13, merges the roles of service administrator and radio operator into a combined one of service telephonist, leaving a separate general administrator post, includes the necessary computing staff and replaces the foreman role with one of local area co-ordinator. With all of the job allocation being performed centrally at the service centre it is no longer appropriate for the line management of the MOs to be directly through the foremen. However, the new local area co-ordinators (LACs) have a significant advisory capacity and it is proposed that MOs operate in a matrix, or dual reporting structure, to both a LAC

TABLE 5.3   *Alternative forms of work organization within the CSU*

	Function	Product	Customer
Description of implementation	Task specialization—separate jobs for different functions, e.g. • job allocation • job administration for all types of work	Effective divisional structure based upon: • gas work • plumbing work, etc. Teams provide all functions for each division	Separate section based upon customer type: • commercial • domestic, etc. Teams provide all functions for each division
Cost	✓ limited, little difference from	x would involve start-up costs	x would involve start-up costs
Productivity	✓ efficient operation of job allocation	x min of tasks (allocation and admin.) may lead to inefficiencies	x min of tasks (allocation and admin.) may lead to inefficiencies
Tradition	✓ no change	x involves change	x involves change
Organizational	✓ practical—maintenance of current system	x product orientation of CSU would clash with multi-functional role of MOs	x product orientation of CSU would clash with multi-functional role of MOs
Health and welfare	x servant role of VDU operator	✓ mix of tasks	✓ mix of tasks
Satisfaction and motivation	x limited task identification	✓ enhanced task identification	✓ enhanced task identification
Summary	✓ although some negative employee issues this is a practical solution	x although practical on employee grounds, overall this option is impractical	x although practical on employee grounds, overall this option is impractical

and the service centre co-ordinator. Elements of an ORDIT responsiblity are given in Fig. 5.14.

Outline job designs

Operations manager

• no change in function
• change in lines of supervision

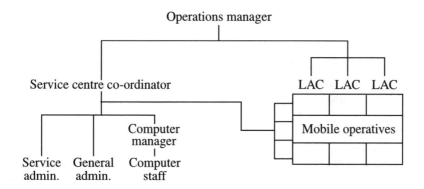

FIGURE 5.13 *Proposed new organizational structure*

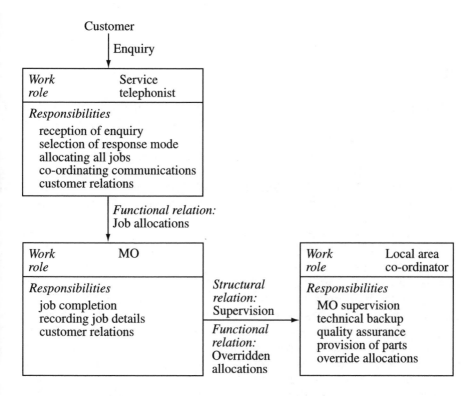

FIGURE 5.14 *ORDIT responsibility for proposed job allocation scheme*

Service centre unit co-ordinator
- no change in function
- change in lines of supervision

General administrator
- undertake administration for jobs after completion

Summary

In this chapter we have reviewed the sociological and organizational issues that inform the design of information systems and have provided a framework for the design of the social system. In particular we have seen:

- The reasons why individuals may resist the introduction of information systems
- That information systems and organizational change are closely related
- How to evaluate the effects of technical solutions on social systems
- An outline process of social systems design
- The determinants of job satisfaction and the criteria for successful job design.

Questions

5.1 How does a study of social psychology pinpoint the limitations in relying on the user classification and taxonomy approach of specifying user needs?

5.2 It has been suggested that individual users have a predispositional attitude to the introduction of computerized information systems. What methods and techniques would you adopt in a practical situation to analyse and describe the predispositional attitude within a whole user group?

5.3 How can an information systems development process mitigate against negative predispositional attitudes and enhance positive predispositional attitudes?

5.4 In which ways can the structure of an organization be affected by the introduction of computerized information systems?

5.5 To what extent are socio-technical design processes being adopted in organizations with which you are familiar? Is the concept of designing for organizational acceptability *understood* and *addressed*? This exercise could be based in a single organization, or through an appropriate survey mechanism that could summarize the results in a number of organizations grouped either by locality, size or function.

References

Beach, L R. (1990), Image Tehory: Decision Making in Personal and Organisational Context, Wiley.

Bentler, P. M. and Speckart, G. (1979), 'Models of attitude behaviour relations', *Psychological Review*, 86, 452–464.

Bramham, J. (1989), *Human Resource Planning*, Institute of Personnel Management, London.

Collinson, D. (1993), 'Introducing on-line processing: conflicting human resource policies in insurance', in J. Clark (ed.), *Human Resource Management and Technical Change*, Sage.

Eason, K. (1988), *Information Technology and Organisational Change*, Taylor and Francis, London.

Eason, K. (1996), 'Division of labour and the design of systems for computer support for cooperative work', *Journal of IT*, 11, 39–50.

Franklin, I., Pan, D., Green, E. and Own J. (1992), 'Job design within a human centred (system) design framework', *Behaviour and IT*, 11(3), 141–150.

Grandjean, E. (1987), *Ergonomics in Computerised Offices*, Taylor and Francis, London.

Hirscheim, R. and Newman, M. (1988), 'Information on systems and use-resistance: theory and procedure', *Computer Journal*, 31(5), 400–405.

Huczynski, M. and Buchanan, D. (1991), *Organisational Behaviour*, 2nd edition, Prentice-Hall.

Hunt, J. W. (1986), *Managing People at Work*, McGraw-Hill, London.

Marcus, M. L. (1983), 'Power, politics and MIS implementation', in R. M. Baecker and W. A. Buxton (eds), *Readings in HCI*, Morgan Kaufman, San Francisco.

Parker, C. and Case, T. (1993), *Management Information Systems*, McGraw-Hill, London.

Porter, M. E. (1980), *Competitive Strategy*, Macmillan.

Robson, W. (1994), *Strategic Management and Information Systems*, Pitman, London.

Tynan, K. O. (1980), 'Improving the quality of working life in the 1980s', Work Research Unit, Occasional paper 16, ACAS, London.

Vaske, J. J. and Grantham, C. E. (1990), *Socialising the Human Computer Environment*, Ablex, Norwood, New Jersey.

Ward, J., Griffiths, P. and Whitmore, P. (1990), *Strategic Planning for Information Systems*, Wiley.

Weber, M. (1947), *The Theory of Social and Economic Organization*, Free Press.

Further reading

Eason, K. (1988), *Information Technology and Organisational Change*, Taylor and Francis, London.

Vaske, J. J. and Grantham, C. E. (1990), *Socialising the Human Computer Environment*, Ablex, Norwood, New Jersey.

Chapter 6

ELEMENTS OF HUMAN– COMPUTER INTERACTION

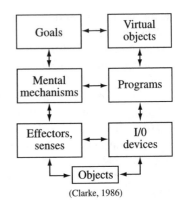

(Clarke, 1986)

Chapter aims

This chapter reviews a selection of techniques that have been developed by human-factor specialists to support the design of usable *human–computer* interfaces. It does so in the expectation that we can later apply such methods in an integrated user-centred interface design method. Specifically through study of this chapter the reader should be able to:

- Place user interactions within a context of goals, activities and tasks
- Describe user tasks using basic techniques
- Recognize the factors that affect interaction design
- Apply design rationale techniques
- Specify interfaces using basic techniques

6.1 HCI and human–computer factors

Thus far in our study of human–computer factors we have focused on the user and his or her role within the development and use of information systems. We have seen that it is necessary to adopt user-centred design principles in order to ensure that all types of user need are identified and addressed. We have noted that we can relate systems success to usability, and in turn, that usability can be described in terms of effectiveness, efficiency and satisfaction.

A number of factors will affect the usability of a system within any given organizational context. In Chapter 4 we reviewed the ways in which different design methodologies address aspects of system effectiveness. In Chapter 5 we saw how the design of the organizational social structure can enhance individual and organizational satisfaction.

In this part of our study we will focus on some of the essential elements of human–computer interaction (HCI), which have been developed in recent years by human-factor specialists, in the expectation that we will be able to apply these later within a user-centred approach to interface design, thereby enhancing the usability of the software interface.

We will not be able to provide a full coverage of the academic discipline of HCI, rather the aim is to focus our attention on a number of techniques which are either central to the study of the interaction between the human and the computer, or are helpful in making explicit the underlying intentions behind approaches to designing for such interaction. The ACM's Special Interest Group on Computer–Human Interaction (ACM SIGCHI) Curriculum Development Group (ACM, 1992) provides a working definition of HCI:

> Human–computer interaction is a discipline concerned with the design, evaluation and implementation of interactive computing systems for human use and with the study of major phenomena surrounding them.

Clearly this definition places the discipline of HCI close to the centre of our analysis. The ACM SIGCHI further clarifies the nature

TABLE 6.1   *ACM SIGCHI content of HCI*

Aspect	Nature	
N	The nature of HCI	
	N1 *	(Meta-) models of HCI
U	Use and context of computers	
	U1 *	Use and context of computers
	U2	Application areas
	U3 *	Human-machine fit and adaptation
H	Human characteristcs	
	H1 *	Human information processing
	H2 **	Language, communications, interaction
	H3 *	Ergonomics
C	Computer systems and interface architecture	
	C1	Input and output devices
	C2 **	Dialogue techniques
	C3 **	Dialogue genre
	C4	Computer graphics
	C5	Dialogue architecture
D	Development process	
	D1 **	Development approaches
	D2	Implementation techniques
	D3 *	Evaluation techniques
	D4 *	Example systems and case studies

of HCI by specifying the content for a *curriculum for HCI* as outlined in Table 6.1. From this we can see that the focus of our study in users and information systems is not identical to that of the discipline of HCI, although of course, there is considerable overlap. In our study we aim to provide a co-ordinated and consistent coverage of all the major user issues in information systems development. The majority of the important general issues with which we are interested are addressed by the ACM curriculum, particularly those which are starred (*) in Table 6.1, but other, perhaps more specific ones are included.

The essential elements in the ACM SIGCHI list on which we will focus in this chapter are interaction analysis, design and specification and relate to the double starred (**) aspects of the ACM curriculum. By studying these aspects it is expected that the reader will develop a sound understanding of the essential elements underpinning interface design that we can apply in the following chapter. Taken together Chapters 6 and 7 constitute our specific coverage of human–computer interaction.

6.2   Investigating user interaction

6.2.1   Activities: goals, intentions, tasks and actions

The starting point for any systematic analysis of human–computer interaction is an understanding of how and why users perform their activities. At a detailed, or elementary level the user performs individual user *actions*. When using a word-processing package, for example, a user may perform the action of *highlighting a sentence* by moving and clicking a mouse. The successful and effective design and development of the software to perform the elementary actions can only be achieved by placing such actions within some clearly defined context of use. Presumably the person using the word processor has some reason to highlight the text; possibly because he or she wishes to perform the *task* of *moving it from one place within a document to another*. Individual tasks only make sense within the context of *goals* that the user is seeking to achieve. The task of moving the piece of text only makes sense within a context or goal such *as writing a letter home to mum*.

Goals and tasks exist in a hierarchical structure and can often easily be broken down into sub-goals and sub-tasks. The goal of *producing a letter to mum* as described above will contain the sub-goal of moving a sentence from one paragraph to another. This goal will be achieved through the accomplishment of the task of cutting and pasting a sentence from one place in the letter to another. One individual action required within the cutting and pasting task is to highlight the sentence by moving and clicking a mouse. The word-processing example is shown in Table 6.2.

When we take a considered view of user activities within HCI we

TABLE 6.2   *Activities, goals, tasks, actions*

	Definition	Example
Activity	Specific user interaction scenario	Using a word processor
Goal	Desired output from a performed task	Goal: writing home to mum Sub-goal: moving a sentence
Task	Set of actions required to achieve a goal or sub-goal	Task: creating and editing a letter Sub-task: cutting and pasting a sentence from one place to another
Action	Lowest level action required to complete a task	Highlighting a sentence by moving and clicking a mouse

notice that we have a hierarchical structure: goals, tasks and actions. Humans perform purposeful, goal-oriented activities (Clarke, 1986). At the highest level, purpose, according to Clarke, may be described as *'a striving towards objectives to do with the self'*. We might, therefore, try to relate purposes with aspirational needs. Goals, however, are to do with things in the real world and are achievable steps to fulfilling some purpose. Goals are achieved through the execution of a number of individual tasks each of which may involve a series of elemental actions.

6.2.2   Norman's model of interaction

Norman (1988) has described a slightly different hierarchy of goals, *intentions* and actions and has used these within the specification of an *execution–evaluation cycle*, also known as the *seven stages of action.* Three of the stages constitute the execution of a specific interaction whereas the remaining four specify the process of evaluating the result of the performed execution. The seven stages are outlined in Table 6.3 together with an example interaction scenario. The scenario chosen represents an error situation, relating to the goal of moving a sentence from one paragraph in a letter to another, and helps amplify another of Norman's concepts; that of the gulfs of execution and evaluation.

The gulfs of execution and evaluation help us understand why in some instances human–computer interaction can be problematic for users. The *gulf of execution* represents the difference between the user's formulation of the actions required to achieve the goal and the actual actions provided by the system. A well-designed interface

TABLE 6.3   *Seven stages of action*

		Stage	Example interaction scenario
Execution	1	Form a goal	Move a sentence from one paragraph in a letter to another.
	2	Form an intention	Use word-processing facilities to move a piece of text from one place in a document to another.
	3	Specify the action sequence	Highlight the text by moving and clicking a mouse, click on cut button, move to new position in document and click on paste button.
	4	Execute the action	An error scenario—the user highlights the text correctly but clicks on the copy button instead of cut button then completes the action.
Evaluation	5	Perceive the resultant system state	User sees new text in correct position, but notices that it is still in the original position as well.
	6	Interpret the resultant state	User realizes that he or she must have copied rather than cut.
	7	Evaluate the outcome	User knows that goal has not been completed and that it is necessary to delete the text in the original position. This leads to a new goal and set of actions.

should attempt to minimize the gulf of execution, thereby making interaction as intuitive as possible. The *gulf of evaluation* is the mismatch between the user's expectations of what should result from the actions performed, and the actual response provided by the system. The gulf of evaluation will be large for both error situations, perhaps as a result of a large gulf of evaluation, and instances where there is poor feedback from the system to the user.

6.2.3   Clarke's three-level model for HCI

The hierarchical nature of user interaction has been described (Clarke, 1986) by a three-level model (Fig. 6.1) which can be used both to further structure our discussion on human–computer interaction, and to support the analysis and design of the software interface. The model specifies at three levels (psycho-social, mental functions and sensori-motor) the human and computer elements within human–computer communication.

The model breaks the overall interaction into three levels. For

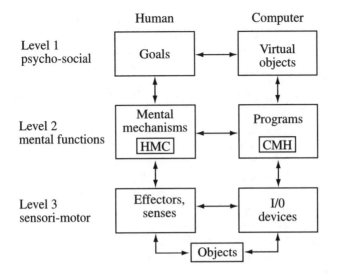

FIGURE 6.1   *Three-level human–computer interface model (*adapted from Clarke, A. A. (1996), 'A three level human–computer interface model', *International Journal of Man-Machine Studies,* 24, 503–517, by permission of the publisher, Academic Press Ltd, London*)*

effective overall human–computer communication there needs to be an appropriate communication between the human and computer elements at each level within the model, together with an effective specification and design through the levels for both elements.

Level 1

At level 1 (psycho-social) the human element of the dialogue represents the goal that the user is pursuing. Within the computer, virtual objects (things that a user can manipulate or know about) exist to support the fulfilment of user goals. In order to fulfil the goal of *writing home to mum* a user will access a document file (the virtual object). For effective communication at level 1 the virtual objects need to closely match the specification of the user's objectives and higher level goals. Both the human and computer elements at level 1 are translated to equivalent elements at level 2.

Level 2

At level 2 (mental functions) the computer element of the communication is represented by the computer programs that enable the user's goal to be accomplished. In order to *write home to mum* a user may use a specific word-processing package. It will access the document file (virtual object) at level 1. The human element at level 2 is described by the mental mechanisms that the user performs to operate the program. We were introduced to the concepts of memory, perception and cognition in Chapter 2. When using any piece of computer software a user will have some idea, or model, in his or her mind about the way in which the program will perform the necessary task. Clarke refers to this as the *human model of the computer* (HMC). In Chapter 8, when we look at user support, we will describe the HMC simply as a *user model*. In the majority of cases users have an accurate model of the system that is much smaller than that which the system capabilities provide. Users often only appreciate, and use, a very small part of a software system. Novice users will have an extremely small accurate model whereas expert users will develop a more extensive one. The nature of interface is an important factor in determining the human model of the computer.

The computer can also be said to contain a model of the human (CMH); or at least a model of the tasks that it is designed to support. We will see in the next section how task analysis techniques can allow the interface developer to build models of user activities. In order for a user to successfully operate the computer program there needs to be an effective match between the human model of the computer (HMC) and the computer model of the human (CMH). Again the elements at level 2 need to be translated to their corresponding features at level 3.

Level 3

At level 3 (sensori-motor) there needs to be an effective match between human effectors and senses (e.g. hands and fingers, eyes) and computer input/output devices (e.g. keyboard, VDU). Both human effectors and senses and computer I/O devices will interact with physical objects within the system, such as the physical document produced by the word-processing package.

Through a detailed study of the Clarke's three-level model we can see the multi-disciplinary nature of human–computer interaction:

- An understanding of psychology is needed for the human elements at levels 1 and 2.
- A knowledge of human physiology is needed for the human element at level 3.
- Computer science is required for the computer element at levels 2 and 3.

We will now study a number of important techniques within HCI that will help us design, document and specify software interfaces. In Chapter 7 we will see how specific implementations of these techniques have been integrated into interface design methodologies.

6.3   Task analysis: building effective models of user activities

It will now be clear that a comprehensive specification of how user goals are broken down into individual tasks and actions is necessary before any detailed consideration can be given to designing the user interface. Task analysis, as this process is generally referred to, is an effective method of building an appropriate model of the user and should be carried out after performing a detailed user study. A variety of study methods such as observation, interviewing, document collection and participation (Chapter 2) can help us identify the activities which users perform. We now require suitable modelling techniques to enable us to describe, in a detailed way, these user tasks.

A variety of potential modelling techniques exist. The reader familiar with systems analysis (Chapter 4) will be familiar with *process oriented* models. Examples of process oriented models include data flow diagrams used in structured methods, conceptual models used in soft systems and functional models used in object oriented analysis. *Data oriented* models such as entity–relationship diagrams and object models provide a second abstraction of an information system. Although important within overall functional analysis and design, process and data oriented models, on their own, do not provide sufficient detail to the interface designer, for whom a range of other techniques has been proposed. As specialists in user interaction we require specific *task oriented* models. Task analysis methods fall largely into two categories: diagrammatic methods and grammatical techniques. Diagrammatic methods such as hierarchical task analysis are probably more widely adopted, whereas grammatical techniques have the advantage of providing significant support in ensuring consistency throughout an interface.

6.3.1   Hierarchical task analysis

Hierarchical task analysis (HTA) is a relatively simple and effective method in which user goals and tasks are decomposed into elemental tasks within a specified hierarchy. A set of plans that describe in what order, and under what conditions, elemental tasks are performed can also be derived. HTA techniques are very useful in the way in which they assist systematic grouping of sub-tasks so that an effective software interface can be provided. One method is outlined below which is adapted from Shepherd (1989).

1. The description is in the form of a hierarchy of operations and plans that describe the attainment of an overall goal.
2. The overall goal has an associated operation which needs to be carried out to achieve this goal, bearing in mind the task constraints.
3. The overall operation is attained by carrying out a set of subordinate operations in accordance with a plan that specifies the conditions when each subordinate operation is carried out.
4. At each redescription, each suboperation is examined in turn to determine whether it needs to be redescribed. If it does, then the operation becomes a candidate for further redescription as in (3) above.
5. The criterion for stopping analysis may vary between applications and contexts.

In order to explore how hierarchical task analysis techniques can be applied we will start by investigating the goal of *getting to work*. In Fig. 6.2 we can see how the goal has been decomposed into individual tasks and sub-tasks with associated plans and further described in an HTA diagram.

The reader familiar with the methods of Jackson (JSP and JSD) outlined briefly in Chapter 4 will recognize the similarity between HTA diagrams and structure diagrams. HTA diagrams can also be described using the selection and interaction notations adopted within structure diagrams.

6.3.2   Formal grammar techniques

The HTA technique can be used to analyse and structure the components of tasks. It does not, however, include any information regarding the knowledge that the user has to acquire to accomplish the tasks, nor can it be used to predict performance of individual user interactions. A number of formal cognitive models have been proposed to meet these needs. Many of these formal methods of task analysis are intended to elicit the user's model of the task rather than the more limited designer's perception as specified in HTA type techniques.

At this stage it might be helpful to emphasize the distinction between a variety of specific HCI 'formal' methods and the more generic formal methods of specification such as Z, VDM, CCS and CSP (Chapter 4), while noting that many of these methods can also be applied to specifications within HCI.

We will look briefly at two of the most well-known formal cognitive methods.

0   In order to get to work
    1   Set the alarm before going to bed
    2   Get up
    3   Get ready for work
        3.1   Wash
        3.2   Eat breakfast
            3.2.1   Eat cooked breakfast
            3.2.2   Eat cereals
            3.2.3   Drink coffee
        3.3   Get dressed
    4   Travel to work
        4.1   Drive to work
        4.2   Walk to work

Plan 0:   do 1 – 2 – 3 – 4 in that order
Plan 3:   do 3.1 – 3.2 – 3.3 in that order
        Plan 3.2:   do 3.2.1 or 3.2.2 or 3.2.3 depending on time available
Plan 4:   do 4.1 or 4.2 depending on weather conditions

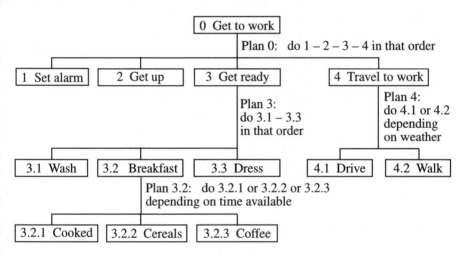

FIGURE 6.2   *'How to get to work'—Hierarchial task analysis decomposition and HTA diagram*

GOMS

The GOMS model for task specification has been proposed by Card *et al.* (1983) and has been discussed by Fountain (1985). The GOMS approach follows from the work that identified the model human processor (see page 47) and considers human cognitive behaviour to consist of four components: a set of goals, operators, methods and selection rules as shown in Table 6.4.

TABLE 6.4 *GOMS*

Goals	Describes what the user wishes to achieve and represents memory points for the user at which he or she can evaluate what should be done next.
Operators	Actions belonging to a user's repertoire of skills—the lowest level of analysis.
Methods	Sequences of sub-goals and operators often carried out in an automatic fashion to achieve a goal—often goals will have a number of different methods.
Selection rules	Used for choosing among different possible methods for reaching a particular goal.

GOMS models tend to operate at a very low level of user interaction and have been used to describe detailed user interactions with word-processing systems. GOMS techniques have been shown to be useful in cases where we know the sequences of operations and want to know how quickly the sequence can be performed. A related technique known as the keystroke level model aims to determine how long it takes expert users to perform routine tasks. According to Preece *et al.* (1994) GOMS models can be used to:

- Predict the quality of an existing system or prototype
- Check for consistency of methods
- Check that the most frequent goals are achieved by relatively quick methods
- Perform quantitative evaluations
- Choose between alternative designs

Cognitive complexity theory (CCT)

Based upon the GOMS model, Kieras and Polson (1985) have developed a framework of *cognitive complexity theory* in which a set of production rules is used to describe user behaviour in which each production rule has the general form:

if *condition* then *action*

A comparison between GOMS and CCT, within part of the specification of user actions for interaction with a text editor, is shown in Fig. 6.3. It should be emphasized that the example provided is only a very small part of a simple interaction scenario. Full real-life formal specifications can get very complex.

GOMS	CCT production rules
MOVE Method	ExecuteMove (IF (GOAL EXECUTE MOVE?OBJ) (NOT(?OBJ SELECTED)))
Goal <1>: Execute Move	(THEN (ADD(GOAL SELECT ?OBJ))
. Goal <2>: Select Object	(CALL OBJ.SEL)))
{use SELOBJ method}	etc.
etc.	
Note that the dot represents a hierarchy of goals	Note that the formal notation could be said to read: *Executing a move can only occur if the user has the goal of moving an object and if the object has not been already selected in which case the user adds the goal of selecting an object*

FIGURE 6.3   *Comparing GOMS and CCT*

Applicability of cognitive task analysis methods

Although cognitive models continue to be developed (Olson and Olson, 1990) such methods have been criticized as being too low level to have general applicability. They tend to be used to specify specific interactions with computer systems, rather than to describe general user domain-based tasks. A further limitation in such approaches is the fact that they only take account of error-free (expert) performance. As a result a number of HCI specialists suggest that a user-centred prototyping approach is a far more effective way of eliciting and specifying the task requirement for an interface.

6.4   Interaction design

Having analysed the user tasks it is now possible for the interface specialist to begin the process of *designing* for human–computer interaction. However, before any detailed interface design can commence it is necessary to identify an appropriate interaction style or styles. The choice of interaction style will be determined by a knowledge of the potential users and tasks. It may also be limited by the hardware and software available for implementation. At the first level of detail we can distinguish between *conversational* and *graphical* styles of interaction, but can further refine the analysis to five broad methods that we will look at in detail later:

- *Menu selection,* the user is presented with a series of alternative actions and can choose among the alternatives.
- *Form filling,* the user enters data on a VDT much in the same way as he or she would do on a paper-based system.

- *Graphical interaction,* through the use of a keyboard and mouse the user directly interacts with graphical objects displayed on the VDT, commonly referred to as a graphical user interface (GUI).
- *Command language,* the user types in commands in some prescribed format.
- *Natural language,* in which either by keyboard or voice input, natural English, or any other natural language, is the input mechanism.

6.4.1   Interaction styles

Factors underlying interaction style

It may be that practical implementation constraints will restrict the choice of interaction style. If a client requires an extension to a current software system, then consistency between elements will be important, and in any case the facilities provided by the software may limit choice. Assuming, however, that the interface developer has a relatively free hand in designing the interface, user issues should be paramount. Five user-related factors have been identified to help determine the most appropriate interface style.

1. **Initiation**   Within any dialogue we can analyse where the initiation of the dialogue rests. In the case of human-to-human communication within a classroom situation, initiation largely rests with the teacher who is controlling the nature and pace of the communication. Although individual students may seize the initiation for a short period, for example by asking a question, the teacher is in control. The software interface is the means through which effective human–computer communication can take place. We can investigate the degree to which the initiation of the dialogue rests with the computer or the human user. In the case of a command language system initiation rests with the user. The user of MSDOS is presented with a set of symbols representing the current disk drive (A>) and is required to instigate one of an almost limitless number of actions by typing in a command (e.g. copy a:file1.doc c:file2.doc). An example of initiation resting with the computer is provided by a structured menu interface where the user selects from a very limited number of options.

2. **Flexibility**   The flexibility of an interaction style is determined by the number of ways in which a user can perform given functions. Flexibility can be built into a system in a number of ways. At one level alternatives can be provided to execute a particular function. In order to print a file within a word-processing system it may be possible to issue the Ctrl + P command (holding down the Ctrl key

and pressing the P key) or to select *Print* from the *File* pull-down menu. At another level flexibility can be increased by allowing for shortcuts within the navigation of an interface.

3. **Option complexity**   At any one time within an example of a user interaction with a software system a number of different actions are possible. The option complexity relates to the number of different options available to the user at any given point in the dialogue. The option complexity of a command language is liable to be high whereas that of a structured menu system is likely to be low.

4. **Power**   Individual commands differ in power: the amount of work accomplished by the system in response to a single user command. Powerful commands such as file deletions are best handled by checking with the user that the action selected is indeed what is intended.

5. **Information load**   Information load is a measure of the degree to which the interaction absorbs the memory and reasoning power of the user. In general the interface developer should attempt to reduce information load. We have noted the limitations on short-term memory: users should not be expected to carry over too much information from one screen or window to another.

Interaction styles and user needs

To a large degree the choice of interaction style should relate to the user requirements under each of the five underlying factors identified above. Each user and/or user group may be suited to a different style. User physical needs in general and user skill levels in particular are likely to be significant. User taxonomies may also be informative here; even though a specific professional user may be a novice, the dialogue design should not compromise his or her task expertise.

In general it is sensible, given other constraints, to rest as much initiation with the user as possible. Users like to feel in control and this is one reason why the graphical user interface (GUI), resting a relatively high level of initiation with the user, is proving to become a standard. Flexibility is normally to be encouraged as long as it does not cause problems with novice users. The appropriate level of option complexity needs to be determined by skill level. Although the aim should never be to provide the highest possible level of option complexity, expert users will soon tire of systems with an option complexity below their level of competence. In some ways flexibility and option complexity are conflicting factors. Information load should be minimized but this does not mean that command languages are to be ignored. In the hand of experienced and expert IT professionals they provide the major mechanisms for the programming of software systems. It is noticeable, however, that visual programming environments are now becoming popular.

In Chapter 2 we identified a taxonomy of users by skill level derived from the three determinants of skill: IT literacy, application knowledge and system knowledge. The eight user types described within the taxonomy are reproduced in Table 6.5 which attempts to relate the factors determining interface style, through the determinants of skill level, to the user types. In developing the table, and in terms of the taxonomy, it has been assumed that:

- Initiation is mainly determined by system knowledge, although IT literacy may be a significant secondary factor.
- Flexibility is related to both application and system knowledge.
- Option complexity is mainly related to system knowledge.
- The power of commands provided should be related to all three, but that system knowledge is of greatest significance.
- Information load is mainly determined by system knowledge.

The comments provided within the table should not be taken to be too prescriptive as other issues, not included within the taxonomy, may be significant.

Metaphors

One way in which human–computer interaction can be enhanced is by the adoption of an appropriate *metaphor* to underpin interaction design. In terms of interface design a metaphor is way of increasing the familiarity between the user and the computer application (Dix,

TABLE 6.5   *Interaction style and user type*

Factor User type	Initiation	Flexibility	Option complexity	Power	Information load
Novice	With computer	Low	Low	Must be low	Low
Parrot	Either/balance	Medium	Can be higher	Should be low	Can be higher
Casual	With computer	Medium	Low	Should be low	Low
Specific	With user	High	Can be higher	Medium	Can be higher
Literate	Either/balance	Low	Low	Should be low	Low
Trained	Either/balance	Medium	Can be higher	Medium	Can be higher
Transferring	Either/balance	Medium	Low	Should be low	Low
Expert	With user	High	Can be higher	Possibly high	Can be higher

1993). Within the *desktop metaphor*, implemented in Windows-based operating environments, the user is made familiar with the concepts of document and file management through the visual metaphor of overlapping windows and iconic representations.

Implemented successfully a metaphor will enhance the interaction at level two of Clarke's three level model (Sec. 6.2.3) as it may allow appropriate human models of the computer (HMC) to be developed. There are, however, a number of limitations in the use of metaphors (Dix, 1993). First not all implementations are equally obvious to all users (e.g. dragging an iconic representation of a file to a wastebasket to eject it from the computer), and secondly some physical operations (e.g. printing a file) do not have an easy metaphorical equivalent. However, a range of metaphor implementations is possible within the design of human–computer interfaces, and perhaps the most striking examples are those which are currently being adopted within virtual reality applications (refer to Chapter 10).

6.4.2   Interface design guidelines

The five factors underlying interaction can help us select an appropriate interaction style. But how do we ensure that we design the interface in the best way possible? The short answer is that we do not yet know! There is an increasing number of methodologies proposed for interface design that attempt to do this, but there is certainly no general agreement on a single approach.

A significant problem with interface design is the fact that there is an extremely large number of possible designs. We often refer to a design space: a conceptual space in which all possible design solutions can be placed. The design space for a human–computer interface is very large as there are a very large number of factors that affect usability. At this stage in our analysis of the user interface we will investigate the empirical evidence that has been gathered by HCI specialists, and which has been shown to assist in enhancing usability. The evidence that is available is often referred to as *heuristics* and is embodied in interface design rules and *guidelines*. Through the application of appropriate design rules we are able to restrict the space of design options.

What makes a good interface?

Without defining the usability of the software interface too strictly, empirical evidence would suggest that there are a number of elements to a successful interface:

- *Ease of use*, interfaces should be *easy to use* in that, through simplicity and consistency, access by the user is made as intuitive as possible.
- *Efficiency,* which can be achieved through the use of short cuts and inherent flexibility.
- *Supportiveness,* which can be provided by a number of mechanisms, including helpful feedback, so that users feel safe and secure when using the system.
- *Acceptability,* by ensuring an appropriate match between user tasks and the functions provided and by meeting user needs in satisfying ways overall *acceptability* can be enhanced.

Design rules

Design rules attempt to provide enhanced formality out of the empirical evidence available. As a result they provide designers with the ability to analyse the usability consequences of their design decisions. Design rules exist at a variety of levels of formality and can be classified both by their *generality* and *authority* (Dix, 1993). Rules that are highly general can be applied to a wide range of situations and are referred to as guidelines. Those which are high in authority place a requirement on the designer, and include standards and codes of practice. The two dimensions underpinning rules are shown in Fig. 6.4 and can be further described:

- *Authority,* one end of the axis represents guidance information whereas the other provides for prescriptive rules.
- *Generality,* generic interface design principles are at one end of the spectrum that can be contrasted with task and domain specific ones at the other.

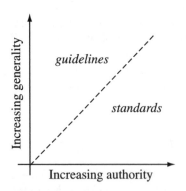

FIGURE 6.4   *Dimensions underpinning rules*

It is important to recognize that it is necessary to apply design rules in a flexible manner. In many cases some of the guidelines will be in conflict, and the designer needs to understand the theoretical basis (psychological, cognitive, ergonomic, etc.) on which they are based before making design decisions.

National and international standards Standards are set by national or international bodies such as the British Standards Institute (BSI) or the International Standards Organization (ISO). A number of standards are relevant to the human–computer factor specialist:

ISO 9241   **Ergonomic Requirements for Office Work with VDTs**
This is the most significant standard and covers a wide range of ergonomic and interface design issues. It comes in 17 parts of which a number relate to interface design:

ISO 9241-10	Dialogue principles
ISO 9241-11	Guidance on usability specifications, measures
ISO 9241-12	Presentation of information
ISO 9241-13	User guidance
ISO 9241-14	Menu dialogues
ISO 9241-15	Command dialogues
ISO 9241-16	Direct manipulation dialogues
ISO 9241-17	Form filling dialogues

ISO 9126   **Software product evaluation— quality characteristics and guidelines for their use**
This provides a set of attributes for software which bear on the effort needed for use, and on the individual assessment of such use, by a stated or implied set of users.

European Directive: Work with Display Screen Equipment
The EU directive (90/270/EEC) specifies minimum requirements for work with VDTs. By conforming to ISO 9241 the designer should be able to meet EU requirements for the human–computer interface. Compliance was required by 31 December 1992 for all new workstations and by 31 December 1996 for all existing workstations.

In-house standards or codes of practice For many human-factor specialists the most important type of design rules are in-house standards or codes of practice, as it is these which are adopted at development level. In order to ensure consistency throughout large systems and across all systems many organizations develop their own standards. For large software supply companies these standards may become a *de facto* industry standard.

Guidelines   At the lowest level of authority there is a vast amount of published guideline material. Shneiderman (1992) identifies eight *golden rules* of interface design:

1. *Strive for consistency*—consistent sequences of actions are required for similar situations, identical terminology should be used for prompts, menus, etc.
2. *Enable frequent users to use shortcuts*—through the use of abbreviations, special keys, etc.
3. *Offer information feedback*—every operation should provide feedback to the user.
4. *Design dialogues to yield closure*—actions should be organized into groups with feedback on completion.
5. *Offer simple error handling.*
6. *Permit easy reversal of actions*—to relieve anxiety and encourage exploration.
7. *Support internal locus of control*—experienced users like to feel in control, place initiation with the user.
8. *Reduce short-term memory load*—keep displays simple, provide help.

Further information on guidelines and style guides can be obtained from Mayhew (1992), Stewart (1991), Apple (1987) and Microsoft (1992).

6.4.3   Comparing interaction styles

Having looked at general issues that determine usability we will now examine and discuss a number of interaction styles in more detail and identify some of the specific guidelines that can enhance their individual effectiveness and efficiency.

Menus

Menus provide the main method by which users are able to navigate through an interface and can be implemented in a variety of interaction styles. Prior to the introduction of the GUI, menus were implemented on alphanumeric VDTs. By typing no more than one or two characters users were able to select from a number of options.

Today's GUI systems implement menus through a variety of different interaction objects.

Structured menus   Early versions of menu-based systems employed the *structured menu* through which the user is required to choose from a series of options by typing a number or character associated with the option. Often as a result of a user selection a further menu is displayed or alternatively further processing may occur. In Fig. 6.5 we take a simple example of a library journal search system. Notice that we show a two-level, tree-structured hierarchy of menus.

With a careful design of structured menus, novice users are able to make effective use of a system, and expert users can enjoy a relatively high speed of interaction. In modern GUI interfaces a structured menu may be implemented thorough a variety of methods including push buttons and radio buttons. The top-level menu of the library journal search system shown in Fig. 6.5 is presented in radio button form in Fig. 6.6.

Flexible, pull-down and pop-up menus   An extension to the structured menu is the facility to provide a *look ahead* facility whereby the user is able to see the next level of menu associated with a particular menu item prior to committing to that choice. This method of interaction reduces the likelihood of the user finishing up in a blind alley. Flexible menus are implemented in most modern GUI

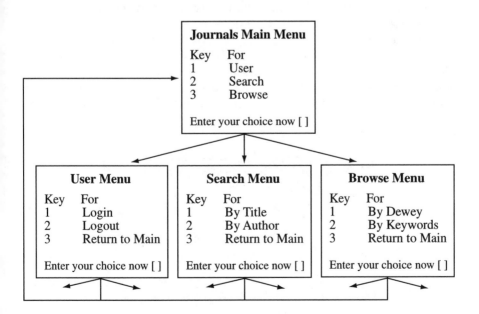

FIGURE 6.5   *Traditional structured menu hierarchy*

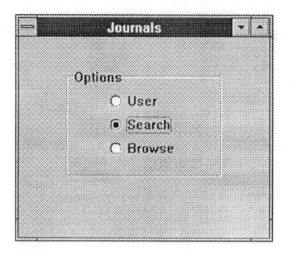

FIGURE 6.6   *Radio button menu*

systems through what is commonly referred to as the pull-down menu. The same library journal search system has been implemented in a pull-down menu as shown in Fig. 6.7.

Menus with graphics   A further extension to the menu interaction style is to make full use of the graphics facilities provided by modern visual display units. Rather than rely exclusively on text, the representation of the application domain through graphics can assist in menu selection. Most users of Microsoft Windows, for example, select the application program from the Program Manager window by clicking on an iconic representation of the application. In a national hotel booking system it would be possible to provide a map with named towns displayed in their appropriate location. Rather than

FIGURE 6.7   *Pull-down menu*

choosing the towns from an alphabetical listing it could be much more intuitive to click a mouse over the correct location on the map.

Menu design issues   Whether menus are implemented in structured or flexible format, with or without graphics, there is a number of generic issues that need to be considered if an efficient and effective implementation is to be achieved. Shneiderman (1992) provides considerable detail covering guidelines for menu design. We will identify two of the most important issues.

1. *Menu system structure*   Menus can be organized in a linear sequence or in a tree structure. Note that the tree structures in Figs 6.5, 6.6 and 6.7 are identical. A rigid tree structure can be modified either by including cyclic elements (by allowing short cut return mechanisms jumping over levels within the tree) or acyclic elements (by allowing more than one screen or node at one level to access another at the next level). One issue to be resolved in menu design is that of an appropriate balance between the number of levels (depth) within the structure and the number of items available (breadth) at each levels. As a general guideline it has been shown to be better to provide broad and shallow network tree structures as opposed to narrow and deep ones.

2. *Semantic organization*   The grouping of menu items between and within menu screens is a more complex issue than it might at first appear. Logically similar data items should be grouped together: it is not by chance that a restaurant menu has the items displayed under courses rather than alphabetically. Many application domains are not either as well known, or as clear cut, as the restaurant situation, and care needs to be taken to ensure a sensible organization. Design should be based upon the task semantics, which is both intuitive to end users, and which covers all possibilities with no unintentional overlap between menus.

We will further illustrate the various interaction styles by referencing the minor case study: Acadmin: a student administration system for UK colleges and universities. In Fig. 6.8 we show the Acadmin main menu screen demonstrating a pull-down menu.

Form filling

The majority of information systems require both data entry and data output. The form filling interaction style allows users to enter and retrieve data from a computer in a manner that closely mirrors a manual, paper-based system. Form filling can be considered to be a relatively inflexible method as a form needs to be designed for each

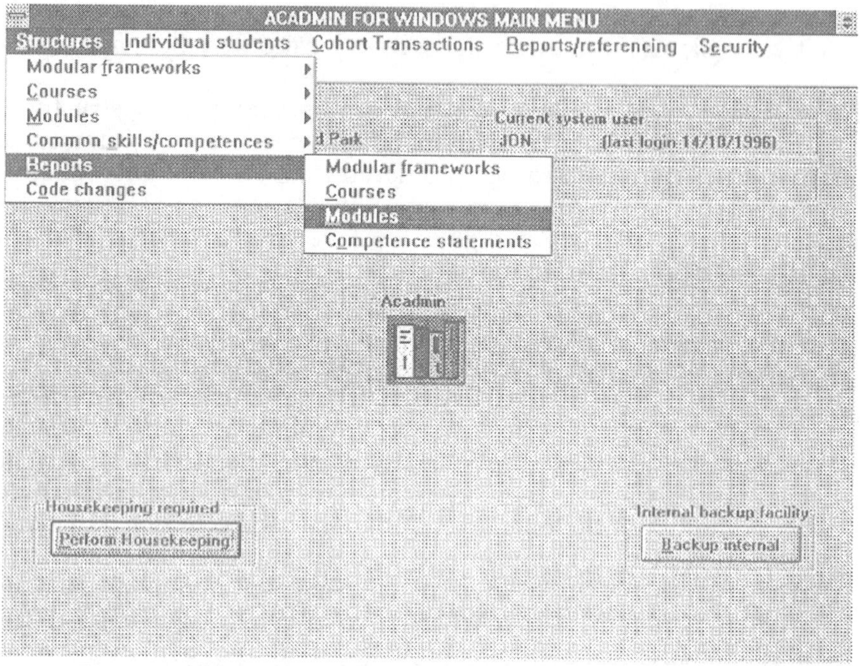

FIGURE 6.8 *Acadmin main menu* (copyright Chalfont Software Ltd)

task scenario. However, in many commercial systems where considerable volumes of data are being handled, it remains the only practical method. Users who are trained in the use of well-designed form-based systems are able to perform their tasks in an efficient and effective way. Successful task analysis is a vital ingredient within the design of form-based systems.

Form filling can be implemented in a variety of software environments from character-based systems to windows-based GUIs. In Fig. 6.9 we show the first of two student details screens for the Acadmin system. Here users, in this case administrators in departmental offices are able to enter basic student data (name, nationality, date of birth, etc.) in character format. Being a GUI interface users are also able to make use of facilities such as radio buttons for gender and a check box for term time address. In a character-based implementation the user would need to type M or F for gender and Y or N for term time address. The window also includes a three item push button based menu (Next, Previous or Quit) to terminate the screen.

As we discussed in relation to menus, there is a number of generic issues that need to be considered if an efficient and effective form filling implementation is to be achieved. Again Shneiderman (1992)

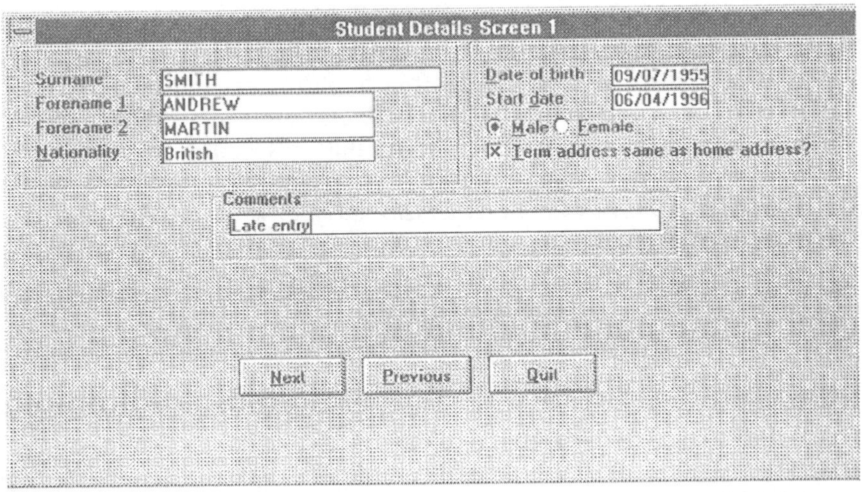

FIGURE 6.9   *Acadmin form filling window* (copyright Chalfont Software Ltd)

provides a comprehensive coverage. We will summarize four of the most important guidelines for form filling:

1. *Form design,* relate design to task, logically group items, etc.
2. *Screen layout,* consider visual appearance and the use of visible space and boundaries.
3. *Consistent cursor movement,* between TAB, mouse click and ENTER.
4. *User support,* provide comprehensible instructions, suitable error handling, etc.

Graphical interaction: direct manipulation, GUIs and WIMP interfaces

We have described a *graphical* interaction style as one in which:

through the use of a keyboard and mouse the user directly interacts with graphical objects displayed on the VDT

and noted that it is commonly referred to as a graphical user interface (GUI). Such an interaction style is also closely related to the term direct manipulation which Macaulay (1995) defines to be:

those in which the user manipulates through button pushes and movement of a pointing device such as a mouse, a graphic or iconic representation of the underlying data

Perhaps the most regularly cited example of direct manipulation is the file deletion action on the Macintosh computer in which the user manipulates a mouse to drag and click an iconic representation of the file to an iconic representation of a dustbin. Feedback is provided by an expansion in the size of the dustbin to show that the task has been successfully achieved. Icons, such as the Acadmin icon shown in Fig. 6.10 are a major feature of direct manipulation systems.

The term direct manipulation was, in fact, first used by Shneiderman (1982) as far back as the early 1980s when he identified five features of such an interaction style:

1. Visibility of the objects of interest.
2. Incremental actions at the interface with rapid feedback on all actions.
3. Reversibility of all actions, so that users are encouraged to explore without severe penalties.
4. Syntactic correctness of all actions so that every user action is a legal operation.
5. Replacement of complex command languages with actions to manipulate directly the visible objects.

The two definitions of *graphical interaction* and *direct manipulation* given at the start of this section would appear to be almost identical, implying the terms to be synonymous. However, there is a view that direct manipulation is a more abstract concept in that the user has access to controls or commands that *directly* relate to the variables which he or she wishes to *manipulate* in order to achieve the appropriate goals. Taking this definition a particular command language interface could be direct and a GUI very indirect. Ankrah (1990) provides an account of *directness* that is distinct from interaction style. We will continue to use the term graphical interaction noting that it relates to direct manipulation within a graphical user interface.

The main claim for graphical interaction is that it is more intuitive. Through graphical interaction users are better able to visualize progress to achieving their goal (for example as based upon Norman's model of interaction) and alter their activities if required. As a result it is further claimed that:

FIGURE 6.10   *Acadmin icon (copyright Chalfont Software Ltd)*

- User anxiety is reduced
- Users learn more easily
- Experts are enabled to work rapidly
- Intermittent users are able to remember more of the system (the human model of the computer is enhanced)
- Error messages are needed less frequently

Graphical interaction is an *interaction style*. Graphical user interfaces (GUIs) are *specific software implementations* which embody the interaction style. GUIs are often referred to as WIMP systems where the acronym stands for windows, icons, menus and pointer. A GUI is composed of a number of interaction objects or widgets (WInDow objEcTs: the 'G' *is* missing) such as push buttons, pull-down menus and scroll bars.

GUIs have a particular *look and feel*. All applications running under Microsoft Windows have the same look and feel, although different from that on a Macintosh. Some windowing systems, such as X Windows, allow for different look and feel for different applications on the same hardware platform. The look and feel of a GUI can be described in terms of its visual appearance (e.g. design of widgets), behaviour (e.g. nature of clicking a mouse) and metaphor (e.g. desktop metaphor).

Acadmin has been developed using a toolkit to run under Microsoft Windows: it is an example of a GUI. While it can be described as embodying a graphical interaction style, being a data intensive information system, it also includes form filling and menu elements.

Command language

While the GUI has much to offer there are many situations where other interactions styles are both desirable and necessary. In many complex systems which act on large database of information a command language system is the most appropriate way through which a satisfactory level of functionality and speed of operation can be achieved.

One example of a command language can be demonstrated through the user of SQL, the major database query language. In SQL, for example, we can investigate the *select from where* statement. The *select* statement corresponds to an output specification and can output an entire tuple (records) or selected attributes (fields). The *from* clause complements *select* by specifying which relation is the scope of the select. The *where* clause adds the qualification.

In the one line command language statement:

select DEPT, MGR from EMPLOYEE where SALARY > 25000

acting on the relational table shown below:

NAME	DEPT	MGR	AGE	SALARY
Peters	Sales	Smith	39	21342
Ali	Personnel	Black	46	35938
Prout	Accounts	Green	21	12098
Barnes	Sales	Smith	29	20928
Holden	Accounts	Green	62	29093
Longman	Sales	Brown	19	34005

The output would be:

Personnel	Black
Accounts	Green
Sales	Brown

In the hands of an experienced user, command language interfaces can prove to be a most efficient means of data retrieval.

Natural language

Being the language of human–human communication it would seem sensible to aim for the development of natural language in human–computer communication. The development of natural language interaction systems has been a major topic for research over the last few decades. There are two possible ways in which natural language input can be implemented: keyboard or voice. Computer voice output, through voice synthesis systems is also under development. At present, relative to other interaction styles, voice input and output systems are still in their infancy and are limited to specific applications where other interaction modes are inappropriate.

Advantages and disadvantages of interaction styles

Table 6.6 provides a summary of the advantages and disadvantages of the various interaction styles that we have looked at.

Earlier we discussed the factors underlying interaction style and related these to user needs and user taxonomies. Having now

TABLE 6.6 *Comparing interaction styles*

	Advantages	**Disadvantages**
Structured menus	• Clear structure for decision making • Few keystrokes required • Minimal learning required	• Deep hierarchial structures can be confusing • Can be slow to navigate
Flexible pull down/pop up menus	• Supports navigation • Easy for novice users	• Inflexible for commands with • many parameters • Frustrating for expert users • Requires manual dexterity
Form filling	• A means of rapid data entry • Straightforward for novices	• Navigation can be confusing
Graphical interaction	• User anxiety is reduced • Users learn more easily • Experts work rapidly	• Swapping between keyboards and mouse can be slow
Command language	• Efficient for experts • User feels in control	• Long time to learn • Requires regular use • Heavy memory load
Natural language	• No specific language training required • Opportunities for the future	• User expectations often too high

analysed the styles themselves it might seem profitable to describe each in terms of the underlying factors in the anticipation of forming a direct link between a user taxonomy and interaction style. Unfortunately this approach would be far too simplistic as it would ignore so many other issues, such as task and domain characteristics and hardware and software considerations. Furthermore many software interfaces will embody a number of interaction styles. The Acadmin system, for example, has menu, form filling and direct manipulation within a GUI.

6.5   Design rationale

6.5.1   The design process and the rationale for design decisions

A range of designers from fashion designers to architects play an important role in the development of the products, or artefacts, which we meet in everyday life. In many cases designers work in partnership with engineers. Architects and structural and civil engineers, for example, need to work in collaboration in the creation of new buildings. The engineering contribution to the overall design process tends to focus on the scientific basis underpinning a design proposal, whereas the design contribution is much more of an artistic one. When designing a new car it is important for it to look good as well as drive well. In our domain of information systems we often refer to *information systems engineers* and *software engineers*, but where does the design element come from? The visual appearance of any information system artefact comes from the human–computer interface, and it is perhaps here, through the work of the HCI *designer,* that the greatest creativity within information systems design is evidenced.

As shown in Fig. 6.11 the design process can be considered to be composed of two elements: *the thought processes* which result in design decisions and the *descriptions* of such processes. Often the latter is neglected and some time after the artefact is produced there is no evident reason as to why the design is as it appears. A formal *design rationale* process can remove this problem.

Design itself gives a result (some artefact) not the rationale that produced it. A *design rationale* is a representation for explicitly documenting the reasoning and argument that makes sense of a particular artefact. Design rationale can be integrated with the design process itself, or used afterwards to document design decisions. Through the use of design rationale techniques we can maintain integrity of the design process and as a result:

- Provide a means of communication between members of the design team (both users and designers)
- Understand at a later stage in the design process earlier design decisions
- Force deliberation in the decision-making process
- Support re-use of, and modification to, both the artefact and the design process

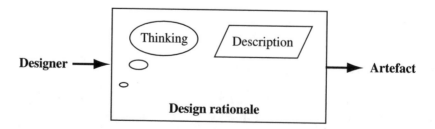

FIGURE 6.11   *Design rationale: thinking and description*

6.5.2   Design rationale and HCI

Within the design of a human–computer interface there is an extremely large design space of alternative solutions. This is one reason why design rationale techniques are particularly suitable. A complex software interface can be implemented in almost unlimited different ways. Although the designer of a bridge over a river will have a number of possible solutions (suspension, cantilever, etc.) once a specific implementation has been decided upon the theories underpinning bridge design (e.g. structural analysis) will greatly limit the number of possible options. In HCI there is no single best design and the designer is often in a trade-off situation. When selecting the method of navigation within an interface a designer may, for example, need to choose between a number of push buttons (on the basis that is obvious to use although it may take up screen space) and a pop-up menu (because it saves screen space although it is less obvious to use). Even if an optimal solution does exist the size of the space of design possibilities may make it too large to find it.

Although we have recognized that there is now a large degree of design rule and methodology support for the interface designer, that which is available is far less rigorous than that provided to the majority of designers and engineers working in other domains. Design rationale techniques can enhance the rigour in which design rules are applied.

A final reason why design rationale is useful to human–computer factor specialists is the fact that the artefact of the interface design process (indeed all software design processes) is very easy to change. Software developers overtly publicize this fact through the various software releases that they produce. This is somewhat analogous to automobile design where new car models appear with major or minor modifications at relatively short intervals, but certainly not to civil engineering where each artefact is unique and not subject to change. Design rationale can support the documentation of interface designs and provides a form of configuration management for the interface.

We may summarize the main reasons why interface design and engineering is significantly different from most other design domains by the following issues:

- Size of the design space of alternatives
- Lack of rigour in design support
- Modifiability in the end product

Three approaches to design rationale have been reported: *process oriented design rationale* methods which are integrated into the design process itself, *design space analysis* techniques which are concerned with the structure of the space of all design alternatives and *psychological design rationale* which attempts to capture claims about the psychology of the user. We will investigate the latter two.

6.5.3   Design space analysis: QOC

One design space analysis method is known as QOC (Maclean *et al.*, 1991) as it involves questions, options and criteria. QOC is concerned with structuring the space of all design alternatives and provides a *complete story of the moment* within the design process. QOC can be used after design has been completed in order to reconstruct, *post hoc*, a variety of design decisions. By using QOC we are able to place artefacts in the design space of all possibilities, and show why the particular design was chosen. QOC is a simple diagrammatic technique and within QOC diagrams:

* *Questions* pose key issues for structuring the space of alternatives.
* *Options* are possible alternative answers to questions.
* *Criteria* are the basis for choosing and evaluating among the options.

In order to illustrate the use of QOC we will explore the rationale which led to the design of the Acadmin form filling window (Fig. 6.9). In this case, as we have already seen, we are performing the analysis *post hoc*, but it is possible that the developers of the system may have integrated it within the design process. From the window we can identify four distinct design decisions:

1. The data entry fields have been created largely in a vertical manner but with a horizontal split after nationality.
2. A considerable amount of space is provided below the form filling boxes.
3. Radio buttons have been used for gender.
4. Push buttons have been used for navigation.

A possible QOC rationale for the design is provided in Fig. 6.12 which identifies the chosen options, among all possible ones, against the appropriate criteria. We notice that the four design decisions listed above are represented by questions and can further see that the second decision is a consequence of the first.

In response to the question *what layout for form filling?* we can see that there are two positive assessments with the *vertical with split* option, whereas the other two options only have one positive assessment each. Having decided upon the *vertical with split* option for form filling it is now necessary to decide where to place the navigation commands. In this case there is one assessment with each

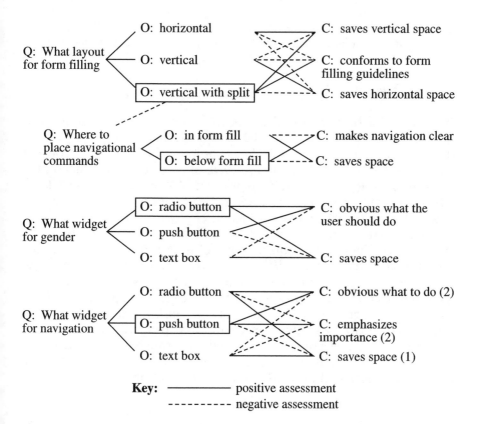

FIGURE 6.12   *QOC diagram for Acadmin form filling window*

option. As the option implemented was *below form fill* we must deduce that making navigation clear was a more important criterion than *saves space*.

A further extension to the QOC approach is to associate weightings to each of the criteria. This is demonstrated within the analysis of the question *what widget for navigation*? If we count the weightings for the positive assessment associated with *push button* we get a total of 4, whereas it is 3 for *radio button* and only 1 for *text box*. Push button is the selected option.

6.5.4   Psychological design rationale

As we have stated *psychological design rationale* attempts to capture claims about the psychology of the user. The method described by Carrol and Rosson (1991, two papers) is based upon the concept of deliberative evolution that is described as:

the connection and transferring of one design to use in another design by means of explicit design rationale and systematic design decisions.

The task artefact cycle

In order to further explore the concept of deliberative evolution it is necessary to appreciate that the design of many artefacts can be described by a task artefact cycle as shown in Fig. 6.13. The concept describes the iterative *product life cycle* of an artefact in which initial tasks define requirements for the artefact. When put into operational use the artefact opens up new possibilities of use that can then inform new tasks and the cycle may start again.

In software terms an example of the task artefact cycle can be shown by the increasing sophistication of the spreadsheet application. Developed initially in the 1970s to handle tables of data, when put into operational use, the spreadsheet emerged as a useful tool for handling *what if projections* which then became a major *raison d'être* for its existence. Further cycles of the task artefact cycle have introduced files and graphics, windows and programming elements. To a large extent it could be said that the spreadsheet package has been engineered by its users in an evolutionary process, rather than having been designed explicitly by software developers.

Design by scenario

In order to attempt to deliberately manage and direct this evolutionary process Carrol and Rosson's aim to *'guide discovery and integration of decision requirements using a scenario based methodology based upon a task artefact cycle for HCI'* is shown in Fig. 6.14. The basis of Carrol and Rosson's psychological design method is the identification, by the interface developer of a range of detailed *usage scenarios* and the development of claims (positive aspects of the

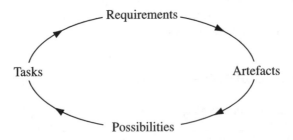

FIGURE 6.13   *Generic task artefact cycle*

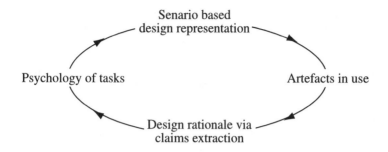

FIGURE 6.14   *Task artefact cycle for HCI*

scenario) and downsides (negative aspects) with the aim of maximizing the claims and minimizing the downsides. If the software developer is to make use of the task artefact cycle as a basis for design (before the artefact is produced) a method is required to identify both the usage scenarios and the claims and downsides. Carrol and Rosson have developed a *typology of user concerns* which can be used to generate the usage scenarios:

• Orienting to appropriate goals
• Interacting with the environment opportunistically
• Searching under a description
• Seeking how to do it procedural information
• Seeking how it works explanatory information
• Reflecting upon and crafting one's own work

By investigating a proposed design under one or more of the user concerns example usage scenarios can be described.

Claims are about the psychological consequences for users and do not relate to the designer's intentions. They capture rich and specific information about design features and therefore contrast with design guidelines that are often very general. By adding a number of questions to each of the stages in Norman's model of interaction, Carrol and Rosson also propose a structure, shown in Table 6.7 through which claims and downsides can be identified.

The process is not as difficult as it might appear on first study. In order to further clarify the method in Fig. 6.15 we describe the *psychological design by scenario* method in the form of a simple flow chart. Given a specific application domain the typology of user concerns can be used to create a series of usage scenarios. By using the questions based upon Norman's model of interaction a number of claims and downsides are identified. As a result the design can be modified to take account of the positive nature of the claims and the negative nature of the downsides.

TABLE 6.7   *Generating claims and downsides*

Norman's stage:	Carrol and Rosson's questions:
1 Form a goal	1.1 How does the artefact evoke goals in the user? 1.2 How does the artefact encourage the user to import pre-existing task goals?
2 Form an intention	2.1 How does the artefact suggest that a particular task is appropriate or otherwise? 2.2 How does the artefact suggest that a particular task is simple or difficult? 2.3 How does the artefact suggest that a particular task is basic or advanced? 2.4 How does the artefact suggest that a particular task is risky or safe? 2.5 What inappropriate goals are most likely or costly?
3 Specifying the action sequence	3.1 What distinctions must be understood to decompose a task goal into methods? 3.2 What planning mistakes are most likely and/or most costly?
4 Execute the action	4.1 How does the artefact make it easy or difficult to carry out the task? 4.2 What slips are most likely or costly? 4.3 How does the artefact indicate progress?
5 Perceive the resultant system state	5.1 What are the most salient features of the artefact? 5.2 What do they communicate to the user? 5.3 What features change as the task is carried out and how are they communicated?
6 Interpret the resultant state	6.1 How does the artefact guide the user to make correct inferences? 6.2 What incorrect inferences are most likely?
7 Evaluate the outcome	7.1 How does the artefact convey the completion of task? 7.2 How does the artefact help the user recognize, diagnose and remedy errors?

Applying scenario based design to the Acadmin interface

We can illustrate the use of psychological design by scenario through one element of the Acadmin system. By selecting *interacting opportunistically* from the typology of user concerns it is possible to create the following scenario:

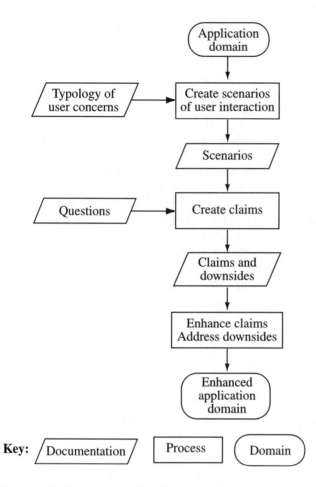

FIGURE 6.15   *Scenario based design—the process*

Scenario: A new user selects *create student records* from the *individual students* submenu of the main menu (Fig. 6.8). As a result the novice user enters the *student details screen* (Fig. 6.9), enters some student data, but is confused about the term time address box.

In fact there is a second student details screen which contains two address fields: one for term time address and one for home address. If the box on screen 1 is checked then the system automatically copies data from the home address field to the term time address field.

By selecting the question *how does the artefact evoke goals in the user?* from Carrol and Rosson's list we can create the following claim and associated downside:

Claim: including term time address in screen 1 evokes possibility of copying addresses in screen 2

Downside: novice users are confused as to why the address is included in this screen at all.

The application of psychological design by scenario is shown diagramatically in Fig. 6.16. From the analysis it seems sensible to move the check box to the start of screen two, thus eliminating the downside while maintaining the positive aspects of the claim.

It should be emphasized that design rationale techniques are relatively new, and are by no means universally applied by interface designers. The selective use of QOC type documentation techniques will, it is suggested, greatly enhance the visibility of difficult HCI design decisions. Although the psychological design by scenario method might at first appear over complicated, on further study it is expected that the reader will appreciate the enhanced rigour that it

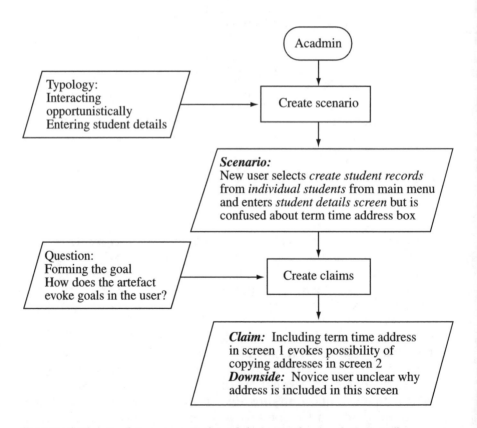

FIGURE 6.16   *Applying scenario based design to the Acadmin interface*

can provide to the interface designer who is seeking to improve usability before building the interface and certainly before any usability testing can be undertaken.

6.6   Interface specification

Design rules help the interface designer restrict the space of design alternatives. Design rationale techniques can also assist and specifically document the reasoning behind design decisions. What neither do is specify the *structure* of the proposed design. This is the role for interface specification techniques.

A variety of diagrammatic dialogue specification techniques have been applied to the human–computer dialogue. While many of these techniques provide the benefit of clear visualization of simple designs, they produce significant difficulties when analysing complex, or even typical, graphical user interfaces. The reader with a detailed interest in interface development will be able to study a range of techniques including standard software engineering formalisms such as state based formal methods (e.g. Z and VDM), algebraic models (e.g. CSP) and status/event analysis. We will investigate one of the diagrammatic techniques referred to as state transition networks.

6.6.1   State transition networks

The state machine approach (Salter, 1976) has been demonstrated to be appropriate for the modelling of real-time systems. *State transition networks* (STNs) have been adapted to some degree of success to dialogue specification. In STNs circles are used to denote a *state* within an interface, and arcs to represent a transition from one state to another. The interaction initiating the transition is written above the arc whereas the response that the system makes is provided below the arc. A full interface can be specified through a hierarchical structure of networks. STNs are, however, weak in their ability to represent certain aspects of graphical user interfaces. Dialogues containing several concurrent processes (e.g. complex toggle switching), in particular, can produce a combinatorial explosion in possible states leading to great difficulty in paper-based specification. In the USE methodology Wasserman *et al.* (1985) cite a number of reasons why STNs on their own are inadequate for anything other than the simplest of interfaces and describe an extended form of STNs with additional textual definition to specify data input, output and linkage to systems operations. In Fig. 6.17 we present a limited STN description of part of the Acadmin system.

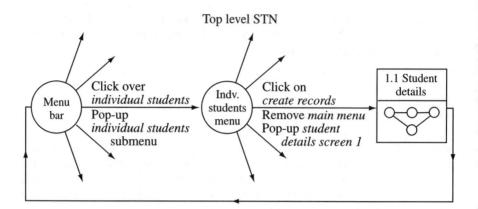

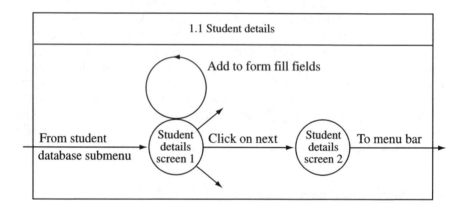

FIGURE 6.17 *STN description of part of the Acadmin system*

6.7 Plumbest plc: an exploratory interface design

6.7.1 Further information

Note: having undertaken social systems design (Chapter 5) we will now refer to the new job titles as specified in Plumbest Solution 5.2:

- Operations manager
- Service centre co-ordinator
- Service telephonists
- General administrators
- Mobile operatives
- Local area co-ordinators

Plumbest have decided to proceed with a version of the pet-plan solution known as the semi-automatic JAS. In this implementation the new computer system will decide an allocation of MOs but will require confirmation from the service telephonist prior to sending data to the MOs. Service telephonists will have the availability to search for current MO work schedules and override the allocation if necessary. Within Usersoft there are a number of strands to the development of the Plumbest's new job allocation system:

- One group, under the control of the *main design team* is developing the functionality within the allocation subsystem that will receive customer call details and, based on MO locations and job schedules, will allocate the optimum MO.
- The *customer communications local design team* is responsible for the development of a suitable software interface for entering and processing jobs.
- The *job completion local design team* is working on the part of the system used by MOs to update the data after jobs have been completed.
- A further group under the direction of the main design team is looking at ways in which effective monitoring of job allocation and completion can be provided.

Customer communications local design team

In this part of our case study work we will focus on the work of the *customer communications local design team*. The team is currently undertaking two tasks:

1. Designing the software interface to JAS that will be used by the service telephonist.
2. Specifying database update and enquiry facilities

The software which the customer communications local design team is co-ordinating will:

- Input details of telephone calls from customers (see Part A of JIF)
- Update relevant tables
- Search a database of currently logged jobs to show the current job situation:
  - by customer number
  - by MO number
- Link to the allocation subsystem being developed under the control of the main design team.

6.7.2   Tasks

Describing the interaction

Plumbest Task 6.1

Within Clarke's three-level model of human–computer interaction what *virtual objects* will there be? Use the model to describe the human and computer elements of interaction between the service telephonist and the JAS.

Task analysis

Plumbest Task 6.2

Describe using heirarchical task decomposition techniques the current manual process for job allocation. You may need to make reference to the soft systems conceptual model derived in Chapter 4. Modify the current manual task analysis to represent the tasks involved in processing a job assuming a semi-automatic job allocation system (one where the computer program selects an MO but the service telephonist is required to confirm or reject the allocation). Draw a hierarchical task analysis diagram.

Interaction style and user needs

Plumbest Task 6.3

By referencing the user analysis data captured in Chapter 2, describe the service telephonist user group's requirements in terms of the five factors underpinning interaction style.

Interface design, specification and building

Plumbest Task 6.4

Draw screen sketches that describe a 'first-shot' exploratory design for a GUI to be used by service telephonists to allocate jobs.

Plumbest Task 6.5

Use the QOC design space analysis technique to document elements of your design.

Plumbest Task 6.6

Depending on the software systems that are available build a limited vertical prototype of the JAS with which the customer communications local design group can interact. You have flexibility in the level of detail within your prototype. It may have very limited functionality as, at this stage in the development you are testing out the interface style. You may decide on a multimedia authoring tool, alternatively you may be able to use a database system such as Oracle or Microsoft Access. Experienced programmers may have access to visual programming languages such as Visual Basic, Visual C++, Delphi or similar systems.

6.7.3   Solutions

Describing the interaction

Plumbest Solution 6.1

The JAS will access a number of virtual objects:

• Job schedule containing details of all current jobs
• MO profile containing details of all MOs and their current location
• Customer list
• Electronic JIF

Fig. 6.18 provides a detailed application of Clarke's three-level model to the JAS.

Task analysis

Plumbest Solution 6.2

The initial manual process of allocating jobs was previously separated between two job roles; the service administrator and the radio operator. The SSM conceptual model derived in Chapter 4 (refer to Fig. 4.9) provides a basis for a logical (unrelated to job roles) specification of the current task allocation process. The hierarchical task decomposition is shown in Fig. 6.19. A modified version representing a semi-automatic job allocation system is provided in Fig. 6.20, and HTA diagrams in Fig. 6.21.

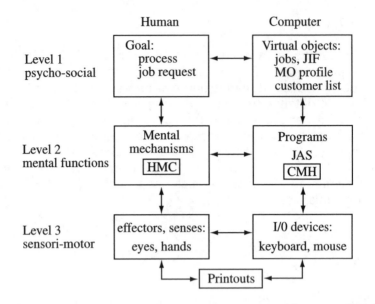

FIGURE 6.18   *Applying the three-level model to JAS*

0		In order to process job
	1	Accept job details
		1.1 Input name and address
		1.2 Enquire about job details
	2	Decide on nature of job
	3	Allocate job
		3.1 Allocate job to emergency MO
		3.2 Allocate job to foreman

Plan 0   do 1 - 2 - 3 in that order
Plan 1   do 1.1 - 1.2 in that order
Plan 3   do 3.1 or 3.2 depending on whether emergency or not

FIGURE 6.19   *HTA —Job allocation task decomposition—current manual system*

Interaction style and user needs

Plumbest Solution 6.3

The two initial job roles (service administrator and radio operator) will need to be merged to form one service telephonist job (with some redeployed as general administrators). The user needs, relevant to the

0	Add job		
	1	Accept job details	
		1.1	Input job type (commercial or domestic)
		1.2	Input customer name
		1.3	Input customer address
	2	Input nature of job (emergency or not)	
	3	Allocate job	
		3.1	Activate functional allocation
		3.2	Process proposed allocated MO
			3.2.1 Confirm allocation
			3.2.2 Cancel allocation

Plan 0   do 1 - 2 - 3 in that order
Plan 1   do 1.1 - 1.3 in that order
Plan 3   do 3.1 - 3.2 in that order
    Plan 3.2   do 3.2.1 or 3.2.2 depending on choice
                Plan 3.2.2 proceed with manual override

FIGURE 6.20   *HTA—Job allocation task decomposition—proposed semi-automatic system*

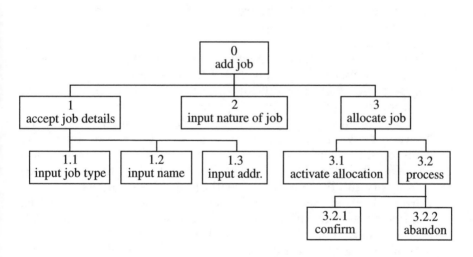

FIGURE 6.21   *HTA diagram for telephonist job processing*

choice of interaction style, identified in the user analysis (refer to Chapter 2) are summarized in Table 6.8.

Having reviewed the user needs and having taken account of the result of effective training programmes, the service telephonist user group's requirements in terms of the five factors underpinning interaction style are summarized below:

TABLE 6.8   *User needs*

Initial user group	User role and needs
Service administrators	Both 'pet plan' and 'minimum solution' would imply data input end user role—relationship to radio operator unclear. Majority of service administrators have some prior IT experience (e.g. word processing, simple database work)—transferring users? *Aspirational:* Experienced users of either JAS will be servants—need to consider motivational aspects. *Functional:* Safety critical nature of system has implications for how this user group will access new system.
Radio operator	*Aspirational:* maintenance/enhancement of job role. *Functional:* majority have very little IT knowledge: potential novice user.

1. **Initiation**   While at present a number of potential end users have little IT experience we have to assume that effective training programmes will enable Plumbest to consider that the service telephonists will be *expert*, or at least *specific*, users (refer to Table 2.1). Current staff unable to meet this requirement will need to be redeployed. Service telephonists will wish to be 'in control' of the JAS and will be able to cope effectively with a relatively high level of initiation.
2. **Flexibility**   The potential *servant* nature of use and the aspirational needs, particularly the implications for motivation, require that a degree of flexibility be built into the system without compromising the importance of a well-defined process for job allocation.
3. **Option complexity**   An effective balance will need to be struck between providing a sufficiently high level of option complexity, commensurate with initiation and flexibility requirements, and ensuring that too high a level does not lead to unnecessary complexity and thereby conflict with safety requirements.
4. **Power**   The service telephonist end-user role will need to use commands with a variety of power levels. The most significantly powerful task that will be required in the semi-automatic JAS is that of the manual override to job allocation. Considerable care will be needed here to ensure that the correct allocation has been made.
5. **Information load**   As with all users information load should be minimized as far as is practical.

Interface design, specification and building

Plumbest Solution 6.4

In Fig. 6.22 we propose an outline sketch of part of a first-shot windows-based exploratory prototype GUI for part of the JAS to be

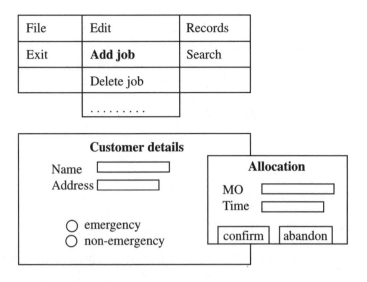

File	Edit	Records
Exit	**Add job**	Search
	Delete job	
	. . . .	

FIGURE 6.22   *Semi-automatic JAS—windows GUI interface*

used by service telephonists to allocate jobs. It includes a pull-down menu and two windows, each of which has been identified from the task analysis undertaken (refer to Figs 6.20 and 6.21):

- Customer details window—to *accept job details* and *input nature of job* (Tasks 1 and 2, Fig. 6.21).
- Allocation window—to decide on the proposed allocation (*allocate job,* Task 3, Fig. 6.21).

In order to allocate a job the service telephonist is required to select *add job* from the *edit* element of the menu bar, after which the *customer details window* will appear. After entering job details either of the emergency radio buttons will be selected which will then trigger the functional allocation system. The proposed allocated MO will be displayed in a second *allocation window* and the operator will either confirm or abandon the proposed allocation.

Plumbest Solution 6.5

The QOC design space analysis design rationale technique has been used (Fig. 6.23) to document why it was decided to implement the confirmation of the allocated MO (Task 3.2, *process*, as shown in Fig. 6.21) in a separate window rather than part of the customer details window. Within the decision it was determined that *emphasizes importance* has a greater weighting than *increases speed*.

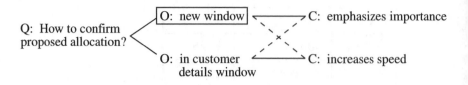

FIGURE 6.23   *Example QOC for JAS*

Summary

In this chapter we have seen:

- That user interactions need to be placed within a context of goals, activities and tasks
- How to describe user tasks using basic task analysis techniques
- How to recognize the factors that determine interface style and usability
- How task analysis can lead to effective design
- How design rationale techniques can clarify interface design decisions
- How to specify interfaces using state transition diagrams

Questions

6.1 Describe how the factors underling interaction style would lead you to propose an interface style for each of the following user groups:
(i)   a computer programmer using a new 4GL package
(ii)   an experienced word-processing operator
(iii) a youth trainee using a sales ordering system.

6.2 Propose designs for the interfaces for the following systems:

Traffic navigation system
In-car traffic navigation systems are now becoming available. You are required to devise the interface to a sophisticated full VDU-based system that will be implemented in lorries owned by a major logistics company. The system will allow for:
- Journey planning in advance of set-off
- Constant directional information (e.g. advance warning of next turning required, etc.)
- In-transit traffic information (jams ahead, etc.)
- Weather information
- In-journey replanning in case of high traffic, poor weather, etc.

Local information system

A regional tourist board has decided to provide information to tourists about the facilities available within the area. The system will be provided on PC format with data distributed weekly to all outlets (which are likely to include hotels, rail and bus stations, travel agents, etc.) by diskette. Information will be required on:
- Physical amenities (historic sites, beauty spots)
- Travel (e.g. rail and bus times)
- Entertainment (theatre, films, etc.)
- Weather

In both cases you will need to consider the following issues:

- Anticipated user group and associated needs
- Interface style selected and why
- Use of design rules
- Detailed design rationale and example screens

References

ACM (1992), 'Curricula for human–computer interaction', ACM.

Ankrah, A., Frohlich, D. M. and Gilbert, G. N. (1990), 'Two ways to fill a bath, with and without knowing', in D. Daiper *et al.* (eds), *Interact-90*, Chapman and Hall, London.

Apple Computer (1987), *Apple Human Interface Guidelines; the Apple Desktop Interface*, Addison-Wesley.

Card, S. K., Moran, T. P. and Newell, A. (1983), *The Psychology of Human–computer Interaction*, Lawrence Erlbaum, New Jersey.

Carrol, J. M. and Rosson, M. B. (1991), 'Deliberated evoloution: stalking the viewmatcher in design space', *Human–computer Interaction*, 6 (3 and 4), 281–318.

Carrol, J. M. and Rosson, M. B. (1991), 'Designing by scenario', *Human–computer Interaction*, 6 (3 and 4).

Clarke, A. A. (1986), 'A three level human–computer interface model', *International Journal of Man-Machine Studies*, 24, 503–517.

Dix, A. (1993), *Human–computer Interaction*, Prentice-Hall, London.

Fountain, A. J. (1985), 'Modelling user behaviour with formal grammar', in *People and Computers: Designing the Interface*, Cambridge University Press.

Kieras, D. E. and Polson, P. G. (1985), 'An approach to the formal analysis of user complexity', *International Journal of Man-Machine Studies*, 22, 365–394.

Preece, J., Rogers, Y., Sharp, H., Benyon, D., Hillard, S. and Carey, T. (1994), *Human–computer Interaction*, Addison Wesley, Wokingham.

Macaulay, L. (1995), *Human–computer Interaction for Software Designers*, Thompson Computer Press, London.

MacLean, A. *et al.* (1991), 'Questions, options and criteria: elements of design space analysis', *Human–computer Interaction*, 6 (3 and 4).

Mayhew, D. J. (1992), *Principles and Guidelines in Software and User Interface Design*, Prentice-Hall, Englewood Cliffs, New Jersey.

Microsoft Corporation (1992), *The Windows Interface: an application design guide*, Microsoft Press.

Norman, D. A. (1988), *The Psychology of Everyday Things*, Basic Books.

Olson, J. R. and Olson, G. M. (1990), 'The growth of cognitive modeling in human–computer interaction since GOMS', *Human–computer Interaction*, 5, 221–265.

Salter K. G. (1976), 'A methodology for decomposing system requirements into data processing requirements', Proceedings, 2nd International Conference on Software Engineering.

Shepherd, A. (1989), 'Analysis and training in information technology tasks', in D. Diaper (ed.), *Task Analysis for Human Computer Interaction*, Ellis Horwood.

Shneiderman, B. (1982), 'The future of interactive systems and the emergence of direct manipulation', *Behaviour and IT*, 1(3), 237–256.

Shneiderman, B. (1992), *Designing the User Interface*, Addison-Wesley, Reading, Mass.

Stewart, T. (1991), *Directory of HCI Standards*, DTI, London.

Wasserman, A., Pircher, P. A., Shewmake, D. T. and Kersten, M. L. (1985), 'Developing interactive information systems with the user software engineering methodology', *IEEE Transactions on Software Engineering*, 12(2), 326–345.

Further reading

Dix, A. (1993), *Human–computer Interaction*, Prentice-Hall, London.

Preece, J., Rogers, Y., Sharp, H., Benyon, D., Hillard, S. and Carey, T. (1994), *Human–computer Interaction*, Addison Wesley, Wokingham.

Macaulay, L. (1995), *Human–computer Interaction for Software Designers*, Thompson Computer Press, London.

Shneiderman, B. (1992), *Designing the User Interface*, Addison-Wesley, Reading, Mass.

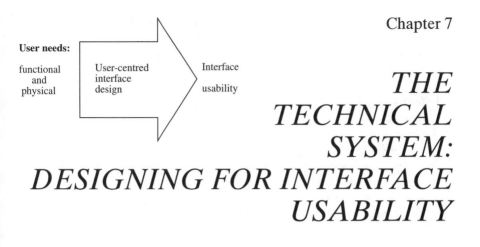

Chapter 7

User needs:

functional
and
physical

User-centred
interface
design

Interface

usability

THE TECHNICAL SYSTEM: DESIGNING FOR INTERFACE USABILITY

Chapter aims

In this chapter we aim to bring together our knowledge in HCI and user-centred design, with our understanding of users, to discuss and propose approaches to the implementation of user-centred methods of interface design that will lead to usable technical systems. Specifically through study of this chapter the reader should be able to:

- Provide a comprehensive definition of usability
- Relate usability and evaluation
- Perform simple user-based interface evaluations
- Evaluate the user contribution to a range of interface design methods
- Describe the essential elements of a user-centred interface development approach

7.1 Introducing interface design

7.1.1 User-centredness and the interface

Central to our whole approach is the principle that user-centredness in information systems development is vital if systems success is to be achieved. A user-centred information systems development approach is one in which all types of user needs (functional, physical and aspirational) are addressed, so that usability inherent in the end product is maximized. Earlier in our study (Chapter 3) we undertook a detailed examination of the generic application of user-centred design to the development of information systems. While the software interface is only one part of the whole information system product, in terms of systems success it is a vital one and can greatly affect all three aspects of usability:

- Effectiveness
- Efficiency
- Satisfaction

It seems obvious therefore that interface design should conform to user-centred principles. In this part of our study we focus on approaches that aim to enhance usability through the production of quality human–computer interfaces.

7.1.2   Integrated interface design

Design vs. engineering

The production of any artefact involves a range of methods and techniques. The developer can exercise a number of skills, gained from personal experience, and apply a number of rules that have been proposed by others working in the same field. The fashion designer, when developing a new dress, will place a very large emphasis on artistic and creative skills whereas a civil engineer, when developing a new bridge, will rely heavily on mathematical and scientific knowledge of the rules underpinning structural design.

Although the development of any artefact can be seen to include aspects of both design and engineering, the balance between the two is different for each artefact. It is, perhaps, for this reason that clothes developers are referred to as fashion designers, but bridge developers are called civil engineers. As with many other artefacts, the development of a software interface includes both design and engineering in an integrated manner. Whiteside, Bennett and Holtzblatt (1988), assume that design is a subset of engineering and define engineering to be: *'the design, planning and construction of artefacts in the real world'*.

Interface design vs. interface engineering

The successful development of the human–computer interface is based upon both creative design and aspects of formal engineering. According to Rubenstein and Hersh (1984) the interface development process should be *integrated* because:

the essence of engineering is creating constructive compromises among many conflicting goals. Integrated design can only occur when all the real issues are allowed to exert an influence, ...creation ... involves elements of engineering, science and art—the practical search for results, the application of theory and the use of skill and taste. Our design philosophy is based upon the view that science and art are as indispensable to design as is engineering practice

There are a large number of influences and issues that need to be taken on board before interface development can be undertaken. Shackel (1986) in describing what he refers to as the *ergonomic approach* to interface development identifies three constituent elements:

1. Systems analysis
2. Workstation analysis
3. Evaluation

In systems analysis he includes the process of allocating tasks between man and machine (Chapter 5). In workstation analysis, through the application of well-known techniques we aim to optimize human–computer interaction (see Chapter 6). The third of Shackel's elements is that of the evaluation of design proposals. It is this area on which we will specifically focus in this part of our study. Throughout this chapter we will seek to review a range of techniques for interface development, the majority of which attempt to be based on sound scientific and engineering principles. We should recognize at the start, however, that interface design is not just a routine or rigorous engineering process, and that artistic and creative flair is also important. It is for this reason that many interface design teams will include specialists in graphic design.

7.2 Usability and evaluation

According to Bevan and Macleod (1994) *'most computer software today is unnecessarily difficult to understand, hard to learn, and complicated to use'*. They state that *'difficult to use software wastes the user's time, causes worry and frustration and discourages further use of the software'*. They ask why *'the usability of most computer software is so poor'* and respond that *'in spite of a recent acknowledgement that usability is an important part of software quality, it has remained a fuzzy concept which has been difficult to evaluate and impossible to measure'*.

We have named this chapter 'The technical system: designing for interface usability' and intend to focus on interface design methods that purport to generate high levels of usability in their end product.

Although we have already discussed usability it is now time for us to undertake a fuller exploration of the term before we can evaluate the differing approaches.

7.2.1   Usability— what is it?

While usability is indeed a fuzzy concept, there is now an increasing number of ways in which interface developers attempt to evaluate the usability of their products. The *fuzziness* problem can be shown by the confusingly large number of different definitions of usability that are in circulation, some of which were introduced in Chapter 1. In Fig. 7.1 we present a spectrum of different descriptions of usability roughly presented in increasing order of *width* and *generality*: those at

general ↓ specific   narrow ↓ wide

	Description	Source
1	'ease of use'	Miller, 1971
2	offering 'functionality in such a way that the planned users will be able to master and exploit (it) without undue strain on their capacities and skills'	Eason, 1988
3	'the quality of a system, program or device that enables it to be easily understood and conveniently applied by the user'	IBM Dictionary of Computing (1993)
4	'. . . effect, learnability, flexibility and attitude . . .'	Shackel, 1986
5	'has multiple components and is traditionally associated with five usability attributes: learnability, efficiency, memorability, errors and satisfaction'	Nielsen, 1993
6	'a set of attributes of software which bear on the effort needed for use and on the individual assessment of such use by a stated or implied set of users'	ISO/IEC 9126 (1992)
7	'the effectiveness, efficiency and satisfaction with which specified users can achieve specified goals in particular environments'	ISO 9241 (1993)

FIGURE 7.1   *Descriptions of usability*

the start of the list take a narrow and general view of usability whereas those at the end take a much wider and, by detailing usability attributes, take a much more specific view of usability.

The reader will already be aware that we have adopted the ISO 9241 definition for usability and have noted that within this definition effectiveness is *'the accuracy and completeness with which users achieve specific goals'*, that efficiency is *'the accuracy and completeness of goals in relation to resources expended'* and that satisfaction is *'the comfort and acceptability of the system'*. It is important to emphasize that usability is only meaningful within a specific context. Normally this context of use includes aspects relating to the users themselves, the tasks they are undertaking, the equipment they are using and the environment in which they are working. One particular system placed in one context will probably display different usability characteristics when placed in a second context. Interface developers need to know the context of use before they start their work. Figure 7.2 describes the context of use for the Acadmin system.

Individual descriptions place usability at different points in a hierarchy of attributes of software quality such as utility, reliability, and acceptability. It could be argued that the ISO 9241 definition equates usability with software quality within a context of use. Nielsen (1993), however, in his hierarchy of attributes places usability as a subset of usefulness that is itself an aspect of acceptability (refer to Fig. 7.3). Note that Nielsen describes usability as one element of acceptability while the ISO (9241) defines acceptability to be one facet of usability! With all these contrasting approaches to usability, it is hardly surprising that to many users and developers of software, it has remained such a fuzzy concept. Specialists may now be beginning to agree on the approach to take and as a result it is to be expected that usability will become easier to quantify.

7.2.2   Usability— how is it measured?

Most users of computer system will easily be able to differentiate between systems that are *easy to use* and those that are not. What they will find more difficult is being able to *quantify* how much more easy it is

---

Users	University administrators
Task	Entering student details
Equipment	PC using Windows-based Acadmin system
Environment	Faculty office

FIGURE 7.2   *Acadmin context of use*

FIGURE 7.3   *A model of the attributes of system acceptability (*reproduced from Nielsen (1993*) Usability Engineering,* with permission of the publishers, Academic Press Inc.*)*

to use one system it is to use another. There are two reasons why the usability of a particular information system software product cannot be directly measured. First, as we have seen, the concept is only meaningful in context. The second reason is that it has a number of different facets. Nielsen (1993) identifies five attributes of usability: learnability, efficiency, memorability, errors and satisfaction. The ISO describe three broad categories: effectiveness, efficiency and satisfaction.

Usability can be measured by identifying metrics associated with the appropriate attributes of usability. For a specific software product, in a particular context of use, a range of usability attributes can be identified. Particular attention should be given to those attributes that are judged to have a significant impact on the quality of use of the overall system (Bevan and Macleod 1994). Depending on the type of attribute an appropriate concept and method of measurement can be chosen. Broadly two types of usability measure can be identified: *performance* measures that can describe both efficiency and effectiveness, and *satisfaction* measures that capture the user's perception of aspects of usability. Questionnaires are particularly useful for satisfaction measures and experiments are necessary for performance measures. Having selected a study and measuring method for each attribute a usability metric can then be chosen. Table 7.1 outlines four potential usability metrics for the Acadmin system.

7.2.3   Usability evaluation

Purpose of testing

Having outlined a method of specifying usability we now focus on the process of undertaking the evaluation process. Hewett (1986) has

TABLE 7.1 *Acadmin usability metrics*

		Task: entering student details	
Usability attribute	Study method	Measuring method	Usability metric
Learnability	Questionnaire	Rating scale	Rating (1–10)
Efficiency	Task/experiment	Observation	Time to complete task
Errors	Task/experiment	Observation	Number of errors made
Satisfaction	Questionnaire	Rating scale	Rating (1–10)

identified two types of evaluation process: *formative evaluation* that monitors the process and product in order to redefine and further develop it, whereas *summative evaluation* assesses the impact, usability, effectiveness and overall performance of user and system. Rubin (1994), however, refines the issue and describes four distinct approaches to testing:

1. *Exploratory tests*, performed early in the development process.
2. *Assessment tests*, undertaken early to midway through the project.
3. *Validation tests*, conducted late on.
4. *Comparison tests*, which can be performed at various times in the development, and which aim to contrast two or more solutions.

Methods of testing

In terms of the techniques and tools that can be used to perform these evaluation tests, five broad methods exist. Three of these (observation, experiments and questionnaire) can be classified as user-based methods and have been introduced in Chapter 2. The other two are expert-based methods that we will briefly discuss before returning to user-based methods. Unfortunately there is evidence (e.g. Dillon *et al.*, 1993 and Smith and Dunckley, 1995) within the mainstream software development community that while awareness of such methods is increasing, their adoption remains largely superficial.

Expert based evaluations In *expert evaluation* human-factor specialists are asked to undertake the user role, and from their expert knowledge provide a description of the strengths and weaknesses of the system. The experts chosen should be independent from the design team as it is very difficult for a designer to evaluate his or her own work. When usability specialists judge whether each dialogue element follows established usability principles the method is referred to as *heuristic evaluation*. Microsoft and other companies are known to have embraced heuristic evaluation and other inspection methods in recent years (Nielsen, 1995). Other interface inspection methods are reviewed in Nielsen and Mack (1994). The other major category of expert evaluation is known as *analytical evaluation* in which HCI formal methods such as GOMS and CCT (refer to Chapter 6) can be used, at the keystroke level of analysis to predict user performance before any software product has been developed.

User based evaluations   In *observational evaluation* end users are studied undertaking real-task scenarios either in the normal workplace or in a specially designed *usability laboratory*. Often usability laboratories are not only deemed by evaluators as necessary for supporting usability evaluations, but are seen as a statement of the organization's commitment to testing the usability of its products and services (Fowler *et al.*, 1994). Often usability laboratories contain at least two rooms including an experimental room (where the user undertakes the task), separated by a one-way mirror from the control room where the evaluators monitor the test. Video-editing suites are used to record both user activity (and non-activity) and VDU interaction. While access to a laboratory can facilitate testing, it can only ensure the production of usable products (Fath *et al.*, 1994), if used for the implementation of a rigorous evaluation process. Such a process will contain a number of stages such as:

- Designing the evaluation
- Preparing to conduct the evaluation
- Conducting the evaluation
- Analysing the data
- Reporting the results

An extension to observational evaluation is *experimental evaluation* in which users are involved as subjects in controlled experiments that aim to provide empirical evidence to support a particular claim or hypothesis concerning a system (Dix *et al.*, 1993). Experiments should be carefully designed and implemented and the results need to be analysed by standard statistical techniques.

With the possible exception of expert evaluation all the evaluation methods discussed so far aim to determine a performance measure. The fifth type of method attempts to elicit user satisfaction measures. Expert evaluation could be said to determine expert satisfaction levels. In user-based *survey evaluation* a questionnaire is designed to specify what users feel about the system they are using. Although generic user-evaluation questionnaires are available (e.g. as provided in Shneiderman, 1992) it is usually necessary to design the survey instrument to match the specific usability attributes that are being investigated. When distributed and returned from a representative, and significantly large, sample of end users, rating scales can provide a considerable amount of useful data. Scales, such as those shown in

Fig. 7.4, grouped together under appropriate headings are useful in determining quantitative satisfaction levels for individual usability attributes. The sum of all rating scales provides an overall measure of satisfaction. In addition to rating scales it is helpful to include questions about the user, such as those which might determine general level of IT literacy and skill level, so that the user sample can be classified and differences in perceptions between user groups analysed. The overall process of user-based evaluation is shown in Fig. 7.5 which has been adapted from Eason (1988).

Learning the system

1 Learning to operate the system was	difficult				easy
	1	2	3	4	5

2 Exploring the system by trial and error is	discouraging				encouraging
	1	2	3	4	5

3 Remembering commands is	difficult				easy
	1	2	3	4	5

4 Tasks can be performed in straightforward ways	never				always
	1	2	3	4	5

5 Help messages are	clear				confusing
	1	2	3	4	5

FIGURE 7.4   *Part of a typical user satisfaction survey instrument*

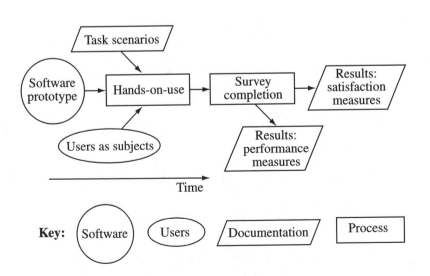

FIGURE 7.5   *The basic process of a user-based evaluation*

7.3   Usability engineering and design

It is generally agreed (e.g. Shackel, 1986; Hewett, 1986 and Nielsen, 1993) that interactive systems should be designed iteratively. Figure 7.5 depicts one pass through the basic cycle of a user-based evaluation. Iterative design (Gould and Lewis, 1985) makes heavy use of early and repeated feedback from representative users. In current approaches this iterative approach is implemented through the construction of software prototypes for proposed systems. The general procedure followed has been to use rapid prototyping with incremental change based around continuous studies of the prototypes in use in authentic tasks. Often approaches to prototyping include a parallel design phase (refer to Fig. 7.6) in which several alternatives are explored at the same time, after which the procedure reverts to the evolutionary approach. One or more of the parallel prototypes can contribute to future development.

Formal user-based evaluation, generating both performance and satisfaction measures, is an essential ingredient in effective design for usability. Nielsen (1993) describes what he refers to as a *life cycle* of usability *engineering* that outlines the processes that need to be undertaken when designing for usability. The usability engineering life cycle should not be considered to be a rigorous sequential series of steps as some of the individual elements interrelate and only make

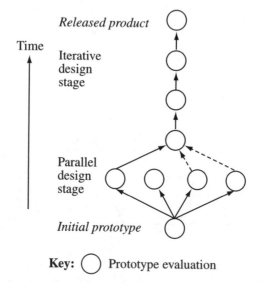

FIGURE 7.6   *Parallel and evolutionary prototyping* (reproduced from Nielsen (1993) *Usability Engineering*, with permission of the publishers, Academic Press Inc.)

sense when undertaken together. The usability engineering life cycle contains the following elements:

1. Know the user
2. Competitive analysis, investigate other competing products
3. Setting usability goals, through usability attributes and metrics
4. Parallel design, where two or more prototypes are compared and elements of one, or more than one feed into future designs
5. Participative design, involve users
6. Co-ordinated design of the total interface
7. Apply guidelines and heuristics
8. Prototyping
9. Empirical testing, measure usability goals established in (3)
10. Iterative design, capturing design rationale
11. Collect feedback from field use

While usability engineering adopts many of the techniques employed in other usability evaluations, the significant issue here is that, through the identification of usability attributes, software developers set clear usability *targets* early on in the design process. This early specification of target values provide a measure of how far the final system meets the specification.

In the usability engineering approach the goals, attributes and metrics are set out in usability specification tables tailored to the needs of individual situations. Usability specification tables define a range of values for each metric from formal failure to state of the art success and are often defined in terms of the worst case, the planned level and the best case. These three components for each metric, are useful in managing the development of complex systems where trade-offs are often needed among the different levels for many attributes (Whiteside and Holtblatt, 1988).

7.4 The contribution from graphic design

We have noted from Rubenstein and Hersh (1984) that the integrated design of computer systems involves elements of engineering, science and art. It is within the interface design element that the artistic element comes to the fore, and it is from the expertise of the graphic designer that such skills are provided.

Graphic design is the discipline of effective visual communication (Baecker *et al.*, 1995). While guidelines and heuristics provide support to the interface developer, effective graphic design can help in their integrated implementation. In terms of our usability criteria graphic design can make a valuable contribution: particularly to *satisfaction*.

Although we can emphasize the benefits that formal graphic design can bring to the interface development process, clearly in this context we are unable to present any more than a cursory overview of the subject. Marcus (1995), however, provides a good introduction to the application of graphic design to interface development. He introduces the term *visible language* which refers to *'all the graphical techniques used to communicate the message or content'*. The term includes:

- *Layout*, formats, proportions and grids
- *Typography*, the selection of appropriate typefaces and typesetting
- *Colour and texture*, which convey complex information and pictorial reality
- *Imagery*, the use of signs, icons and symbols
- *Animation*, dynamic displays which are especially important for the video elements of multimedia systems
- *Sequencing*, the overall approach to storytelling
- *Sound,* or aural cues, which are now often referred to as earcons
- *Visual identity*, the rules that lead to consistency

Marcus describes the basic task of interface design based upon three principles:

1. *Organize* by providing the user with a clear and consistent conceptual structure
2. *Economize* by maximizing the effectiveness of a minimum set of cues
3. *Communicate* by matching the presentation to the capabilities of the user

Care needs to be taken when attempting to integrate the work of graphic designers with others involved in interface design. Technical specialists and graphic designers have different priorities. Computer scientists, for example, value their program and how it works; graphic designers value the picture and how it looks (Kim, 1995). For interface design to thrive many disciplines must co-operate through participative structures (Chapter 3).

7.5   User interface design methodologies

Throughout our study we have noted the great many tools and techniques which constitute the discipline of human–computer interaction, and which inform interface design. Although we have seen how many of these techniques can be integrated into life cycles for usability engineering, we have yet to mention any specific design methodologies: well-documented approaches that developers can follow. Compared to software development methodologies (SSADM, etc.) interface design methodologies are at a much earlier stage in development. A number of specific integrated interface design methods have, however, been proposed in the last decade, which to varying degrees integrate HCI tools and techniques into a coherent whole.

7.5.1   User software engineering (USE)

Wassermann *et al.* (1985) describe one of the earliest integrated interface design methods known as the *user software engineering (USE)* methodology and show how it is supported by automated tools. It is proposed that USE gives particular attention to effective user involvement in the early stages of software development, concentrates on *external* design (as perceived by users) and on the use of rapidly created and modified versions of the user interface. User interface design is dependant upon user characteristics, functional requirements and design guidelines. Emphasis is placed upon the use of state transition diagrams to specify the refined prototype versions. The overall approach can be seen from the following steps that comprise the full USE methodology:

- Requirements analysis, activity and data modelling and the identification of user characteristics
- External design, dialogue and interface specification
- Prototype creation, with revisions as necessary
- Functional specification completion
- Preliminary database design
- Functional prototype creation
- Formal specification of the system
- Detailed design
- Implementation

7.5.2   Method for usability engineering (MUSE)

Lim and Long (1994) describe the *method for usability engineering (MUSE)* which consists of three phases:

1. *Elicitation and analysis*, which covers system study and the creation of a generalized task model
2. *Design synthesis,* through which a statement of user needs is derived followed by a composite task model used to prepare user and system task models
3. *Design specification*, which creates a user specification consisting of an interaction task model made up of an interface model and display design

7.5.3 HUFIT PAS

Although not strictly a methodology the *HUFIT PAS* toolset (Human Factors in IT—Planning Analysis and Specification) aims to provide tools and techniques which enable the wide variety of (non human-factor experts) personnel involved in the design of generic (i.e. off the shelf) IT products to take account of ergonomic/human-factor issues for themselves, as a normal part of their role, within whatever design process they are currently operating. Caterall (1991) and Allison *et al.* (1992) describe the HUFIT PAS and specifically review the user computer interface design tool. In recognition of these constraints generated by non-specialists the (mainly paper-based) tools are high level, relatively simple in format and highly tailorable, thereby enabling product designers, planners and marketeers to adopt a user-centred design approach. HUFIT PAS contains five elements:

1. User mapping
2. User and task characteristics
3. Usability specification for evaluation
4. User requirements summary
5. Functionality matrix

7.5.4 HUFIT user interface design tool

As part of the HUFIT package the user computer interface design (UCID) tool follows from the use of the user and task characteristics and functionality matrix tools of PAS. It aims to assist the designer in selecting relevant interaction styles and helps to design the overall appearance of the system and create interface/dialogue structure. The UCID tool attempts to present the vast amount of guideline material in an acceptable format for non human-factor specialists. It provides a step-by-step guide to interface design including five stages:

1. Choose relevant style
2. Design overall appearance
3. Design dialogue structure
4. Design detailed aspects
5. Provide user support

7.5.5 MUSiC method

The MUSiC (metrics for usability standards in computing) project at the National Physical Laboratory in the UK has worked in close conjunction with industry to develop methods and tools for the specification and measurement of usability. According to Bevan and Macleod (1994) the MUSiC methodology is the first comprehensive approach to the measurement of usability and reinforces the principles in ISO 9241-11. Within the project, tools have been developed for the user-based measurement of usability, user performance, user satisfaction, and for analytical measures of aspects of usability. A usability context analysis guide is used to identify the key characteristics of the users, tasks and environments and an evaluation design manager guides the choices being made when planning and carrying out an evaluation.

7.5.6   Supportive evaluation

Supportive evaluation (Robinson and Fitter, 1992) is an iterative, formative evaluation methodology, which provides rapid feedback to designers, and has been developed within the healthcare domain. Issues such as functionality, usability and clinical and social impact are the primary focus of the evaluation. A key element in the approach is the formative assessment workshop in which potential users of the system test the system in simulation of their usual environment. Evaluation is carried out by a team independent from the designers of the prototype being tested.

7.5.7   STUDIO

STUDIO (Browne, 1994) is an acronym for structured user-interface design for interaction optimization and was developed:

> in response to the inadequacies of existing systems development methods, particularly their lack of ability to meet the needs of computer users.

It addresses the software development life cycle from project planning to the production and engineering of an operational prototype. There are five main stages:

1. Project proposal and planning
2. User requirements analysis
3. Task synthesis
4. Usability engineering
5. User interface development

7.5.8   Logical user-centred interface design (LUCID)

While Hartson and Boehm-Davis (1989) in a review of user interface development processes and methodologies, recognize that *'in one sense considerable progress has been made'*, they also identify a number of specific key research areas where there remains the need for *'real breakthroughs'*. In terms of iterative methodologies Hartson and Boehm-Davis state that:

(i) research in the area of formative evaluation needs to focus on iterative evaluation techniques that, in fact, lead to a convergence on a good or at least an improved design

(ii) there is especially a need for techniques that can assign credit and blame, pinpointing why user performance is not up to expected levels in terms of specific interface flaws and shortcomings.

In recognition of these issues, Smith and Dunckley (1996) outline the early stages in the development of a new approach to interface development which is referred to as the logical user-centred interface design (LUCID) method. LUCID is a prototyping methodology that implements Taguchi techniques from the arena of total quality management to ensure that the final prototype is the optimum version. The method proposes to exploit the systems and tools developed for rapid prototyping but follows an entirely different philosophy and practical approach.

Within LUCID, users are involved in establishing factors (and levels) together with quality characteristics and subsequently evaluating a number of prototypes created by designers on a 'design by experiment' basis. The whole process aims to provide the answer to the following three questions. What is the optimum interface design? What factors and associated levels give the optimum design? What is the expected quality characteristic (usability metric) for the optimum interface? The main phases in the LUCID method are shown in Table 7.2.

7.5.9   Comparing interface design methodologies

The individual user interface design methodologies themselves have yet to receive sufficient practical implementation for an extensive comparative evaluation. We can, however, identify three design concepts underpinning the methods that can be used as a basis for comparison and evaluation:

1. User focus (involvement of real users in design)
2. Formal design (task analysis, interface specification, etc.)
3. Iterative nature (parallel, iterative and evolutionary prototyping)

Although individual methods address all three concepts they place a different emphasis on each. In Table 7.3 we attempt to contrast the

TABLE 7.2   *Phases in the LUCID method*

	Phase	Activities
1	Functional analysis and design	• Requirements capture • Task analysis, etc.
2	Exploratory investigation	• Exploratory prototypes developed, • Through brainstorming sessions users and developers identify key factors, associated levels and performance criteria
3	Taguchi design	• Investigate interaction between factors • Design of experiments
4	Taguchi testing	• User testing • Analysis of results • Selection of optimum design
5	Refinement	• Confirmatory testing • Further iterative refinement

TABLE 7.3   *Comparing interface design methodologies*

Method	User focus	Formal design	Iterative nature
USE	High	High	
MUSE		High	
MUSiC	High		High
Supportive evaluation	High		High
STUDIO	High	High	
LUCID	High	High	High

methods by highlighting the underpinning emphasis in which they are particularly strong. The table could be used as *one* factor in determining the appropriateness of each method for a particular application. There will be other issues which will be important such as the nature of the application domain, the process model and methodology being adopted, and the degree of accessibility to individual users. Although the author would never shy away from selling the positive benefits of the LUCID method he would not try to implement it in an organization committed to the waterfall approach and ill-disposed towards user involvement.

We should again emphasize the relative immaturity in the development and specification of interface design methodologies. Many of the approaches described above have enjoyed very little application outside of university research departments or human-factor laboratories. All software developers must, of course, use some method to produce their interfaces, even if they achieve their task in an unplanned and non-rigorous manner. We will now try to describe a generalized, comprehensive, yet non-specific approach to user-centred interface design.

7.6   Towards a comprehensive approach to user-centred interface design: requirements of a method

Before we can propose a comprehensive approach to user-centred interface design we should identify what previous researchers have found the necessary ingredients to be. In addition to Nielsen's (1993) life cycle approach there are three useful sources to investigate:

7.6.1   Features of designing for usability (Shackel)

Shackel (1986) describes five fundamental features of designing for usability:

1. *User-centred design*, the focus should be on the users
2. *Participative*, design teams should include *users as designers*
3. *Experimental design*, formal tests should be performed with *users as subjects*
4. *Iterative design*, design, test, measure and recycle
5. *User supportive design*, aim to provide training, help facilities, etc.

7.6.2   Attributes of a method (Johnson)

When describing the requirements of a general method for interface design, Johnson *et al.* (1989) state nine attributes:

1. *Systematic*, it should be straightforward and routine to apply
2. *Based upon existing criteria*, it should be derived from empirical and theoretical work
3. *Iterative*
4. *General*, it should work in a range of settings
5. *Participative*
6. *Sensitive*, to the users
7. *Simple* to use
8. *Face valid*, it should relate to realistic use
9. *Reasonably exhaustive*, it should cover most of the issues that constitute usability

7.6.3   Categories of user-centred design (Smith and Dunckley)

While the software interface is only one part of the whole information system product, in terms of systems success it is a vital one. The design of the interface should therefore conform to well-established user-centred design principles. To repeat: a user-centred information systems development approach (Chapter 3) is one in which all types of user needs (functional, physical and aspirational) are addressed so that usability (effectiveness, efficiency and satisfaction) is maximized in the end product. It will be useful at this stage to reproduce a slightly modified version of the user-centred design model as provided in Fig. 7.7.

We will look first at the *input* to the design process. The design of the software interface needs to take account of both functional and physical needs, although it is unlikely to greatly affect aspirational needs that are addressed by organization and job design (Chapter 6). The functional needs can be specified through task analysis techniques while physical needs will be identified in user studies. The user interface as *output* from the design process will affect all three aspects of usability. In terms of the design *process* itself we have seen how Smith and Dunckley (1995) evaluate user-centredness in terms of the three categories of structures, processes and scope:

1. *Structures* that either support or inhibit the way in which the user is able to contribute to the design process.
2. *Processes* in which participating users need to engage.
3. *Scope* which describes how far the analysis reflects a socio-technical, as opposed to just a technical, solution.

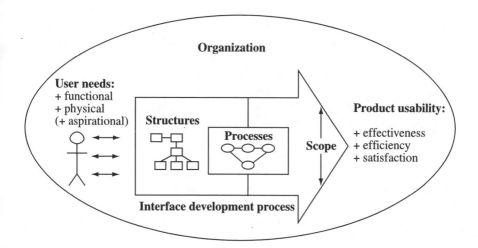

FIGURE 7.7   *The three categories and user-centred interface design*

Looking specifically at these concepts for interface design we can see that:

- Appropriate participative **structures** need to be in place so that representative users are engaged in both design and evaluation.
- The range of design **processes** (task analysis, design rationale, specification techniques) should include those in which the user can participate.
- **Scope** is not specifically addressed, although job design will be informed from the man-machine task allocation element of task analysis.

7.7 The process of interface design

As with social systems design the process of interface design is not one that should be too rigorously specified, as it should be flexibly implemented in each individual situation. Accepting this, and having noted that a considerable number of interface design methods do now exist, it will be profitable to place the theories of interface design within a coherent context of information systems development. Two approaches to the specification of the interface design process will be explored: a hierarchical checklist and an outline activity model. Both the hierarchical checklist and the activity model for user-centred interface design are complemented by similar frameworks for social systems design which can be found in Chapter 5.

Hierarchical checklist In Fig. 7.8 we will attempt to set out some rules of interface design that can be applied in roughly chronological order under each of the categories of user-centred design (structures, processes and scope). The rules themselves are not original as they are derived from the sources identified in previous sections, although it is expected that their presentation will provide enhanced understanding of UCID. It is not suggested that every interface development project should include all rules, rather that they can be used as a checklist to evaluate the potential effectiveness of a proposed or current interface design process.

Outline activity model In Fig. 7.9 we present a generic activity model of user-centred interface development. As with the checklist it should not be considered to be too rigorous but it provides a pictorial representation of the main stages in interface design. Note that one input is a technical task specification that is derived from task analysis and human–computer allocation as described in Chapter 5 and documented in Fig. 5.10.

The interface design process is underpinned by two aspects of

1   Establish participative structures which will enable effective user participation:

      1.1   Establish main and local design teams
      1.2   Ensure that users as designers should be members of all design teams
      1.3   Ensure users as designers are supported and trained
      1.4   Select different specialist for design and evaluation
      1.5   Select sufficient representative users as subjects for evaluations

2   Adopt processes which lead to usable solutions and with which users can engage:

      2.1   Perform comprehensive user analyses:
            2.1.1   Determine user physical needs
            2.1.2   Determine user functional needs
            2.1.3   Perform task analysis:
                  2.1.3.1 Analyse tasks by formal and semi-formal methods
                  2.1.3.2 Separate man and machine tasks
            (2.1.4   Determine user aspirational needs, used in organizational design)
      2.2   Set usability goals, through usability attributes and metrics:
            2.2.1   Ensure metrics are exhaustive:
                  2.2.1.1 Specify efficiency metrics
                  2.2.1.2 Specify effectiveness metrics
                  2.2.1.3 Specify satisfaction metrics
      2.3   Undertake formal design:
            2.3.1   Apply guidelines and heuristics
            2.3.2   Use design rationale to document decisions and force deliberation
      2.4   Use parallel prototyping techniques:
            2.4.1   Adopt rigorous methods to gain maximum benefit from prototypes
      2.5   Use iterative prototyping: design, test, measure and recycle:
            2.5.1   Adopt formal usability evaluation tests using users as subjects
            2.5.2   Ensure tests are face valid
      2.6   Co-ordinated design of the total interface
      2.7   Collect feedback from field use

3   Ensure that wide scope is informed

      3.1   Ensure personnel working on social systems design are informed of man-machine task allocation
            (note that designing for scope is the remit of social systems design)

FIGURE 7.8   *Hierarchical checklist for user-centred interface design*

systems analysis which can be undertaken concurrently. By conducting a formal user analysis a detailed *user specification* can be set out (Chapter 2) and by applying rigorous task analysis techniques based upon the requirements definition a *comprehensive task specification* can be produced (Chapter 5). Together with other

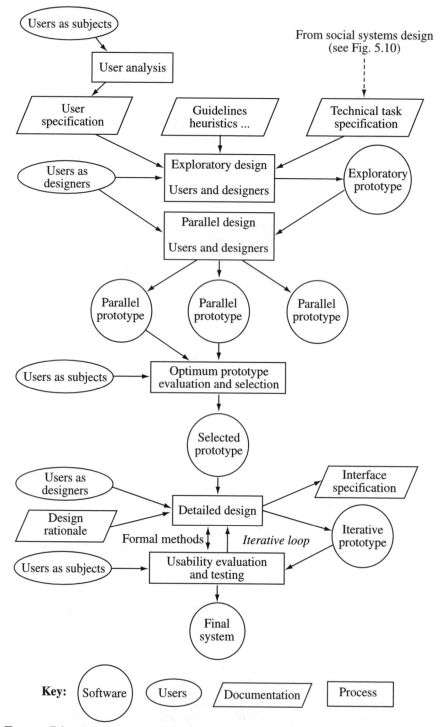

FIGURE 7.9   *An activity model of user-centred interface design*

interface design support material such as design guidelines, the task and user specifications are taken forward to the design stages.

In exploratory design, users and developers can jointly produce an exploratory prototype that can be used to tease out aspects of design after which it may be possible, and appropriate, to move to a parallel design stage through which a number of different prototypes can be produced.

By conducting formal evaluation studies with users as subjects, perhaps using the LUCID approach, one or more of these parallel prototypes may feed into a selected prototype. Development may now follow an iterative model whereby users and developers produce iterative versions of the interface, which is incrementally improved by formal usability evaluation tests. Formal methods (e.g. GOMS, CCT, etc.) may also be useful in predicting user performance. Design decisions can be documented using design rational techniques (e.g. QOC) and the final version specified using appropriate techniques such as state transition networks.

7.8   Plumbest plc: evaluating the interface

7.8.1   Further information

Plumbest Task 6.6 required the reader to build a limited vertical prototype of the JAS. Not all readers will have the time or resources to undertake this task. In the following figures we present some windows from an exploratory design for the JAS that has been developed in Visual Basic to run on a PC:

• Figure 7.10—Login window

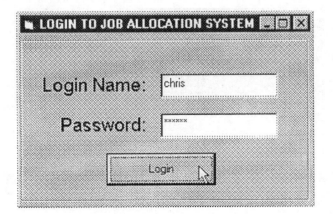

FIGURE 7.10   *Login window*

- Figure 7.11—Job instruction window
- Figure 7.12—Job instruction window, showing pull-down menu structure
- Figure 7.13—Job activation window

The design represents an enhancement on the 'first shot' design proposed in Chapter 6 (refer to Fig. 6.22) but essentially follows the same design approach. After logging-in to the system the service telephonist will be provided with the *Job Instruction Form* window. This has a menu bar at the top, the main elements of which are described below:

- *File* option, includes option for *Exit*

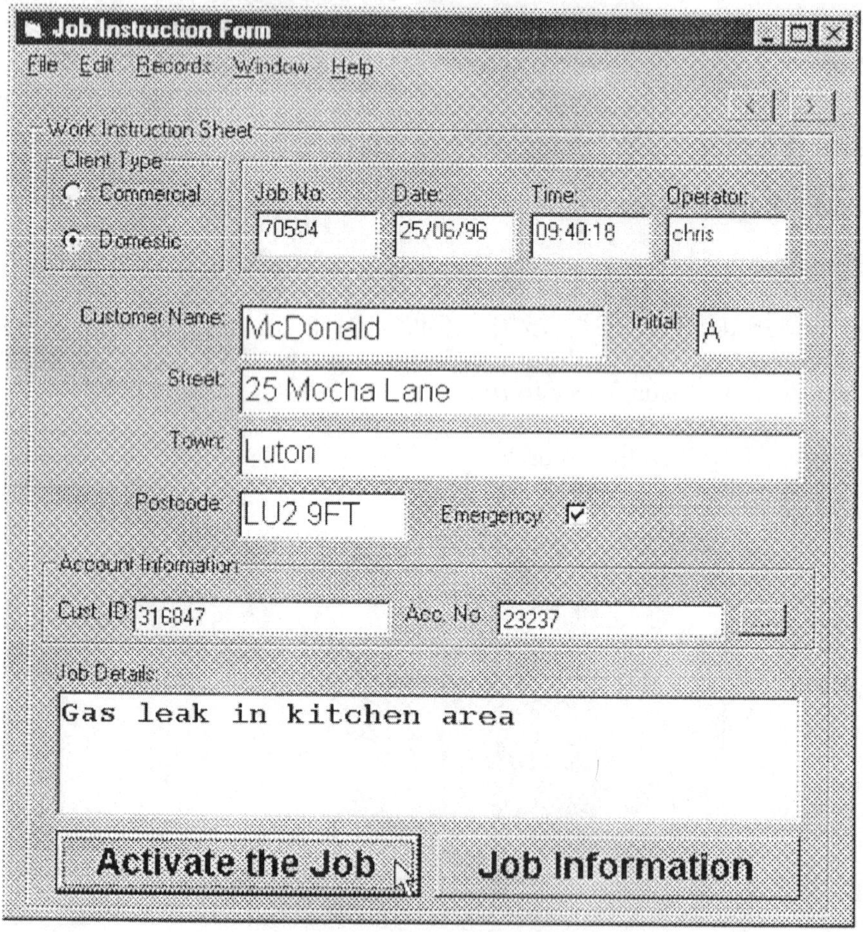

FIGURE 7.11   *Job instruction window*

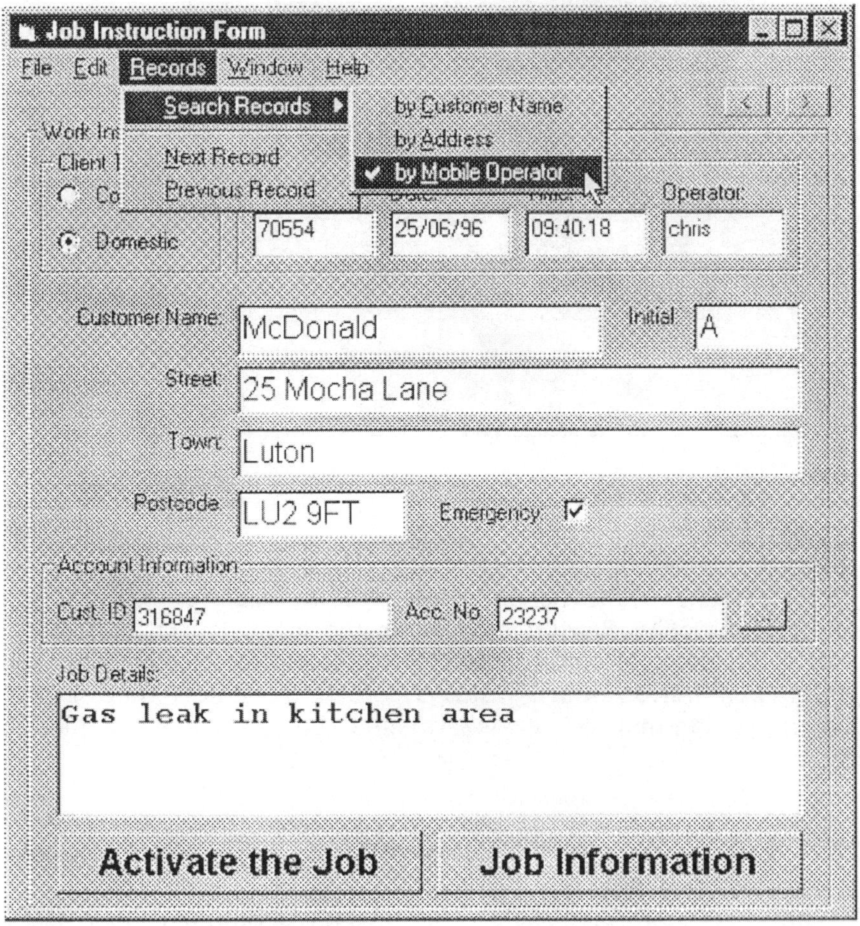

FIGURE 7.12   *Job instruction window showing pull-down menu structure*

- *Edit* option, includes options for *Add job* and *Delete job*
- *Records* option, includes options for *Search*, by customer *Address*, customer *Name* and *MO* number

For new job processing, customer and job details can be typed into the various fields on the form fill interface. Alternatively the system can search for pre-recorded information, for example by name or account number if the customer already exists on the system. The functional allocation system is activated by clicking the *Activate the job* button. The proposed allocated MO is displayed in the *Job Allocation* window and provides an estimated time of arrival. The service telephonist can either confirm (*Okay*) or reject the allocation (*Cancel*).

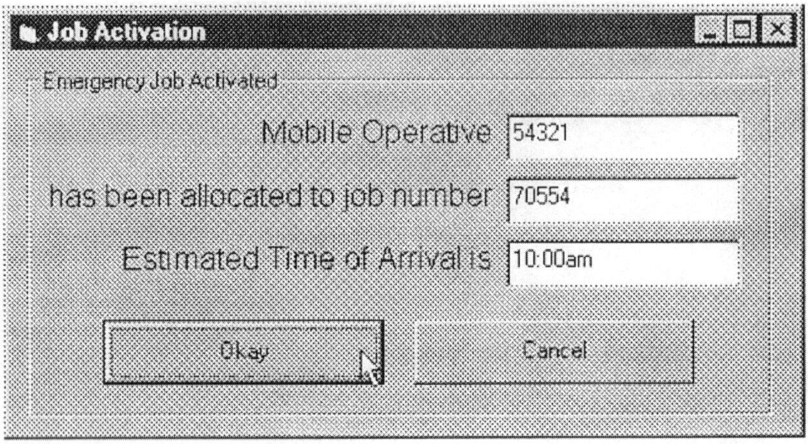

FIGURE 7.13   *Job activation*

The same *Job Instruction Form* window can be used for job interrogation. The <u>*Records*</u> element in the menu bar can activate a search. Further job information is available by clicking the <u>*Job Information*</u> button which displays a further window (not shown) containing data that was previously contained on the Job Completion Form.

7.8.2   Tasks

It is now necessary to evaluate either the system outlined above or the individual one that the reader has developed. Because of the flexible nature inherent in this stage of the analysis it is not possible to provide solutions to the following tasks.

Plumbest Task 7.1

Design a user satisfaction survey to be distributed to potential service telephonists, which will evaluate specific aspects of the JAS and provide an overall measure of satisfaction.

Plumbest Task 7.2

Decide which usability metrics you will use for your usability evaluation. Ensure that measures are available for efficiency and effectiveness consideration.

Plumbest Task 7.3

Design appropriate task scenarios in which you can determine the usability metrics that you have decided upon in Task 7.2.

Plumbest Task 7.4

If you do have a working, albeit limited, prototype version of the JAS conduct a formal user-based evaluation with a number of people playing the role of users. Determine performance and satisfaction measures of usability. What conclusions can you draw?

Summary

In this chapter we have focused on user-centred interface design and on ways in which usability can be enhanced. Specifically we have seen:

- The relationship between usability and evaluation
- How usability can be measured
- How a range of user interface design methods design for usability
- An outline process of interface design.

Questions

The following exercises requires individuals or groups to perform a usability study of a chosen information system. One possibility might be a library information system.

7.1 Identify the information system that you wish to study.
7.2 Which usability attributes of the system will you investigate? Which usability metrics will relate to each usability attribute? How will you access users for your evaluation?
7.3 Devise an appropriate task for users to undertake. Design a suitable user satisfaction survey instrument.
7.4 Perform the usability study. Determine individual metrics. What conclusions can you make about the effectiveness, efficiency and satisfaction of the information system that you have chosen?

Author's note   *The author would like to acknowledge the contribution of Chris Carline to the development of the JAS interfaces shown in this chapter.*

References

Allison, G. *et al.* (1992), 'Human factor tools for designers of information technology products', in M. Galer, S. Harker and J. Ziegler (eds), *Methods and Tools in User Centred Design for Information Technology*, Elsevier Science.

Baecker, R. M. *et al.* (1995), *Human Computer Interaction; towards the year 2000*, Morgan Kaufman, San Francisco.

Bevan, N. and Macleod, M. (1994), 'Usability measurement in context', *Behaviour and IT*, 13(1 and 2), 132–145.

Browne, D. (1994), *STUDIO*, Prentice-Hall.

Catterall, B. J. (1991), 'Three approaches to the input of human factors in IT systems design, DIADEM, the HUFIT Toolset and the MOD/DTI human factors guidelines', *Behaviour and IT*, 10(5), 359–371.

Dillon, A. *et al.* (1993), 'A survey of usability engineering within the European IT industry— current practice and needs', in J. L. Atly *et al.* (eds), *People and Computers VIII, Proceedings of HCI-93*, Cambridge University Press.

Dix, A., Finlay, J., Abowd, G. and Beale, R. (1993), *Human-computer Interaction*, Prentice-Hall, London.

Eason, K. (1988), *Information Technology and Organisational Change*, Taylor and Francis, London.

Fath, J., Mann, T. L., and Holzman, T. (1994), 'A practical guide to using software usability labs: lessons learned at IBM', *Behaviour and IT*, 13(1 and 2), 94–105.

Fowler, C., Stuart, J., Lo, T. and Tate, M. (1994), 'Using the usability laboratory: BT's experiences', *Behaviour and IT*, 13(1 and 2), 146–153.

Gould, J. D. and Lewis, C. (1985), 'Designing for usability: key principles and what the designers think', *Communications of the ACM*, 28(3), 300–311.

Hartson, H. R. and Boehm-Davis (1993), 'User interface development processes and methodologies', *Behaviour and IT*, 12(2), 98–114.

Hewett, T. (1986), 'Role of iterative evaluation', in M. D. Harrison and A. Monk (eds), *People and Computers: Designing for Usability*, Cambridge University Press.

Johnson, G. I., Clegg, C. W. and Ravden, S. J. (1989), 'Towards a practical method of user interface evaluation', *Applied Ergonomics*, 20(4).

Kim, S. (1995), 'Interdisciplinary co-operation', in R. M. Baecker *et al.* (1995), *Human Computer Interaction; towards the year 2000*, Morgan Kaufman, San Francisco.

Lim, K. Y. and Long, J. (1994), *The MUSE Method for Usability Engineering*, Cambridge University Press.

Marcus, A. (1995), 'Principles of effective visual communication for graphical user interfaces', in R. M. Baecker *et al. Human Computer Interaction; towards the year 2000*, Morgan Kaufman, San Francisco.

Nielsen, J. (1993), *Usability Engineering*, Academic Press, London.

Nielsen, J. (1995), 'Getting usability used', in K. Nordby *et al.* (eds*), Human-Computer Interaction, Proceedings of INTERACT-95*, Chapman and Hall.

Nielsen, J. and Mack, R. L. (eds) (1994), *Usability Inspection Methods*, Wiley, New York.

Preece, J., Rogers, Y., Sharp, H., Benyan, D., Hillard, S. and Carey, T. (1994), *Human-computer Interaction*, Addison Wesley, Wokingham.

Robinson, D. and Fitter, M. (1992), 'Supportive evaluation methodology: a method to facilitate systems development', *Behaviour and IT*, 11(3), 151–159.

Rubenstein, R. and Hersh, H. (1984), *The Human Factor: Computer Systems for People*, Digital Press.

Rubin, J. (1994), *Handbook of Usability Testing*, Wiley.

Shackel, B. (1986), 'Ergonomics in designing for usability' in M. D. Harrison and A. Monk (eds), *People and Computers: Designing for Usability*, Cambridge University Press.

Shneiderman, B. (1992), *Designing the User Interface*, Addison-Wesley, Reading, Mass.

Smith, A. and Dunckley, L. (1995), 'Human factors in software development—current practice relating to user-centred design in the UK', in K. Nordby *et al.* (eds), *Human-Computer Interaction, Proceedings of INTERACT-95*, Chapman and Hall, London.

Smith, A. and Dunckley, L. (1996), 'Towards the total quality interface—applying Taguchi TQM techniques within the LUCID method', in M. A. Sasse *et al.* (eds*), People and Computers XI, Proceedings of HCI-96*, Springer.

Wasserman, A. I., Pircher, P. A., Shewmake, D. T. and Kersten, M. L. (1985), 'Developing interactive information systems with the user software engineeiring method', *IEEE Transactions on Software Engineering*, 12(2), 326–345.

Whiteside, J., Bennett, B. and Holtzblatt, K. (1988), 'Usability Eegineering: our experience and evolution', in M. Helander (ed.), *Handbook of Human-computer Interaction*, ENorth Holland, Amsterdam.

Furthur reading

Dix, A., Finlay, J., Abowd, G. and Beale, R. (1993), *Human-Computer Interaction*, Prentice Hall, London.

Preece, J., Rogers, Y., Sharp, H., Benyan, D., Hillard, S. and Carey, T. (1994), *Human-Computer Interaction*, Addison-Wesley, Wokingham.

Macaulay, L. (1995), *Human-Computer Interaction for Software Designers*, Thompson Computer Press.

Nielsen, J. (1993), *Usability Engineering*, Academic Press, London.

Chapter 8

SUPPORTING THE USER

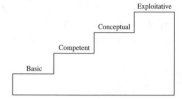

with Sunila Modi

Chapter aims

In this chapter we focus on the ways in which users can be supported during the final two stages of the systems development life cycle. Specifically through study of this chapter the reader should be able to:

- Identify levels and domains of user understanding
- Appreciate the need for, and nature of, user support systems
- Design outline training programmes to meet user needs
- Describe the types and distinguishing features of support materials
- Recognize the reasons for the growth of end-user systems and identify the specific support requirements of those who implement such systems
- Understand the issues associated with the organization and management of training and user support

8.1　Support and training aims

The growth in the use of interactive computer systems and the associated dramatic increase in the number of direct computer users has produced the need for the provision of a range of support mechanisms to enable users to maximize effectiveness. Users in all types of operational situations need access to support systems but the issue is particularly crucial in the implementation of new systems.

Before embarking on our analysis it will be profitable to emphasize the distinction between organizational (corporate) systems and end-user systems as described in Chapter 1. Users of both types of information system have many support needs in common, but we can identify a set of such needs unique to those working with end-user systems.

An adequate understanding of the current knowledge and skills of the potential users of an information system is central to the design of an effective support and training provision. Earlier in our study (Chapter 2) we investigated user *skill level* and identified three underpinning elements:

1. The knowledge or skill in the underlying application domain
2. The knowledge or skill in the specific software system
3. IT literacy and general computer knowledge

In this section of our analysis we wish to focus on specific software system knowledge and skill and investigate what this may tell us about the ways in which users need to be supported and trained in the use of specific software applications.

8.1.1   Levels of understanding

User skill level increases in line with usage. Over time a novice user will become an expert. In Chapter 2 (Table 2.2) we described an eight member taxonomy based upon user skill level using the three underpinning elements given above. So that we can effectively analyse support needs we need to look specifically at software system skill level and should seek a more finely grained categorization than the high or low approach adopted within the skill taxonomy.

Bailey (1989) notes that skill development takes place for most activities as a three-stage process. First performance is almost totally under *conscious control*. Secondly, the performance is under *shared control*; some activities require conscious deliberation and others are automatic. Finally, in the third stage, performance is totally under *automatic control* leaving the person free to monitor and improve performance. Another way to investigate skill level is to identify a theoretical model of a software skills hierarchy in which four levels of skill from *basic* to *exploitative* can be described:

1. *Basic usage skills,* this is the lowest level in the hierarchy where the user has limited appreciation of the computer and application package but is able, none the less, to perform simple tasks.
2. *Competent usage skills,* in which the user has developed a greater appreciation of the facilities provided by the systems and is able to undertake a range of tasks.
3. *Conceptual usage skills,* in which the user has a comprehensive understanding of the system, and the *generic concepts* that underpin it, and as a result is able to obtain maximum benefit from the system within a *specific and predetermined* context of use.
4. *Exploitative usage skills,* in which the user is able to implement the full potential of the system within a *wide and flexible* context of

use, and is therefore able to exploit it to modify the working environment in ways that have not been previously conceived: the development of *end-user systems* is a typical example.

The aim of user support and training is to ensure that all users are brought as far as possible up the skills hierarchy so that they are able to operate at maximum efficiency. This does not mean that all users need to reach the exploitative level. While data input clerks, for example, will be able to operate successfully at the competent/ conceptual level, the manager implementing an end-user system will require exploitative usage skills.

8.1.2   Domains of understanding

A potential problem has been identified as the problem of *plateauing* whereby users stop progressing in skill level and remain in possession of an incomplete understanding of the systems that they are using. Overall users of complex systems have been shown to exploit around only 40 per cent of available functionality provided by a computer system (Wasson and Akelson, 1992). The mismatch between the reality of the functionality provided and the user perception of that functionality has been described by Wasson and Akelson who specify distinct domains of understanding. In Fig. 8.1 we provide a modified version of these and describe the two main elements as:

1. *System capabilities:* Area A represents the knowledge required for the complete system and equates to the knowledge for which training and support should be available.
2. *User model:* equating to the human model of the computer identified in Clarke's three-level model of HCI (Chapter 6), Area B represents the user's complete view (both correct and incorrect) of the system, indicating his or her expectation of the system functionality.

There are three subdivisions of the overlap between areas A and B:

1. Area B is outside Area A: these user expectations can never be correct as they represent an inaccurate perception of available functions.
2. Area A is outside Area B: the user is unaware of these aspects of the system, but they are available.
3. Area B overlaps with Area A: user expectations are met in that the system is capable of performing the tasks that the user thinks it will, and in which there are three further subdivisions:
   (i) *Accurate knowledge:* Area C represents the user's full and accurate knowledge about this part of the system and uses it

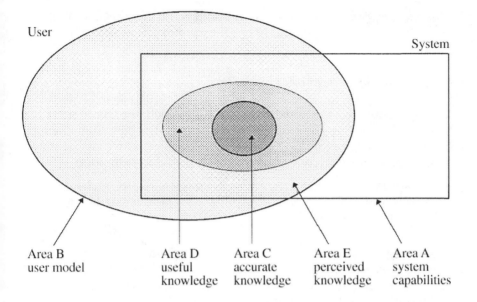

User

System

Area B	Area D	Area C	Area E	Area A
user model	useful	accurate	perceived	system
	knowledge	knowledge	knowledge	capabilities

FIGURE 8.1   *Domains of understanding (*adapted from Wasson, B. and Akelsen, S. (1992), 'An overview of on-line assistance: from on-line documentation to intelligent help and training', *The Knowledge Engineering Review,* 7 (4), with permission of the publisher Cambridge University Press*)*

regularly with no problem; the user's expectation and systems capability are matched.

(ii) *Useful knowledge:* Area D represents the user's correct but only partial knowledge about this part of the system and only uses it occasionally, not understanding it fully.

(iii) *Perceived knowledge:* Area E represents a correct user perception of what this part of the system will do but the user has never used it, and/or does not know how to use it.

Another way of looking at support and training aims is, the need to modify the domains of understanding for each user so that the four areas can be brought as close together, enabling the user to make full and effective utilization of all facilities provided. Without planned training, or effective user support, the user model is likely to vary greatly from the system capabilities and users would be unlikely to progress to conceptual or exploitative usage levels.

8.1.3   Organizational acceptance

An effective user support and training provision is also necessary to mitigate against any negative predispositional attitudes to computer systems (Chapter 5) so that the possibility of user rejection can be minimized and the likelihood of organizational acceptance enhanced.

8.1.4   Training vs. support

In this chapter we will review the ways in which computer users can be helped to rise up the skills hierarchy, through which their domains of understanding may be enhanced. Specifically we will analyse approaches to two related mechanisms: training and support:

> *Training* is the systematic acquisition of skills, knowledge, and attitudes that will lead to an acceptable level of human performance on a specific activity in a given context.
>
> (Bailey, 1988).

Training is a vital element in the successful implementation of new socio-technical information systems. As such it should aim to improve, or change the user in some task-related way, not merely to add to his or her store of knowledge.

> A *user support* system enables individual users to access a range of documentation, help and advice so that they can enhance their operational use of a specific application.

8.2   The learning process

8.2.1   Theories of learning

Effective training in the use of computer systems should be founded on established theories of learning. Piaget, for example, is well known for identifying stages of learning in his studies of children and adolescents and has specifically documented:

- A *concrete operationalism* stage, in which steps are undertaken by rote with little resource to any underlying theory and,
- A *formal operationalism* stage, in which principles are understood and applied.

Until an individual reaches the formal operationalism stage incorrect conclusions may be drawn from specific situations experienced. Other more recent cognitive psychologists have added a third *meta-cognitive* stage in which adult learners monitor, evaluate and direct their own learning. Harmon (1985) assumes that users of information systems engage in these three stages (concrete, formal and meta-cognitive) in sequence. The implication for trainers is that it is necessary to train people to the concrete operational level before attempting more formal thinking and problem solving.

Broadly speaking two separate learning processes can be described. In one situation a learner is able to perform a task in a real-life, or simulated environment, and over a period of time assimilates the necessary skills and concepts. We will refer to this as *learning by doing*. In the alternative *learning by instruction* process, a facilitator or instructor guides and directs the learning process.

8.2.2   Skills, knowledge and attitude

Support can relate to three different learning entities:

1. *Skills* are needed for structured task-related activities and are necessary for the user to operate at the basic and skilled levels.
2. *Knowledge* provides a deeper understanding of the underlying concepts, purpose and functionality within the whole system and is needed for operation at the conceptual level.
3. *Attitudes* may need to be modified for effective skills and knowledge to be developed.

The difference between skills and knowledge can be illustrated by our minor case study the Acadmin system. The university administrator may be skilled in inputting student data but has little knowledge or concept of the underlying data structures accessed. Skills may be developed within a user at the concrete operational stage, but conceptual knowledge will not be appreciated until the user is at, or above, the formal operational stage. The three learning entities need to be addressed differently. Knowledge can be delivered through *learning by instruction* but active *learning by doing* is required for the successful inculcation of skills. Attitudes, particularly predispositional attitudes, are difficult to change as they are largely determined by experience. However, as we saw in Chapter 5 (Sec. 5.1.2) training and user support can make a positive contribution to the modification of attitudes and to the determination of user behaviour.

8.2.3   Learning curve

In order to explore the learning patterns of computer users, Eason (1988) describes a learning curve of full-time and intermittent (occasional) users. Underpinning this learning curve is the assumption that users start off with a period of system *exploration* after which they move on to effective *usage*. The elapsed time spent and the use

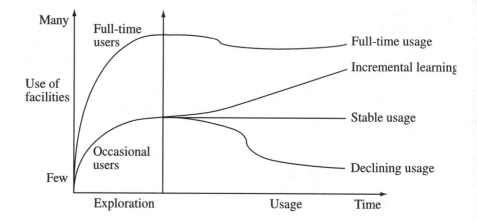

FIGURE 8.2   *Learning curve for full-time and intermittent users (*source: Eason, K. (1988), *Information Technology and Organisational Change,* Taylor and Francis, London*)*

of facilities made, by both full-time and intermittent users, maps the user onto one of the curves of the graph shown in Fig. 8.2.

Note that following complete exploration full-time users broadly remain at a constant level of usage. Intermittent users, on the other hand, are in danger of falling into a situation of *declining use*. Studies have indicated that only a minority of intermittent users progress to *incremental learning*.

8.3   User analysis

8.3.1   User classifications and support requirements

The provision of user support and training should be designed to meet the needs of the individual users. We have seen (Chapters 2 and 5) the many dimensions on which users diverge and some of the methods that have been employed to analyse and document the characteristics and needs of a user population. Rockart and Flannery (1983) show how:

> diversity in the end-user population ... (generates the) ... need for strongly differentiated education, training and support for the quite different classes of user

As we noted, in terms of user support and training, a useful starting point is to break the user population down into two groups:

1. Regular or full-time users
2. Occasional or part-time users

As is evident from the learning curve these two distinct types of user have differing needs. Occasional users are highly oriented towards task completion and tend to underutilize the facilities at their disposal (Eason, 1988). Occasional users tend to undertake only limited training. This often amounts to only short familiarization sessions through which the user rarely gains a fully organized understanding of what the system contains, what benefits it can provide and how to use it. They also experience limited exploration, tending not to devote sufficient time to trial and error exploration. Also, by following familiar procedures occasional users tend to make *'implicit judgements'* concerning the system and do not recognize the *'unknown benefits'* available.

8.3.2   Training needs analysis

Regan and O'Connor (1994) document the goals of an effective training program and from this we can summarize that training should result in:

The right users learning the right things in the right way for the right reasons.

For this to occur a *training needs analysis* needs to be carried out to survey the users and ascertain what training and support is needed. The analysis should cover all three learning entities: skills, knowledge and attitude. One way of carrying this out is to distribute questionnaires to potential trainees and to analyse the results. Other *user study methods* such as observation, interviewing and the use of focus groups are also appropriate (Chapter 2). A training assessment should be based on the user groups involved and upon the tasks that they will be carrying out. It should identify the pre-existing knowledge and skills together with the capabilities, characteristics and attitudes of individuals within the user population. The bigger the user community the longer and more costly this analytical process tends to be. However, it is to be expected that the effort would be repaid by ensuring users get the right training for their needs.

8.4   Training

An effective training program is one that, under particular conditions, will provide an effective and efficient mechanism through which an identified group of users can acquire necessary skills, knowledge or attitudes at identified levels. If training providers prove unable to identify accurately the nature of the training requirements for individual users the result tends to be the implementation of training across the board, with large groups of users receiving the same training according to a pre-set schedule. This blanket approach to training can be acceptable if the users are learning from scratch; for example in the late 1980s when PC users were upgrading from DOS to Windows. However, nowadays user groups within organizations have vastly different skill sets, and identifying who needs training, and at what level, is the key to the problem of successful training.

8.4.1 Criteria for training delivery

In terms of training delivery a number of generic criteria have been identified. While each particular training method will have distinct emphasises in general training should be:

- *Task-centred,* as opposed to system-centred so that users are able to work through tasks which are based on their own work and not on generic activities.
- *Learner-centred,* providing the user with opportunities for exploration and discovery.
- *Paced,* ideally users should be encouraged to work at their own pace rather than be expected, as a whole class, to achieve specific goals by a specified time.
- *Structured,* spreading the necessary training over a number of elements of training; no attempt should be made to cram all the necessary learning into one training course.
- *Assessed,* so that both learner and trainer can recognize the learning outcomes for individual participants.
- *Evaluated,* by the training provider to identify the success and failures within a particular training initiative.

8.4.2 Training methods: off-the-job training

We should acknowledge that a great amount of learning occurs in an unplanned manner. In what we might formally refer to as *on-the-job* training the user is able to increase his or her skill level with access to a range of resources from documentation, to on-line support, to help from colleagues. This type of training is sometimes, more informally, referred to as *sitting-by-nellie.* In this section we are more interested in the variety of methods are now available for the delivery of *off-the-job* training. Essentially these methods separate into two distinct types:

1. *Course-based training,* in which a number of users engage in a tutor-led group session, and
2. *Mediated training,* which benefits from a range of recent technological developments leading to methods which replace

tutor-led training with:
    (i)   Computer based training (CBT)
    (ii)   Multimedia training
    (iii) Internet training
    (iv) Virtual reality training

Course-based training

Course-based training comprises a training specialist providing *learning-by-instruction* to a group of learners supported by traditional visual aids. It is suitable for the training of underlying *concepts* and if backed up by hands-on *learning-by-doing*, exercises can be used to reinforce practical *skills*. Having identified the training needs for the users concerned individual courses can be developed along one of the following lines:

- *IT literacy training*, providing general information on hardware and software systems as underpinning material for future courses.
- *Familiarization courses*, short flexible programmes mainly for occasional users to enable a minimum platform of expertise to be established.
- *Structured training*, which covers the majority of the facilities within a software system and remains an effective and efficient way in which individual *user models* can be brought close to the *system capabilities*.

Although classroom-based training has the disadvantage that users have to wait for the next appropriate course (it is not *on-demand*), when training is being undertaken users can gain immediate access to the training specialist thereby gaining rapid feedback on progress. It should be emphasized that training courses are not the only solution to the provision of skills and concepts. Often they can increase rather than minimize the fear in prospective participants. This is especially the case in older workers (Eason, 1988).

According to Bailey (1989) training courses should be:

- *Relevant*, in that the skills, knowledge and attitudes being addressed should match the job requirements.
- *Effective*, so that participants achieve course outcomes.
- *Efficient*, so that time is not wasted for either trainer or trainee.

Course-based training is a particularly expensive form of training, particularly in terms of course development. It is important therefore to place an emphasis on assessment and evaluation of the learning process so that the three criteria above can be analysed.

Mediated training

The three types of mediated training that we will discuss have one element in common: the computer. Within this study there are two aspects to our interest in mediated training:

1. As part of successful information systems implementation
2. By providing and additional application domain for human–computer factors (training)

Computer-based training (CBT)   Computer-based training (CBT) adopts the computer as the training vehicle. In CBT, the user is taken through a series of exercises in which the computer is not just a tool the user can employ to sample work, but is also the co-ordinator of the training process. The CBT package usually consists of authoring programs, presentation programs and courses. The course creator uses an authoring program to develop a series of presentations and learning exercises for potential students. The data file created by this program is called a course. Each user needs to access a presentation program in order to play back the course on his or her screen.

British Airways have reported use of CBT (Little, 1995) in a situation where they had to train quickly 2000 cabin crew in customer service techniques as they were moving crew to new aircraft types. The programs were found to have the advantage over formal training courses because they are permanently available on demand in BA's learning centres—both in UK and abroad. CBT should not be seen as a mechanism to replace classroom training, however, *'CBT together with a workshop can be very effective, because people can use the CBT in their own time'* (Trull, 1996).

Multimedia training   An extension to CBT, multimedia training is becoming popular because the training programs provided are both rich in presentation and interactive in nature. The trainee can receive rapid feedback and learn at his or her own speed which helps with concentration and information retention. Sartorius (1995) states that:

> multimedia training is well suited to process or procedural-driven training where simulations, drill and practice and 'soft skills' such as role plays and scenarios are part of the education requirement

Multimedia is particularly effective for providing consistent training to large numbers of people across a wide geographical spread and at different times. Hall (1995) claims that through the use of video, CD-ROM and laserdisk, future *personal learning systems* will provide video-based training on demand thereby providing on-the-spot customized support.

Internet training   The Internet provides an additional mechanism through which training can be provided. Indeed some supporters would suggest that it is set to offer the main non classroom-based method. According to Wimpress (1996):

> the Internet provides a new era for training by offering an interactive distance learning facility, where each student is allocated an on-line lecturer with whom he or she can overcome any learning difficulties, and receive assignments, assessment and feedback. Students can also communicate with their 'classmates' via interactive discussion

It may be that the future of training will be heavily affected by technological developments but many training providers feel that if the instructor is replaced something of great and measurable value is lost. Lawton (1995), however, feels that the training industry is only just recognizing the possibilities of new technology:

> it is important that we do not get carried away with the technology for its own sake ...it's a sobering thought: by the time 2010 arrives the kind of technology we are able to conceive of now may well be obsolete.

Virtual reality training   One of the more recent technological developments has been the introduction of virtual reality (VR) techniques. These will be discussed in more detail in Chapter 10. VR is proving to be an effective form of mediated training in a number of situations. According to Leston (1996):

> VR is being used extensively to train staff and to simulate working environments. These types of applications include staff familiarisation, equipment operation, assembly and production line training. Significant cost savings can be achieved by using VR instead of training off-site

8.4.3   Organization of training

Those with the responsibility for organizing training need to consider a range of questions before they can move towards implementation:

Who should deliver the training?

A range of different personnel can be engaged in the delivery of training:

- In-house computer specialists
- Product suppliers
- End users
- External training providers

The weakness of both computer specialists and product suppliers is that neither party are training experts and that although they may have the right material packaged, it may be in a very poor instructional format. An alternative is to ask a user representative to deliver the training, however, this requires considerable user commitment and time. A further option is to outsource the training to external providers.

The case for user-centred training: how should the training programme be designed?

Whoever delivers the end training, there is a significant benefit in involving users in the development of the training programme. Without end-user involvement there is a danger of focusing solely on what the new system does (the technical system), and neglecting how it will affect the user roles (their social system). The users after all are the customers of the training and to them the critical issue is not the system itself, but how it is to be implemented and the manner in which it might affect their job. Within the training arena this has been confirmed by White (1995) who suggests that an *impact analysis* (refer to Chapter 5) should be carried out in order to take into account all aspects of the changes faced by the organization and its staff. Depending on the implications of the impact analysis, resultant change can be brought about most effectively through a number of mechanisms of which training is just one component.

How will users be grouped for training?

If training is in support of a cross-organization, or corporate, system (as opposed to an individual end-user system) it is necessary to decide how to group users into manageable units. Possible criteria for selection include grouping by organizational level, by function or by deliberately mixing users.

How will the training be evaluated and monitored?

Feedback from learners is an essential element in the evaluation of training performance. It can be either written (through tests, questionnaires or unstructured comment), verbal (through the trainer or the learner's line manager) or observational (during training or on the job afterwards). After completion of a training programme there should be an ongoing monitoring of user performance to ascertain that the medium- to long-term objectives have been fulfilled.

8.5   User support

Although training can be provided for users throughout their operational use of an information system it is an especially important element within the implementation of a new system. During operational usage, training is just one element within a range of individual user support services. The other support mechanisms can be classified as either *support materials* (both on- and off-line support) and *support roles* provided by information centre and help desk facilities. Support roles are particularly important in relation to end-user systems.

8.5.1   Support materials

User support materials are an important part of the total user-system interface and often constitute the user's first encounter with a system. According to Mayhew (1992):

> users may form impressions of the usability of a system through reading the manual or accessing the on-line help or tutorial. If the manual or tutorial is easy to use, users will assume that the system itself will be easy to use...the quality of user documentation thus determines in large part both the perception, and the actual ease of learning and use, of the system

Support materials can therefore be seen to either enhance or degrade the overall usability of the system. They are provided in either on- or off-line mode.

Off-line support: using the manual

Since the first computer applications were developed the manual has been a major vehicle to assist learning. Manuals, particularly those for off-the-shelf applications have a number of limitations. Fundamentally they are system, rather than user or task oriented; the same information is available regardless of the tasks or capabilities of individual users. Manuals also lack the immediacy and interactive capacity of on-line methods.

Manuals are too often badly designed and lead to difficulty in location of the necessary help facility. Users have also been found to suffer from cognitive overload as too much information may be available. Both these factors may be minimized by effective indexing and cross-referencing. As we have seen it is common for users to continue to use a subset of a system's functionality because they find it daunting to explore new facilities on the basis of the available documentation (Browne, 1994). The overall quality of the manual is an important factor in increasing user's useful and accurate domains of knowledge (Fig. 8.1).

For bespoke systems the success of a manual may be enhanced by involving users in its development. By relating the content of the manual to the users and the specific task that they are undertaking some of the limitations inherent in manuals can be addressed. Guidelines and standards for the production of manuals are available.

Minimum manual   In a study of novices attempting to learn to use commercial word-processing systems by means of the commercial self study books that accompany them, Carrol (1992) found that user behaviour and learning was *'chaotic, halting and non-convergent'*. Essentially users tend to resist rote descriptions and practice and prefer a task oriented, *learning-by-doing*, approach based upon the problems they encounter (e.g. how do I do this?). From this discovery Carrol developed what is known as the *minimum manual* approach. A much briefer document than the full version a minimum manual's main features are:

- *Less to read,* by eliminating repetition summaries and reviews it is typically one-quarter of the size of its original counterpart.
- *Greater task orientation,* it is directed at real-work activities.
- *More learner initiative,* it places the user in a much more active role and by giving only abbreviated specification of procedures leaves much more for the learner to discover.
- *More error information.*
- *Use for reference purposes after training.*

In a study Carrol found that the minimum manual approach proved to be 40 per cent faster than the other manuals for the basic topic areas which it covered, and produced a learning achievement at least as good as the other methods.

On-line help and support

With the increasing capacity of on-line storage devices it is now common practice to provide all traditional manual material in on-line format. On-line documentation, as this is known, is only one of a number of examples of on-line help and support systems:

- *Command help,* by requesting help on a particular command the user is presented with a help screen or page of the manual. The problem here is one of vocabulary: what if the user does not know the name of the command? Gwei and Foxley (1990) for example, identify six separate command names (rm, del, el, era, decatalog, dltf) for the deletion of data files in different operating systems.

- *On-line help,* through menu (pull-down and push-button) and hypertext access the majority of recent applications provide enhanced flexibility within access to help facilities.
- *On-line tutorials*, a form of computer-based training, on-line tutorials allows the user to work through the basics of an application within a test environment so that progress can be made at individual speed and so that parts of the tutorial package can be repeated as needed.
- *Intelligent help systems,* by monitoring user activity and constructing a *user profile* (Gwei and Foxley, 1990), and knowing the domain in which the user is working, the intelligent help system is able present help information in a format relevant to the user's current task and suited to his or her experience.

Usability issues are probably even more crucial to the design of on-line help systems rather than to the applications to which they relate. Users who are in a situation requiring help require their needs to be met in an efficient and effective way. Unfortunately the task of help system design is often left until rather late in the overall development process. According to Dix (1993) the ideal on-line help system should possess the following characteristics:

- *Availability,* the user needs to access help at any time during an interaction with the system: he or she should not have to quit his application to obtain help.
- *Accuracy and completeness,* the help facility should be kept up-to-date and represent an accurate reflection of the current state of the main system which it supports.
- *Consistency*, within the help system, between the help system and the main application and with paper-based equivalents.
- *Robustness,* help systems are required by users when they are in difficulty, therefore it is important that they should be robust.
- *Flexibility,* help systems should not be rigid; a flexible or intelligent help system should not produce the same help message regardless of the expertise of the person seeking it.
- *Unobtrusiveness,* it should not prevent the user from continuing with normal work, nor should it interfere with the user's operation of the main system which it supports.

Carroll's training wheels approach

Following the development of the minimum manual, Carrol (1992) identified a paradox within its use as a means of support to learn a *maximal* system. Often advanced functions can create problems for the learner who is not ready for them. In the resulting *training wheels* approach, by closing off many areas of functionality, a software system is provided which limits the learner to simple actions only. The advantages proposed for this method of support can be summarized as:

- *Ability to learn simple things first,* learning something that is simple (the training wheels system) is easier than learning something that is complicated (the full system).
- *Promotes a high transfer of learning,* through the provision of safety in system exploration and a reduction in the likelihood of side tracks and frustration.
- *Removal of common error states,* by blocking novice users from states which are known to cause errors.

8.5.2 Support roles

User support is also available through access to individuals who are expert in the system concerned. Personal support is available either through face-to-face contact, telephone conversation or electronic communication. A *help desk* is a support facility that consists of a group of highly trained employees who are knowledgeable about the hardware and software systems that their users operate. By helping to solve individual user problems the help desk aims to ensure that expensive computing resources are as productive as possible for as much of the time as possible (Robson, 1994). Help desks are an essential part of an organization's information centre (see below) or can be part of a software suppliers after sales service. The majority of bespoke software supplies offer hotline support. Help desks can also play an important role in facilitating user-to-user support and communication through the establishment of user groups and the production of newsletters.

8.6 Support requirements for end-user systems

8.6.1 Defining end-user computing

The 1980s involved many changes in the use of organizational computing. One of the most striking of these changes was the rise of the phenomenon that has come to be known as end-user computing (McLean *et al.*, 1993). Driven by the backlog of applications being serviced by central IT departments, and made possible by access to inexpensive hardware and easy to use software, users were prepared to take the technical plunge and develop their own *end-user computing* (EUC) systems. A vast array of differing software systems are available for end users to exploit to meet their perceived needs.

Many of the end-user developed and operated applications are not merely personal or private in nature (Alavi and Weiss, 1985). A survey has shown (Rockart and Flannery, 1983) that over half of applications cover operations relevant to an entire department. Topping the popularity list of end-user implemented systems is the spreadsheet which, in the right hands, is now able to offer the user sophisticated development opportunities. Other notable applications include database and office automation systems, word processing, decision support, process control, desk-top publishing and expert systems.

A variety of definitions for end-user computing are available (e.g. McNurlin and Sprague (1989); Robson (1994) and Gupta (1996)). We will define end-user computing as:

> The direct use, development and maintenance of information systems by those whose primary role is to achieve a business purpose rather than the indirect development and management through information systems professionals.

A number of researchers have attempted to classify those involved in end-user computing. Perhaps the most useful for us is the one provided by Rockart and Flannery (1983) which identifies six types of development personnel of which the *middle four* can be considered to constitute the domain of end-user computing:

1. *Non-programming end user,* someone with limited computer skills who is not capable of undertaking software development but is able to perform structured tasks.
2. *Command level end user,* someone using, for example, limited 4GL and database query commands to produce unique reports to meet their work needs.
3. *Programming level end user,* a computer literate user who is capable of developing his or her own application to suit perceived functional requirements.
4. *Functional support personnel,* a specialist who is assigned to a functional business unit in order to develop systems within the unit and to provide user support and training.
5. *End user support personnel.*
6. *DP programmer,* the IS professional developing large complex systems.

8.6.2   Benefits and problems of EUC

In terms of the organization as a whole a number of benefits and risks have been associated with the expansion of end-user computing. On the positive side the backlog of applications waiting to be implemented by central MIS is reduced, thereby releasing specialist IT skills to address problems which are not amenable to the end-user solution. It also enables end users to receive their IT solutions in a much shorter time scale.

A major problem with end-user computing, at the organizational level, is that of *duplication*: both in terms of effort and data:

- Often a number of users within an organization will develop similar applications thereby duplicating *effort*, such systems would be more efficiently deployed centrally.
- Individual users are able to set up their own databases without any co-ordination between users and departments, and with no simple mechanism for checking for consistency between the *data* sets.

A further negative factor relates to the questionable quality of the end-user systems that are established.

8.6.3   Supporting EUC

Effective organizational management of EUC is necessary so that the positive aspects can be maintained while the negative ones can be addressed. Gupta (1996) summarizes three broad activities that an organization needs to undertake:

1. *Co-ordination,* of all resources associated with EUC.
2. *Support,* for end users so that they can manage, implement and maintain their systems.
3. *Evaluation,* providing management and end users with feedback so that they can resolve existing problems and identify potential problems before they arise.

In our study of human–computer factors we are more interested in the user perspective (as opposed to the organizational or management one) and will therefore focus on support issues. Mirani and King (1994) show how end-user support is seen to be the critical factor to user satisfaction and EUC effectiveness, and hence, to organizational effectiveness. McLean *et al.* (1992) in a survey of EUC identify the most frequently provided support services. Notable among the list are the following eight user-related issues:

1. Product evaluation
2. MIS managed training
3. On-site hardware support
4. On-site end user assistance

5. Help desk
6. Newsletter
7. User groups
8. Training library

8.6.4 Information centres

One of the most commonly adopted mechanisms for managing end-user computing is the provision of information centres. According to Robson (1994) an information centre is:

> an organizational construct that exists to support the development and operation of the personal or small group systems generated by end user computing

Since end-user support is so important, and the information centre is the primary mechanism in many organizations for providing end-user support, a major responsibility of information centre staff is to accurately assess and fulfil the diverse support needs of their end users (Mirani and King, 1994). Information centres extend the concept of a help desk (and indeed many include a help desk facility) by providing a range of user-support services such as those identified by McLean *et al.* Effectively they attempt to *promote, control, support and mange* EUC (White and Christy, 1987).

8.7 The steps of user support

So that we can summarize the range of training and user-support services that we have discussed within this chapter we shall return to the levels of understanding and theories of learning introduced earlier. We defined a theoretical model of a *software skills hierarchy* in which we specified four levels of skill from *basic* to *exploitative*. Table 8.1 repeats the four levels and associates with each a number of services that can support the user at that level and assist him or her to move to the next level. Taken together, and with the addition of preliminary literacy and general education, the four levels can form the basis of the *steps of user support* (Fig. 8.3) which users need to climb if they are to progress to exploitative use.

8.8 Designing a user-support system

A comprehensive user-support system should be developed as an integrated part of the whole information system: it should not be seen

TABLE 8.1   *Skill level and support requirements*

Level	Description	Appropriate support services
Basic usage	User has limited appreciation of the computer and application package but is able, none the the less, to perform simple tasks	• Familiarization courses • Training wheels • Minimum manuals
Competent	User has a greater appreciation of the facilities provided by the systems and is able to undertake a range of tasks	• On-line documentation • Structured training • On-line help • Manuals
Conceptual usage	User has a comprehensive understanding of the system, and the generic concepts that underpin it, and as a result is able to obtain maximum benefit within a specific and predetermined context	• Structured training • On-line help • Help desk • User groups
Exploitative usage	User is able to exploit the full potential of the system within a wide and flexible context of use and is therefore able to develop end-user systems in support of identified needs	• Product evaluation • Hardware support • Development support

as an add-on to the design of the main system. Three key issues need to be considered in the design of an integrated user-support system:

1. *Content,* selecting the key components (training, on- or off-line support materials, support roles).
2. *Interaction,* deciding on the way in which users will access the support provided: considerations can vary from the structuring and design and presentation of an on-line help system to locating and structuring a help desk or information centre facility.
3. *Implementation,* managing the establishment and monitoring of the whole support system.

8.9   Plumbest plc: training the employees

From the proposed social-technical system outlined in previous chapters it is now necessary to specify in more detail how individuals within Plumbest will interact with the new job allocation system (JAS) and through this specify the training and support requirements of each user group.

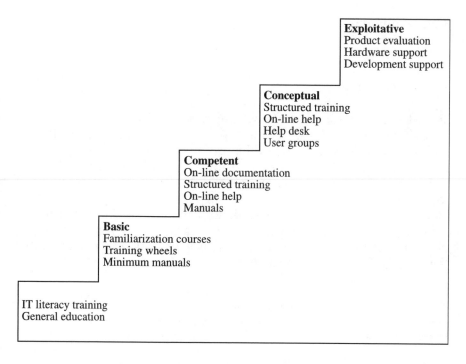

FIGURE 8.3   *Underpinning the steps of user support*

8.9.1   Tasks

Needs analysis

Plumbest Task 8.1

- Describe in general form the tasks that each user group will need to undertake through the new JAS.
- At what level within the software skills hierarchy are individuals within each user group likely to operate?
- Outline the training needs of each group in terms of skills, knowledge and attitude.

  Summarize your results in a training needs analysis.

Training for different user groups

Plumbest Task 8.2

Propose the outline content of a number of elements of training (courses) which meet the combined training needs of Plumbest. Map each user group to the elements of training.

8.9.2   Solutions

Needs analysis

Plumbest Solution 8.1

Table 8.2 provides a summary training needs analysis.

It should be emphasized that both the service centre co-ordinator and the three local area co-ordinators play an important role in the monitoring of job progress and overall performance. With the introduction of the new computer systems both these groups will need to fully understand all major aspects of the system: they must operate at conceptual usage level. The other user groups (particularly the MOs and service telephonists) are accessing a safety critical system and will require skilled usage levels. However, they only need to know their respective parts of the system.

TABLE 8.2   *Plumbest training needs analysis*

User group	JAS tasks	Skill level	Training needs
Service centre co-ordinator	• Monitoring all MOs and jobs • Allocation overriding	Conceptual usage	*Skills:* job allocation, performance monitoring *Knowledge:* of whole system, for monitoring and management of error situations *Attitude:* supportive
Service telephonist	• Inputting and allocating jobs	Competent usage	*Skills:* job allocation process *Knowledge:* limited to allocation only *Attitude:* largely supportive
General administrator	• Administration after job completion	Competent usage	*Skills:* job completion administration *Knowledge:* limited to relevant facilities only *Attitude:* potential difficulty
Local area co-ordinator	• Monitoring relevant MOs and jobs • Inputting job completion details	Conceptual usage	*Skills:* performance monitoring, job completion details *Knowledge:* of majority of system, for monitoring and management of error situations *Attitude:* need to enhance overall perception for this important role
Mobile operative	• Receiving jobs • Inputting job completion details	Competent usage	*Skills:* job receipt, job completion details *Knowledge:* limited to relevant facilities only *Attitude:* needs persuading of benefits

Training for different user groups

Plumbest Solution 8.2

It is proposed to develop five elements of training:

1. General IT literacy course, for those who have no experience of computer equipment
2. JAS overview course, outlining broad functions and purpose
3. Job allocation sub-system course
4. Job completion sub-system course
5. JAS monitoring and control course

An outline mapping between user groups and training elements is shown in Table 8.3.

TABLE 8.3   *Training courses and user groups*

Course	Service centre co-ordinator	Service tel.	General administrator	Local area co-ordinator	MO
General IT			✓	✓	✓
Overview	✓	✓	✓	✓	✓
Allocation	✓	✓		✓	✓
Completion	✓		✓	✓	✓
Monitoring	✓			✓	

Summary

In this chapter we have reviewed a range of user-support systems and attempted to relate them to users' interaction needs. Specifically we have seen:

- That support should be based on user needs specified through a formal training needs analysis
- That the three main type of support mechanisms are:
    - training
    - user support
    - support roles
- How support can enhance levels and domains of understanding
- That support should relate to user needs and the tasks that they are undertaking
- That users developing end-user systems have particular needs

Questions

8.1 Users need supporting in enhancing their skills, knowledge and attitude. Which user support and training methods are suitable for each of these entities?

8.2 Compare the relative amounts of accurate, useful and perceived knowledge as the user climbs the steps of user support and moves from basic to exploitative use.

8.3 Discuss the role of the user in the development of a comprehensive training and support system.

8.4 Compare the training and support needs of users of organizational (corporate) systems with those of end-user systems.

References

Alavi, M. and Weiss, I. R. (1985), 'Managing the risks associated with end-user computing', *Journal of Management Information Systems*, 2(3), 5–20.

Bailey, R. W. (1989), *Human Performance Engineering*, 2nd edition, Prentice-Hall, Englewood Cliffs, New Jersey.

Browne, D. (1994), *STUDIO*, Prentice-Hall, New York.

Carroll, J. M. (1992), *The Nurnberg Funnel: Designing Minimalist Instruction for Practical Computer Skills*, MIT Press, Cambridge, MA.

Dix, A. (1993), *Human–Computer Interaction*, Prentice-Hall, London.

Eason, K. (1988), *Information Technology and Organisational Change*, Taylor and Francis, London.

Gupta, U. (1996), *Management Information Systems: a managerial perspective*, West Publishing, St Paul, Minneapolis.

Gwei, G. M. and Foxley, E. (1990), 'Towards a consultative on-line help system', *International Journal of Man-Machine Studies*, 32, 363–383.

Hall, J. (1995), 'Flexibility is the Key', *IT Training*, December/January 1995.

Harmon, P. (1985), 'Training: psychology meets technology', *Computerworld*, 19 May.

Lawton, J. (1995), 'Training 2000: the future of IT training', *IT Training*, December/January 1995.

Leston, J. (1996), 'Virtual reality: the IT perspective', *Computer Bulletin*, 8(3), 12–13.

Little, B. (1995), 'British Airways Win with CBT', *IT Training*, April/May 1995.

Mayhew, D. J. (1992), *Principles and Guidelines on Software User Interface Design*, Prentice-Hall, Englewood Cliffs, New Jersey.

McLean, E. R., Kappelman, L. A. and Thompson, J. P. (1993), 'Converging end-user and corporate computing', *Communications of the ACM*, 36(79–92).

McNurlin, B. C. and Sprague, R. H. (1989), *Information Systems*

Management in Practice, 2nd edition, Prentice-Hall.

Mirani, R. and King, W. (1994), 'Impacts of end-user and information center Characteristics on end-user computing support', *Journal of Information Systems*, 11 (1).

Regan, E. A. and O'Connor, B. N. (1994), *End-user Information Systems*, Macmillan.

Robson, W. (1994), *Strategic Management and Information Systems*, Pitman, London.

Rockart, J. F. and Flannery, L. S, (1983), 'The management of end-user computing', *Communications of the ACM*, 26(10), 776–784.

Sartorius, P. (1995), 'Building a multimedia strategy', *IT Training*, February/March 1995.

Ttooulis, B. (1996), 'Making Training Count', *IT Training*, April 1996.

Trull, H. (1996), 'The changing face of IT training', *IT Training*, April 1996.

Wasson, B. and Akelsen, S. (1992), 'An overview of on-line assistance; from on-line documentation to intelligent help and training', *The Knowledge Engineering Review*, 7(4).

White, T. (1995), 'Realising the vision', *IT Training*, February/March 1995.

White, C. E. and Christy, D. P. (1987), 'The information centre concept: a normative model and a study of six installations', *MIS Quarterly*, December 1987.

Wimpress, D. (1996), 'A new era for training', *IT Training*, February 1996.

Further reading

Eason, K. (1988), *Information Technology and Organisational Change*, Taylor and Francis.

Gupta, U. (1996), *Management Information Systems: a managerial perspective*, West Publishing, St Paul, Minneapolis.

Gunton, T. (1988), *End User Focus*, Prentice-Hall.

Nelson, R. R. (1989), *End-User Computing*, Wiley.

Robson, W. (1994), *Strategic Management and Information Systems*, Pitman, London.

Chapter 9

HUMAN–COMPUTER FACTORS: THEORY AND PRACTICE

Chapter aims

In this chapter we aim to look at the reasons why human-factor issues are not being uniformly and successfully addressed across organizations. Specifically through study of this chapter the reader should be able to:

- Relate the theory and practice of human–computer factors
- Identify problems experienced in practice
- Describe the major influences on user-centred design
- Recognize the growing importance of human-factor specialists within, and external to, user organizations

9.1 Theory and practice

This study has attempted to provide a co-ordinated and consistent coverage of all the major user issues in information systems development. We have seen how important it is to involve users, within both design and evaluation processes, right from the conception of an IS project, through feasibility study and exploratory interface design, to user support and training. However, by studying a range of human–computer factors techniques and placing an emphasis on how they have been shown to assist in attempts to increase systems success rates, we may be at risk of neglecting the problems experienced by practising information systems developers trying to adopt such methods within mainstream organizational settings.

Throughout our approach we have focused on the importance of socio-technical design and on how the development process can be made user-centred. To readers who are not practising information systems developers, it is possible that, in trying to discuss the techniques in a positive manner (in a way to *sell* user-centredness) we may have generated the ideas:

1. That the application of the methods proposed will *automatically* lead to effective user involvement and thereby to enhanced systems success, and
2. That all information systems developers in general, and interface designers in particular, are routinely adopting such techniques as part of their work.

Unfortunately neither of these suggestions would appear to be true. Chapter 3 of this book reviewed user-centred design throughout the life cycle, and having looked at surveys and case studies of user-centred design, we found that user-centred techniques were indeed not being implemented extensively across commercial IT systems development. To repeat part of the summary:

> User-centred principles are not being adopted uniformly across the IT industry. There is a disparity in the speed and depth of the adoption of the different aspects or concepts within UCD. While structures are increasingly common, and processes are developing, organizational issues are largely ignored. Blocks to the further development of UCD include management policy and styles, user skills and priorities together with a lack of resources.

There are many excellent examples of organizations with a commitment to human-factor considerations and to user-centred design. Clearly some large software suppliers providing generic software (particularly PC) products place HCI issues high in their agenda. Even some commercial user organizations have now established usability services within their organization to address human-factor needs. However, there are still very many mainstream supplier and user companies which, although they may be adopting some standard HCI methods, are by no means providing a total user-centred development environment.

9.2   Practical experience

It will be useful to provide some further detailed results from the survey of user-centred design discussed in Chapter 3 (Smith, 1993 and Smith and Dunckley, 1995). The survey itself involved postal questionnaires and individual discussions with IT managers in a significant number of medium to large UK user commercial organizations. Only 30 per cent of organizations said that they established local design groups of users working with developers, and only 36 per cent replied that they thought that their approach could be described as *active user involvement*. In respect of prototyping, although 88 per cent used the technique in some form, 55 per cent of the sample used it for testing system functionality, and only 38 per cent for interface design. The percentage of organizations that set up local design groups and used evolutionary interface prototyping (i.e. those who could reasonably be expected to be undertaking at least a minimum form of user-centred interface design) was only 11 per cent.

Why are so few organizations managing to implement the ideas suggested in this book?

What are the problems associated with user-centred design?

In attempting to answer these questions it will be illuminating to investigate some of the case study material. In the following section we present some edited summaries of the discussions with practising IT managers. They are presented in ascending order of user-centredness as determined by the survey's analysis method.

Organization A is a relatively small medical organization where time and money are very important issues within systems development. It gained an overall score for user centredness of 20 per cent. It finds SSADM, together with a CASE tool to be both effective and cheap. The organization feels that users can be trained to be effective participants in the process, although problems with user involvement relate to the users' unrealistically high expectations of IT solutions. Designers do not fully understand business needs, while users take a far too simplistic view of IT opportunities. Prototyping is not possible because of a lack of resources and available time.

Organization B is a well-known chain of supermarket retail outlets. It gained an overall score for user-centredness of 25 per cent. The management information systems department is very centralized and does not make a significant attempt to engage end users or individual stores in the design of systems. A traditional approach is used with little emphasis on prototyping. In general systems are imposed on stores from the centre.

Organization C is a medium-sized organization specializing in truck rental, distribution and logistics. It gained an overall score for user centredness of 29 per cent. The organization is moving away from traditional systems analysis and design towards a new structured method. A major contribution to this decision has come from the fact that the organization is a subsidiary of a larger American company. The organization feels that having users actively involved in design can have both advantages and disadvantages, but on the whole it is felt better to attempt to involve users. Problems relate to apathy on behalf of the users and their lack of ability to relate to IT issues.

Prototyping tends to be limited to paper-based techniques. Organizational issues are becoming increasingly part of its overall development process.

Organization D provides IT services centrally to a range of subsidiary companies. It gained an overall score for user-centredness of 36 per cent. Systems engineering is used (an SSADM-like approach) and this is seen to be very helpful in communication with users, for example through the use of data flow diagrams. The organization is very keen on the secondment of users to the design process, but feels that finding the 'right' person is often difficult. Problems with communicating with end users rest with line management within the user department. Prototyping is difficult as the end-user department often has unrealistic time expectations.

Organization E is a well-known, medium-sized provider of energy facilities. It gained an overall score for user-centredness of 37 per cent. The organization is fairly traditional in its approach to analysis and design but has found that SSADM helps to formalize design and aid communication. Prototyping is seen to be very useful for user communication. There has been no real attempt at wider organizational issues within design, mainly because of the lack of senior management support.

Organization F is a nationally known regional electricity supplier. It gained an overall score for user-centredness of 45 per cent. They have standardized on a structured methodology, which has been found to be useful in communicating with users, particularly through the use of formal diagrams. Overall though, some IT staff are 'luke warm' to the whole process of user involvement. Partnership in design is enacted at managerial level but there is not much engagement with end users; mainly because of the politics within the organization. What engagement there is, is limited by the difficulty in finding the right people and overcoming their knowledge gap. User groups are being set up so that organizational implications can be identified, but currently the wider organizational view is not gaining appropriate recognition.

Organization G is a medium-sized property and investment company. It gained an overall score for user-centredness of 47 per cent. A total of 200 staff are employed with approximately 150 at head office and the rest at regional outlets employing an average of six personnel. The relatively small size of the company is seen to be a limiting factor to user involvement. It has standardized on an 'SSADM-like' methodology, which is seen to be quite effective in involving users at appropriate points. Considerable emphasis is put on structures to support design. Overall control rests with a permanent project steering group which co-ordinates the activities of an IT quality assurance group, which in turn manages individual user groups. The company finds it difficult to second users to projects but is keen to make demands from users of their commitment, in advance, to the project in terms of *man-days required*. Much of the actual design is done by external suppliers, but users are very much involved in IT tendering and tender evaluation. The organization feels that it is not large enough to fully address organizational issues, which tend to occur as an 'afterthought'. It is aware of human factors input to the process but have no specific experience of employing human-factor specialists.

Organization H is an international pharmaceuticals company. It gained an overall score for user-centredness of 48 per cent. There is no company-wide method as it has project standards for each department. This particular case study involved a 'sawn-off' version of SSADM augmented with additions at the early and latter stages of the life cycle. The method is perceived to meet the needs of users, but the organization is aware of different levels of user. They recognize the need to involve personnel at all levels. Users are certainly involved as designers. In this case study, financial personnel were particularly keen on the development of, and quality assurance relating to, the end product. Problems relating to user involvement include the user comprehension of the size of the analysis and design process and their lack of knowledge. Users are heavily involved in the analysis of vendor solutions, a process which is perceived to be close to that of prototyping. The organization is moving towards fully addressing organizational issues. Design is seen to reside within the user department and as a result a debate about organizational issues is possible.

Organization I is a manufacturer and distributor of commercial vehicles. It gained an overall score for user-centredness of 51 per cent. A traditional approach to systems analysis and design has been adopted by choice. Individual personnel feel that the main criterion for success lies not in the design method but in the skills of individual analyst personnel. The organization is highly aware of organizational needs and resulting organizational change, but finds difficulty in finding staff with appropriate skills for a fully user-centred design engagement. They are keen on secondment of users for this to be achieved. Prototyping is seen to be useful and evaluation of prototypes does involve real-life data and scenarios. The IT role is seen to be crucial and can often lead to overall organizational development. Business needs inform an IT solution which often prompts organizational change.

Organization J is well-known provider of brochure-based home shopping services. It gained an overall score for user-centredness of 58 per cent. The chosen project relates to a large database system. There is a high degree of commitment to user involvement, but the nature of the system means that the engagement is limited to requirement specification and signing-off, together with informal evaluation of prototypes. The new IT director has initiated structures to encourage the coverage of organizational implications of IT systems, which are fed through an IT planning committee and permanent cross-organizational IT steering committee. This move is in line with a general 'openness' within the organization.

Organization K is a multinational oil company. It gained an overall score for user-centredness of 62 per cent. The particular project cited is in some ways a 'one-off' within the organization as in this case it proved difficult for the end user to envisage what was required. An evolutionary prototyping method was therefore adopted, which is not the case in all IT projects. In general the company has a considerable 'open' style and this feeds into IT design. Although users do not get actually involved in design they are often seconded to projects on a half or full-time basis and the result seems to be an increase in project success rates. Problems involve finding the right person, overcoming their reluctance and limiting their expectations. Prototypes are evaluated in real-life scenarios with real data. There is some movement toward a wider organizational scope in design. The appointment of a business re-engineering consultant will assist this process and will help to address human-factor issues.

Organization L is a small to medium-sized company involved in wholesale beer distribution. It gained an overall score for user-centredness of 81 per cent. It adopts a very user-centred method with the systems manager particularly committed to such processes, and was recruited as his approach to systems design fitted well with the general organizational ethos which is 'highly organic, dynamic and participative'. The methods chosen, a mixture of information engineering and object orientation together with an emphasis on prototyping, address user issues fully, with users being involved all the way through the design and implementation process. Issues which mitigate against this include user resistance to change and fear of contribution to the technical design.

9.3   The issues

There is a remarkable degree of similarity between the case studies in relation to the issues which inhibit a fully user-centred approach to information systems development. From the evidence it is possible to identify four main themes:

1. User issues
2. Organizational commitment
3. Developer skills
4. Resource constraints

9.3.1   User issues

Within a fully user-centred approach users are involved both as:

- *Users as designers,* as participants in design teams, and as
- *Users as subjects,* in user-centred evaluation studies, particularly usability evaluations

Problems that are inherent to users themselves mainly fall into the former category and it is primarily these which we will now address.

User selection and recruitment to design teams

While we have clearly shown how user participation in design is important to the successful and usable development of information systems, it is certainly not sufficient just to involve *any* users. Finding the *right* people to contribute is both crucial and unfortunately often very difficult. By the right people we mean those who:

- *Have the prerequisite personal skills*, particularly communication skills that are important if users are to maintain an effective collaboration with technical experts.
- *Have relevant practical experience and knowledge*, of both the domain/application under analysis and any necessary computing and IT skills (see below).
- *Are viewed favourably*, by the whole user organization (users and management), and will therefore be able to make a representative contribution.

A major obstacle to user selection and recruitment stems from resourcing constraints, which we will study later. However, even given sufficient resources and assuming that the right people, as defined above, are available, further hurdles need to be negotiated before a full range of representative users can be recruited to design teams. User *apathy* is often an issue. End users in particular may not appreciate the importance that their contribution could make to development, and as a result *overcoming user reluctance* to participate can be difficult.

User experience and knowledge

Once a range of users have been identified for participative design the next major problem involves overcoming their knowledge gap and integrating them into the design process. Users seconded to main design teams in particular will need considerable support and training in order to make an effective contribution. Even users contributing at a specific and local level may experience considerable difficulty in relating to IT issues. These difficulties may manifest themselves in a range of ways. While those who have no prior experience of information systems development often have difficulty in comprehending the size and complexity of the analysis and design process, others demonstrate a fear of contributing to the technical design.

User expectations

Users often have an unrealistically high expectation of what IT solutions can offer and tend to take a far too simplistic view of IT opportunities. Sometimes it is necessary to try to limit their expectations. An alternative and conflicting aspect to be considered under this category is the problem of user resistance to change. Striking a balance between these two disparate aspects of expectation is not always easy.

User contribution and agreement

Further complications to participative design relate to problems inherent to all types of group work. Groups can, for example, exert strong pressure on individual members to agree to majority decisions, even if the decision is wrong. User representatives on design teams are in danger of being marginalized. On the other hand, vocal minorities, even minorities of users, can sway a decision not through the underlying power within their argument but because of the strength in which it is presented.

User diversity

A further issue exists that is relevant to all aspects of user involvement, both *users as subjects* and *users as designers*. Obtaining a representative sample of users may not be simple. Users vary in many dimensions. In Chapter 2 we focused on some issues (such as skill level and IT knowledge) which can be analysed and specified, and noted others such as adaptability which cannot be analysed. We augmented the latter category in Chapter 5 by adding cognitive differences and variations in predispositional attitudes. User needs also differ widely and again some, particularly functional needs, are easy to identify, whereas others, notably aspirational needs, are much more difficult.

User diversity is immense, it encompasses many facets some of which cannot even readily be measured. Information systems developers should recognize such diversity, do their best to engage representative users in both design and evaluation, but crucially should recognize the limitations inherent in extrapolating results from the user sample to the whole user population.

9.3.2   Organizational commitment

Commitment within the organization as a whole is necessary for human-factor issues to be successfully integrated into information systems solutions. Two specific issues can be identified:

1. Management support and ethos
2. Organizational IS structure

Management support and ethos

At organizational and senior management level a positive commitment to employee participation is important. Participative management in its generic form attempts to reduce conflict between workers and management and gives employees the opportunity to influence all the policies that affect their work. The degree of participation within an organization will vary and is much more prominent in some countries than others. Scandinavian countries are particularly well disposed towards the human-factor approach. Unless the ethos of the organization, and the practice of senior manages within it, is conducive to the generic practice of participation, its specific embodiment within user-centred design, and the successful integration of human-factor issues within development, will be difficult if not impossible.

Organizational IS structure

Further negative factors flow from the form of organizational structure and the way in which the IT/IS department is integrated within it. Organizations that provide only central IT/IS services tend to impose systems from the centre with only limited user involvement. There is a trend nowadays to disperse the IT function within user departments. This has been accompanied by the growth in what is known as *hybrid managers;* individuals with both domain and computing expertise. Such an approach is clearly likely to support user engagement. However, communication problems are still often shown to exist between developers and end users, and in many cases the cause can be put at the door of end-user department management.

9.3.3   Developer skills

Further impediments to the expansion in the human-factor approach to information systems development relate to the knowledge, skills and experiences of individual technical experts. Human–computer interaction and participative design are relatively recent initiatives. Although the majority of professional qualifications now address human-factor issues, and as a result many newer recruits to the profession will have been trained to a basic level, other more established, and therefore senior, staff may not yet fully appreciate the potential benefits.

In response to this Dunckley and Smith (1995) have developed a self-assessment template which enables individual software developers to evaluate their user centredness. The template has three specific aims:

1. To raise awareness within the design community about what constitutes user-centred design.
2. To enable individuals and organizations to identify their strengths and weaknesses in respect of user-centred design.
3. To provide a sign-posting facility that will direct software development managers to the many tools and techniques that are currently available to integrate human-issue factors within the development process.

9.3.4   Resource constraints

The final restraining influence stems from financial and time constraints. The iterative or evolutionary approach to development is often seen as problematic particularly as end-user departments have been known to possess unrealistic time expectations. Iterative prototyping encourages the perception that software will not be delivered within the necessary timescale, even though studies show that it takes no longer than other methods. To quote from one of the survey organizations: 'prototyping is not possible because of a lack of resources and available time'.

Resourcing user contribution to design *(users as designers)* and evaluation *(users as subjects)* can be highly significant. User secondment (full or part-time) to a main design team is obviously very expensive and even the release of users for usability evaluations requires additional temporary staffing support.

9.4   Improving the development process: enhancing human–computer factor expertise

The arena of information systems development is awash with new initiatives. Whether it be object orientation, business process re-engineering or rapid applications development there are plenty of new techniques calling at the door of the IS developer. It is therefore within the context of *initiative overload* and within the constraints identified in the previous section that we attempt to sell the human-factor approach. Based upon the work of Franklin (1995) we can perhaps identify four reasons why the take-up has not been as large as we would like:

1. *Academic emphasis,* many tools and techniques have been developed in universities and research laboratories but there has been comparatively little commercial emphasis.
2. *Minimal marketing,* compared to the more visible developments in say SSADM or object orientation there has not been a great amount of selling user centredness, again outside of the academic community.
3. *Unproven success,* although well-considered interface design is seen as important, and some general case study evidence concerning user participation does now exist, to date there has been limited documentary *proof* that the integrated human-factor/user-centred approach to socio-technical systems actually leads to better information systems solutions.
4. *Inappropriate zeitgeist,* because the business ethos of today is more related to economic efficiency than worker participation there is an inherent barrier to overcome.

We are, to some extent, in a *chicken and egg* situation: without greater commercial application of human-factor techniques it will be difficult to sell the positive documented evidence of success. One of the keys to unlocking the door to expansion may lie in the establishment of a specialist human factor or usability services group within the commercial organization. This can act as a catalyst for the mainstream adoption of human-factor techniques. During the period in which this book was being written a number of recruitment notices were broadcast on the British Human–Computer Interaction Group email news service demonstrating that an increasing importance is being placed by commercial software developers to this area of study. Two edited versions of these job opportunities are shown in Fig. 9.1.

Considerable support is now available for commercial IS development departments wishing to become more user-centred. For example:

- HUSAT (Human Sciences and Advanced Technology), based in Loughborough, UK is 'Europe's largest independent centre focusing exclusively on shaping technology to the ways people and organisations use it'. It has an objective to see that 'user-centred approaches become a normal part of systems development and implementation' (HUSAT, 1995).
- NPL (National Physical Laboratory) Usability Services, based in the UK, is 'an independent organisation with a proven record in user-centred design'. 'Consulting NPL Usability Services early in the design process can bring significant time and cost advantages' (NPL, 1995).
- HUSAT and NPL are both part of a European network of Usability Support Centres which has been set up, with EU funding, to provide

---

User Centred Designer

ABC specialises in technical software for engineers and is committed to a user centred approach to software development. As one of our HCI designers you will be a key team member with responsibility for user needs analysis, HCI, prototyping and user interface design, through to user evaluation and acceptance.

We need your ability to 'think HCI' and to produce a good design in a commercial environment. ABC's particular strengths are in business analysis and analysis of the front end of the software development life cycle, user modelling and HCI, and advanced engineering modelling as well as state of the art Windows applications on client-server networks

---

Human Factors Specialist

XYZ Ltd needs a senior Human Factors Specialist. We already have a small team of Human Factors Specialists working in a multidisciplinary environment. Work areas include training analysis, interface design and research.

We want to hear from people who:
- have a degree in psychology, ergonomics, human factors or equivalent
- could obtain chartered status or equivalent
- are able to communicate with specialists in other professions

---

FIGURE 9.1   *Human–computer factor job opportunities*

TABLE 9.1   *European Usability Support Centres*

Name	Tel:	Email
NPL Usability Services, Teddington, UK	+44 181 943 6993	nigel@hci.npl.co.uk
SINTEF REHAB, Oslo	+47 22 06 73 00	jan.heim@si.sintef.no
Nomos, Stockholm	+46 8 7536220	nigelc@nomos.se
University of Glasgow, Multimedia Comms Gp.	+44 141 330 5424	annemari@mcg.gla.ac.uk
University College Cork, Human Factors Gp.	+353 21 902636	hfrg@ucc.ie
HUSAT, Loughborough	+44 1509 611088	m.c.maguire@lboro.ac.uk
Lloyd's Register of Shipping, Croydon	+44 181 681 4040	tcsjve@aie.lreg.co.uk
WITlab, Delft	+31 15 2783753	a.g.arnold@wtm.tudelft.nl
CB&J, Paris	+33 1 45 55 57 15	73064.4426@compuserv.com
Fraunhofer-IAO, Stuttgart	+49 711 970 2315	pualus.vossen@iao.fhg.de
Data Management SpA, Milano	+39 39 6052 488	l.binucci@finsiel.it
Sistemas Expertos, SA, Madrid	+34 1 359 69 45	sysnet@bitmailer.net
SIEM, Athens	+30 1 9240923	athous@siem.ath.forthnet.gr

companies with advice on how to ensure that their products and systems offer 'greater cost effectiveness and meet the needs of their intended users'. The full list is provided in Table 9.1.

• Human Centred Computing Group. The author leads the Human Centred Computing Group at the University of Luton which provides training and consultancy in a range of user issues (Email:andy.smith@luton.ac.uk).

Summary

In this chapter we have seen that:

• The theory of human–computer factors is not always easy to apply in practice
• Problems can be categorized by user issues, organizational commitment, developer skills and resource constraints
• Usability services groups are providing support within organizations
• A range of usabilty support centres exist providing external support

Questions

9.1 Why do organizations experience difficulty in adopting the human-factor approach to information systems development?

9.2 What are the obstacles to user-centred design within the organization in which you are based? How and in which ways are they being overcome?

9.3 Section 9.2 presented some case study evidence of the obstacles to user-centred design. The evidence was gathered in 1993. Are the results of the survey still valid?

9.4 If the IT director of a large multinational corporation asked you for ten reasons that support the move towards the user-centred approach how would you respond?

References

Dunckley, L. and Smith, A. (1995), 'A template to assess user-centredness in software quality management', in M. Ross, *et al.* (eds), *Software Quality Management III, Proceedings of SQM-95*, Computational Mechanics.

Franklin, I. (1995), 'Noddy's guide to participatory design', *Interfaces*, (29), British HCI Group.

HUSAT (1995), 'Human Factors Research and Consultancy at Loughborough University', HUSAT.

NPL (1995), 'Usability Services', NPL Usability Services (ref NPLUS/Training/950512).

Smith, A. (1993), 'A survey of user centred design', M.Sc. Thesis, Interactive Computing Systems Design, Loughborough University of Technology.

Smith, A. and Dunckley, L. (1995), 'Human factors in software development— current practice relating to user centred design in the UK', in K. Nordby, *et al.* (eds), *Human–computer Interaction. Proceedings of INTERACT-95*, Chapman and Hall, London.

Chapter 10

USERS AND INFORMATION SYSTEMS: CURRENT DEVELOPMENTS AND FUTURE ISSUES

with Andrew Tinson and Mick Baldwin

Chapter aims

In this, our final, chapter we attempt to review some of the more recent ways in which the introduction of new technology has led to the development of new types of information system. We will study how such systems are affecting, and might continue to affect, the user role. Specifically, through study of this chapter, the reader should be able to:

- Appreciate the implications of data communications on the user role
- Evaluate the contribution of, and recognize the difficulties associated with, computer supported co-operative working systems
- Assess the potential applications of virtual reality to information systems

10.1   Introducing the future

There are two important features of modern computing that have enabled society to become so dependent on the computer: size and speed. In 1959, one megabyte of memory required a space equal to the size of a room more than two metres square by two metres high. Today, the same amount of memory requires little more than a cubic centimetre of space. In 1959 one megabyte of memory cost about $25 000, in 1996 it costs less than $50 (Fitzgerald and Dennis, 1996). Processor chip speeds are similarly impressive. Today's high-speed chip's dynamic random access memory takes only 80 billionths of a second to access stored data. At this speed, the single chip can read a 2200 page document in only one second (Fitzgerald and Dennis, 1996). These dramatic technological developments have enabled a rapid evolution in new computer applications and innovative ways of working for the users of such systems.

In the 1960s data processing was by means of off-line batch processing systems. There was no technological connectivity between 'users' (through whom data was captured) and the computer (where processing occurred). In the 1970s communication links were established between remote (dumb) terminals situated in user departments and mainframes operating in the DP department. The spread of standalone personal computer systems in the 1980s moved much of the emphasis to end-user processing.

Nowadays in the late 1990s there is again a resurgence in communications, in this case with an emphasis on the linkage between intelligent workstations and the use of systems to communicate and co-operate between users and groups of users. The Internet is enabling a vast amount of information to be shared on a global basis and virtual reality applications are offering the potential of a *paradigm-shift* in human–computer interaction.

While there are many predictions available concerning the impact of new technologies, foretelling the future has never been easy. However, the combination of developments is potentially immensely significant to the human users of computer systems, and it is on three current and future opportunities that we will complete our study of users and information systems:

1. *Telematics,* the application of communications technologies to information systems.
2. *Computer supported co-operative working,* the study of specific software systems to support group working.
3. *Virtual reality systems*, which represent a computer-generated simulation of a world in which the user is immersed.

10.2   Telematics

Before being able to assess the potential impact of communications technology it will be helpful to share a common understanding of the nature of the network technology itself and how it is developing. According to Gupta (1996) a network is:

> a system that transmits data to and from a number of locations which are geographically dispersed.

Before assessing the current and future impact of telematics we will now review some details of the underpinning technology.

10.2.1   Networking: the enabling technology

Speed and capacity constitute the central elements that steer the development of network technology. For those not fully conversant with terminology we present some basic definitions as they will be useful for us in assessing the potentials and limitations of networking:

Bit—the smallest unit of representation within a computer, a Binary digIT, denotes a zero or one.

Byte—a collection of eight bits, sufficient to store one character of information.

Mega—approximately one million (10^6), a megabyte is approximately one million bytes.

Giga—ten to the power 9 (10^9).

Classifying networks

We can identify four broad types of computer network:

1. *Local area network (LAN)*—A LAN comprises a group of microcomputers or terminals located in the same general area and connected by a quite cheap twisted-pair or coaxial cable so they can exchange information and computer hardware resources. LANs are typically used within the same building or a set of buildings situated close together.
2. *Backbone network (BN)*—A large central network that connects all the terminals, microcomputers, mainframes, local area networks and other communication equipment on a single site; sometimes called a campus area network (CAN).
3. *Metropolitan area network (MAN)*—A network spanning a geographical area that usually encompasses a city or county area; it interconnects various building or other facilities within this city-wide area.
4. *Wide area network (WAN)* —A WAN is a network spanning a large geographical area in which its nodes (microcomputers) can span cities, states, or national boundaries. It interconnects computers, LANs, BNs, MANs, and other data transmission facilities on a country-wide or world-wide basis.

Data transmission

A variety of techniques are available to connect outside a single site. The telephone network provides the cheapest method of connection, using *modems* to change digital computer signals into analogue signals that can be carried over the *public switched telephone network* (PSTN). Dramatic increases in speed have been achieved over recent years so that lines that could only support 300 bits per second can now handle 14 400 and 24 000 bits per second using better and indeed, cheaper modems. Nevertheless, because of the increasing demand for data within modern software applications, these speeds are only suitable for connecting single users to remote sites.

Wide area networks are usually provided by specialist telecommunications companies who lease lines to firms requiring high volume data transmission. Until recently, the X.25 packet switching protocol, generally running at 64 000 bits per second, was thought to provide a good service. Much higher speeds are, however, now possible using better equipment at the ends of the existing lines, and also through the use of fibre optic cables that can handle speeds in excess of 200 mega bits per second (Halsall 1995).

Integrated services digital network (ISDN) has been developed as a digital successor to analogue telephone networks. At present, price and availability are holding back the widespread use of ISDN by companies although the service is predicted to gradually gain hold. The basic ISDN line provides two channels of 64 000 bits per second giving a total of 128 000 bits per second. The primary ISDN connection provides 30 channels of 64 000 bits per second and this will assist its take-up. (Kyas, 1995).

Electronic data interchange (EDI) is the 'direct computer to computer exchange of data over a telecommunications network' (Gupta, 1996), and represents a significant step forward towards the paperless transmission of orders, invoices, and other business documents between users and organizations. Any company using EDI will have networks to interconnect its micro-computers and computer systems at other sites. These connections will allow them to initiate transactions electronically, and then to transmit the transactions to another company where the order can be supplied. It has been predicted that only the transfer of real goods will occur outside of electronic systems, all other aspects will be handled through the network connections.

Bandwidths: the current limiting factor

We have stated that modern software applications have an increasing demand for data. In fact larger and more complicated software, such as multimedia and virtual reality applications, can be said to be highly *data hungry*. This requirement for more and more data means that the network infrastructure supporting such data transfer must continually be improved. When simple text was sent, line speeds of 300 bits per second were possibly acceptable, but to transfer graphics files, voice and video, so that end users are not waiting for the next packet of data to arrive, is going to continue to require more transmission lines of ever greater *bandwidth*.

The bandwidth requirements for multimedia applications vary between 10 megabits per second for video and 900 megabits per second for high definition television (HDTV). These figures are high because of the need for real-time updating of screen images. A screen contains about one million points, or pixels, of information with each colour pixel using three bytes (24 bits) of storage. Simple mathematics indicates that 24 million bits must be transmitted to achieve a full screen picture. Using a connection running at 64 000 bits per second (X.25), it would take six minutes to generate the screen!

Asynchronous transfer mode (ATM) is a data transmission method under further development, it was designed to address the problems associated with the demand for high speed, high data rate transmission. Each connected user can expect speeds of 155 and 622 megabits per second. A link of 155 megabits per second reduces the time to generate a screen to 0.15 seconds (Kyas, 1995).The latest ATM switches that route this high speed data are designed to process data flows of 10 gigabits per second and above. It is expected that in time, ATM will provide the mechanism for handling both local and wide area traffic (Kyas, 1995).

Network applications

Networks are becoming all pervasive. Banks, for example, are already using data networks to link branches and automatic teller machines (ATMs) with their central headquarters. The reservation systems used by large companies such as American Airlines' SABRE and United Airlines' APOLLO are totally dependent on the underlying networks that connect head office with the outlying booking offices. Large hotel chains and car rental firms could not currently function effectively without reservations systems that rely on network technology.

The developments in networking technology has enabled the *Internet* to be established. The Internet is a network of networks, the world's largest group of connected computers. Some of these networks belong to government bodies, some to universities, some to businesses, some to local communities and some to schools (Kent 1994). Usually each connected network that is part of the Internet has a number of computers that act as *servers* for incoming enquiries. We will focus on the Internet in the following section. However, we can highlight the potential for networking through one recent view that network and Internet connectivity will be so widely available, so reliable and so cheap, that holding data locally and running software from individual hard disks will be pointless. The following vision is provided by the chair of Oracle Corporation, Larry Ellison (*The Guardian*, 21 May 1996):

> In order to open up a truly mass market, Oracle has stripped the PC of most of its expensive clothes like hard disk drives and expensive internal chips. Instead Oracle is planning to introduce a 'network computer' (or NC) which wouldn't even need today's pricey shop-purchased computer programmes. The NC links up to the world-wide Internet network of computers through a modem and will receive all of its software—from games to spreadsheets—from the Net.

With luck there is likely to be one winner from this battle of giant technology companies: the user, who will see prices continue to fall. The prospect is that the digital revolution will continue to spread to people who until now have felt themselves too poor to buy a computer of their own.

10.2.2   The Internet and the World Wide Web

The *Internet*, or just *net* as it is often referred to, evolved from ARPANET, a research project in the USA subsidized in the 1960s by the Defense Department and the National Science Foundation to link research institutions and government agencies across the world. The Internet can be considered to be a vast repository of information on any topic imaginable, and through which users across the world can:

- Search for information
- Provide information
- Exchange views
- Conduct transactions

In order to access the Internet users have individual *Internet addresses*; the writer's current Internet address, for example, is andy.smith@luton.ac.uk. The term *information superhighway* is also currently heavily used in association with the Internet. The term *intranet* has been coined to relate to internal organizational information networks developed using the hypertext techniques associated with the World Wide Web.

The Internet

The Internet is based on interconnected wide area networks (WANs). There are a large number of WANs in existence serving diverse and different needs. They allow users to gain access to services that are geographically distant. Usually access controls to the network ensure that only fee paying businesses can gain access. These are the *private* WANs often constructed around public lines or leased lines that use packet switching techniques to handle large volumes of data. WANs have been widely developed and used within the academic community across the globe. ACSnet in Australia connects universities, government agencies and private organizations; BARRNet (San Francisco Bay Area Regional Research Network) connects several University of California campuses with Stanford University and Lawrence Berkeley and Livermore laboratories; JANET (Joint Academic Network) connects universities and research institutions in the UK and offers file transfer, mail, remote login and remote job entry.

The size and number of users connected to the Internet is impossible to determine but it is known that the Internet is growing at an incredible rate. One recent estimate was that 1000 new machines were being added every day. In 1993 the Internet connected 45 000 networks. Currently (1996) it is estimated that between two and four million computers are connected to the Internet and that 10–20 million people have access to the Internet, 7–15 million of them in the USA alone. The Internet is expected to continue growing from about 3.2 million computers today to over 100 million machines on all six continents. By the year 2000, there may be more than one million networks connecting one billion users, with the majority of these users connecting to the Internet from their homes. (O'Leary and O'Leary, 1996).

Nobody owns the Internet as a whole and so it develops and expands in an unplanned manner and this is part of its strength as a system that hangs together through mutual interest. The disadvantage of unplanned development is that no single user or organization dictates what the network should look like and what user interface should be provided. Two significant problems with the Internet are its current lack of control and unreliability in the information provided. For the Internet to be the site for a *commercial revolution*, rules governing its operation will need to be established. Despite the fact that the net lacks any central authority, rules are emerging piecemeal, pulled and prodded by the often conflicting interests of business, governmental agencies, and traditional net users.

The World Wide Web

A number of *tools* are available on the Internet to facilitate user access to the technology. All readers will no doubt be aware of email and the more interested reader will be able to locate details on *ftp, gophers, telnet* and *usenet*. By far the most significant tool is the *World Wide Web* (or just WWW or *Web*), which is a hypertext-based Internet tool allowing users to access and display documents, graphics, video and audio stored on any server on the Internet. In order to search for information on the Web the user requires access to a *Web browser* (such as Netscape). In order to establish an individual *Web site* organizations or individuals need to set up their own *Web server* to control the passage of information on and off the Internet. Through mark-up languages such as HTML (hypertext mark-up language) or VRML (virtual reality mark-up language) a home page and subsequent pages can be developed.

At the time of writing (July 1996) the Web is growing at an amazing pace and is fast becoming an integral part of the business landscape. In the summer of 1994 the number of Web servers was doubling every 56 days. In March 1996 there were 200 000 Web sites and by the end of 1996 there will be over 1 000 000. Access to the Internet is currently multiplying by a factor of 10 each year.

Organizations can set up a Web site for one of three purposes:

1. *Promotion,* to act as a form of on-line advertisement
2. *Content,* to provide information perceived to be of value to the reader
3. *Transaction,* to provide ordering or booking of services or products

There are some conflicting views concerning the Internet and the Web. A positive perception is provided by Nicholas Negroponte, the director of MIT's Media Lab:

> I think that the Internet is one of the rare, if not unique, instances where 'hype' is accompanied by understatement, not overstatement. I estimate that the net will have one billion users by the year 2000. I don't think we know what has hit us.

As described by Nielsen (1996) other experts have predicted the impending collapse of the web. Certainly at the time of writing the limitations inherent in currently implemented communication technology can severely limit performance and hence usability. Ed Krol, one of the world's leading Internet experts when responding to the many sceptics who see the Internet as a triumph of hype over quality of service says (Krol, 1996):

> I think that this is nothing new, it happens with every new technology. If you look at television in the 1950s, the quality of service was awful with fuzzy black and white pictures....as the technology matured the service met the hype's expectation. So will the Internet go.

10.2.3   Telematics: user needs

With such a massive spread in telematics and Internet/Web usage comes a wide range of user issues with which human–computer factor specialists are particularly interested. In the following section we will review the implications in relation to the distinct types of user need identified in Chapter 2:

- *Functional needs,* the requirement for the information system to perform the specific tasks that the users require it to do in the operational situation.
- *Physical needs,* the requirement of the information system to perform the tasks in a manner that is well suited to the physical characteristics of the user.
- *Aspirational needs,* the requirement of an information system to support the medium- to long-term personal goals of the user.

Telematics: implications for user functional needs

The major implications of the spread of telematics on user functional needs relates to the degree to which the new technology can affect the way in which users have control over the data, and to a lesser extent processes, that they manage. The safety and security of data is a paramount concern.

The increased prevalence of computer networks is leading to a whole new range of security issues that must be addressed and solved if users are to maximize the potential of electronic interaction. Information system security must resolve the critical problems relating to *confidentiality and privacy, availability,* and *integrity.* Users require a level security for their data that inspires sufficient confidence. If data that is held remotely is lost, either accidentally, through hardware failure, or by malicious attack, users will feel disinclined to trust the network. There are emerging *security standards* for electronic commerce with some new suggestions for *cryptography* and *electronic key management.* Shay (1995) describes how the use of a *publicly known key* for encryption can provide quite secure data transfer given that the decryption algorithm is private. An encryption key is an algorithm that converts plain textual data into ciphertext so that only the sender and receiver can decode and understand the data being transmitted. The basic principle is that the decryption key cannot be derived from the encryption key and so many users can employ the publicly available key, while only the recipient has the correct decryption key. This approach is being widely used on the Internet to protect data from interception, but it is not yet secure enough to allow fully electronic trading to take place. The eventual need is to make some data, sums of electronic money for instance, completely tamper proof.

For users and system managers, deciding on the level of security needed for any given piece of data will also be important so that time and money is not wasted on indiscriminate, blanket coverage. There are a few considerations to keep in mind when developing a comprehensive policy for protecting the information within an organization:

- Initially it is necessary to decide what information really needs protecting, rather than wasting money protecting everything, as though every bit of data were equally important and confidential.
- It is then possible to decide the real value of each piece of information, not spending more money on protecting information than the information is worth.
- Finally a high-level management policy can be developed, that can be clearly understood, and then communicated throughout the whole organization.

One way of ensuring that only valid users are allowed access to sensitive systems is to further exploit innovative technology. MasterCard International, for example, are testing a 'smart card' that includes information about a user's fingerprint in a chip embedded in the plastic. The company evaluated several other techniques, including voice prints, but decided to go with the 'finger minutiae' approach because it was so simple. If the tests are successful, card readers in stores and banks will include a pad that scans the cardholder's fingertip and compares it with the information on the card (*Business Week*, June 1996).

Networked systems bring a new and rather nasty set of risks for their users. Any data or software that is downloaded, or even just accessed, may result in *virus* attack. Connections between computers and access to electronic bulletin boards make the existence of worms and viruses a serious problem. The .exe and .com files on DOS-based machines are common targets for viruses. A virus is a collection of instructions linked to an executable file that carries out some action that the executable file was not designed to do. Once the virus has attached itself, the file is described as *infected*. *Worms* are similar to viruses but usually appear as separate files. The virus code is executed by a batch command in the executable file, so that when the file is run, the virus code runs too. The damage infected depends on the malicious intentions of its author. Minor, even benign problems are quite common such as the screen display showing a pattern or picture. However, others are designed to be much more damaging by wiping the user's hard disk or corrupting the file system (Shay, 1995).

Telematics: implications for user physical needs

In terms of user physical needs usability issues are paramount. Dunckley and Zajicek (1996) show how usability is being compromised by physical difficulties and the problems of providing complex facilities within an environment that is aimed at the non-computer expert. With the explosive growth in the number of Web sites, users now have so much choice that they are not going to waste time on Web sites that are poorly structured, confusing to navigate, difficult to understand or unattractive (Nielsen, 1996). Usability is a central issue in the design of effective Web sites.

The Web is highly interactive in nature, combining as it does text, graphics, audio and video. The visual design of a Web site is increasing in importance, both in terms of usability and publicity. The public image that a Web site provides of the organization that has created it is increasingly important. Information technology related organizations are placing considerable investment in their Web sites. Visual metaphors (refer to Chapter 6) are increasingly being adopted: especially on the home page and early pages. As users progress through a Web site they may expect a lowering in the visual material and an increase in textual information as shown in Fig. 10.1.

Navigation issues are paramount within the design of a Web site. A usable Web site is one in which the user is easily able to locate the information or services required. Current Web browsers include the following facilities to navigate a Web site:

- *Go to an absolute address*, by typing in its URL (uniform resource locator)
- *Use hypertext links*, by clicking on underlined text
- *Landmarks*, directory buttons such as 'what's new'
- *Backtracking*, to previous pages

The developers of Web sites for large organizations place a great importance on designing for usability. Many of the techniques that we

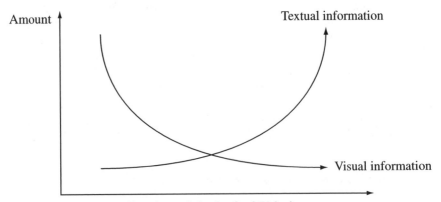

FIGURE 10.1   *Visual and textual information in a typical Web site*

discussed in Chapters 6 and 7 are particularly relevant to Web design. The design of a Web site should be:

* *Iterative,* and evolutionary
* *User-centred,* particularly for intranets
* *User-tested,* using performance and satisfaction metrics

At the time of writing, bandwidth limitations are causing problems with response time on the Web and this is a major usability concern. Many multimedia elements are big and take a long time to download with the horribly low bandwidth available to most users (Nielsen, 1996). Current technology prevents moving television images from being viable on the Web and this can have a profound impact on its potential new 'audience'. Basic usability guidelines that have been developed since the 1970s tell us that systems response times of fewer than 10 seconds are needed to keep the user's attention. On the Web, current users have been trained to endure so much suffering that it may be acceptable to increase the limit to 15 seconds. It is to be expected that with the current increase in Web usage the problem of low response time will not disappear in the short term.

Telematics: implications for user aspirational needs

Telematics presents the potential for major changes in the way society is organized. In Chapter 1 we were introduced to the effects of the IT revolution as documented by Tofler. Within our analysis we noted predictions such as the *collapse of the city*, the *global village* and the *electronic cottage*. This group of effects were noted as being caused by the communications revolution. Here we will summarize such effects under the concept of teleworking which we will define as:

> The ability to work remotely from the normal business location while maintaining, through telecommunication facilities, access to the data and information services of the organization.

Teleworking offers the opportunity to affect user aspirational needs in a number of ways, both positive and negative in nature. By removing the necessity to travel, for example, greater leisure time may be provided, but by limiting the worker to home-based activities, affiliation and status may be diminished (refer to Maslow's hierarchy of needs, Fig. 2.8). We will briefly review a number of aspects of teleworking before returning to an evaluation of its potential effects.

Teleconferencing   Business meetings occupy a considerable part of managers' time. Many of these, possibly over half, could be handled by voice communications only. With cheaper communications across wide area networks, teleconferencing is likely to increase significantly into the early part of the 21st century. Through teleconferencing, people from diverse geographic locations can 'attend' a business meeting in both voice and picture format without the need for travel. In America, 90 per cent of all air travel is for business purposes and increased fuel costs and the need for fast decisions make high mileage travel less sensible and teleconferencing the preferred option (Fitzgerald and Dennis, 1996).

Telecommuting   The changing nature of business and manufacturing, together with the increased acceptance of distributed working, means that information workers will be able to reduce their travelling time and benefit from improved quality of life by *telecommuting*. In addition working at home often provides greater time flexibility and staff can give higher levels of concentration because of fewer distractions. The dramatic increase in subcontracted staff since the mid-1980s is a trend that is likely to continue. Large firms have reduced their own head-count and are tending to hire expertise only when necessary. As a result many overheads of large personnel departments, such as sickness and maternity benefits and the company pension scheme, are reduced. It is to be hoped that individuals will be able to optimize their work and personal life scheduling and thereby reduce levels of stress.

Telecottaging   A *telecottage* is a local centre for any user who is remote from their company headquarters to access better services than those available in their own homes. It provides the opportunity for contact with other professionals who use the telecottage and who are probably working for many different clients. The group is fluid and will probably contain a wide range of disparate skills. The key reason for meeting is that all the members of the group choose to live in an area away from the firms or clients who employ them. One of the effects of telecottaging may be to create stronger neighbourhood groups.

Evaluating the effects   Teleworking can have drawbacks as well as benefits for the aspirational needs of workers. In the UK, the Manufacturing Science and Finance (MSF) trade union for skilled and professional people has issued *a code of practice* to help avoid exploitation by 'greedy' employers trying to cut overheads (*Computing*, 10 November 1995). The abbreviated guidelines are:

• Teleworkers should be employees of an organization rather than self-employed.
• To avoid isolation contracts of employment should require workers

to attend the office periodically with weekly liaison meetings between employees and their supervisor.

- There should be a separate room available at work for teleworking, a separate telephone, and employers should pay the additional costs.
- Teleworkers should enjoy the same rates of pay, employment benefits, child care facilities and working hours as other workers.
- All equipment should be paid for and serviced by the employer.
- Access to trade union representation should continue.
- Teleworking should be voluntary.

10.2.4 Telematics: the future

The next generation of computing software will be designed to make the best use of the networks that end users are able to connect into. Future technological developments, including the potential of the superconductor, allow data to be transmitted at previously unimagined rates and are expected to have a major impact on the ability of data communications to change the way we work in the future. Both the number of users accessing telecommunications facilities, and the range of facilities they have available, is set to increase. The market for personal telephones, for example, has expanded considerably over recent years and it is reasonable for users to assume that soon all the facilities of a fully networked PC may be available *anywhere at any time* providing immediate access to information and services on a global basis.

The predictions being made today about the future capabilities and impact of communication systems on working practices and users may seem exotic and fantastic but they are probably no more strange than today's technology would have appeared decades ago. Television pictures and telephone conversations were science fiction not long ago. Using light to transmit voice, music and pictures was total fantasy and the prospect of computers talking to each other and even controlling each other seemed ridiculous.

10.3 Computer supported co-operative working (CSCW)

A prevalent theme of modern industrial societies is that group activities are an economically necessary and efficient means of production. Group activities are also important in the reinforcement of democratic values (Kraemer and King, 1988). The modern society could not survive on individual effort alone. In spite of this obvious fact information systems that support group, as opposed to individual work, have only been proposed in recent years and are still at an early stage in their development. Such systems are generally referred to as either computer supported co-operative working (CSCW) systems or group decision support systems (GDSS), depending on whether the focus is on the human factor or the management support element of the system. The specific software products are also known as groupware. We will use the term CSCW.

There are perhaps three reasons why CSCW systems are currently being implemented. First, because of the increased complexity of organizations, and the environment in which they operate, management decisions in the late 20th century require the participation of many more people than they did earlier (Mallach, 1994). Secondly changes in organizational culture have led to an increased use of participatory management methods. The third reason is a technological one. As we have seen fast wide area telecommunication links have enabled the rapid transfer of text, graphic and video based data. The combination of these three factors has promoted the development and commercial exploitation of CSCW systems. CSCW systems focus on group work that potentially can be supported by some kind of technology, be it for communication among group members, or for supporting the conduct of the work itself. Examples of such systems include: email, video conferencing, shared editors, co-authoring systems, co-operative development systems.

CSCW systems are defined by Ellis *et al.* (1993) as:

> computer-based systems that support groups of people engaged in a common task (or goal) and that provide an interface to a shared environment

If the discipline of human–computer interaction can be said to be founded upon an understanding of the combination of psychology and computing, then the study of CSCW could equally be said to be based upon a comprehension of both sociology and computing. HCI focuses on the individual interaction between one computer and one user, whereas CSCW concerns groups of users. It involves the development of software to support individuals working in groups and on the study of how the use of group technology solutions can affect modes and patterns of work. It is therefore easy to see why we need to understand and evaluate the contribution that CSCW is bringing, and might continue to bring, to the enhancement of information systems at the disposal of the user.

10.3.1   Defining groupwork and co-operation

As CSCW systems propose to support, and hopefully enhance co-operation, it is appropriate for us to discuss what we mean by *co-operation* between *groups* of individuals before we can evaluate the contribution that information systems might provide. According to Clarke and Smyth (1993) co-operation is:

> a group behaviour that can have distinct, even critical, advantages in problem identification and problem solving

Olson (1993) defines a group as:

> a set of people who are knowingly collaborating on a common goal, who require communication and co-ordination among group members

Elements of co-operation

Deutch (1962) identifies that for successful co-operation there must be one agreed common goal towards which the parties are working. Birenbaum and Sagarin (1976) investigate patterns of behaviour in group work and Marwell and Schmidt (1975) identify aspects of the content of successful co-operation between individuals. From these and other studies in sociology we can summarize the main criteria for, and elements of, co-operation:

- *Goal directed behaviour,* there must be one agreed, common goal towards which the parties are working.
- *Behavioural norms*, legitimate socially shared standards or guidelines must exist for the accepted and expected patterns of conduct of participants.
- *A reward system*, each party involved in the co-operation should receive a reward as a result: successful task completion may be sufficient reward, or higher issues such as money, power and knowledge may be involved.
- *Distributed responses*, all parties must receive a response from the act of co-operation.
- *Effective co-ordination*, there must be a division of labour and the specified relation between activities.
- *Appropriate timing*, synchronization of component responses is important: if any party does not respond in time then co-operation may be jeopardized.
- *Effective communication*, there needs to be a common language between the participants.

Having discovered that there is perhaps more to co-operation than there might at first seem, we may also note that Deutch provides us with a more specific definition of co-operation:

> co-operation is the situation where the movement of one member towards the goal will to some extent facilitate the movement of other members toward the goal

Framework of co-operation

Figure 10.2 provides a diagrammatic representation of a framework for the generic co-operation between two participants (not necessarily related to information technology), and the interaction between themselves and their artefact of work (Dix, 1993). We can use the model to describe the co-operation inherent in an example situation of co-operation:

> *Situation*: Two estate agents are asked to measure a very large room, and are only provided with one two-metre extending tape rule.

> *Description of co-operation*: Both estate agents are *participants* in the task and the rule is their *artefact of work*. They have a shared *understanding* of how to measure a room. They will be in *direct communication*, talking about the problem at hand, and will *control* the use of the rule, receiving feedback, especially when the rule reaches its maximum extension. Somehow they will reach an agreed way of measuring the room.

The framework will be useful in evaluating the contribution that CSCW systems can make to the co-operation between individuals.

10.3.2   Classifying CSCW and groupware

CSCW systems have been characterized in many ways (e.g. Nunamaker (1993); Rodden, (1991) and McGrath and Hollingshead (1994)). We will find it sufficiently informative to note two main methods by which these types of information system have been be classified. We can analyse CSCW either by the *time and place* of co-operation or by the *nature of functionality* afforded by the system.

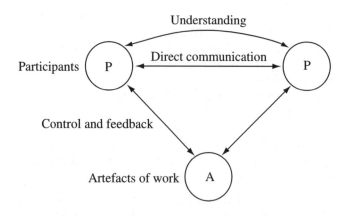

FIGURE 10.2   *Framework for co-operation*

By time and space

One way in which CSCW/groupware products can be categorized is to establish *where* and *when* the participants are performing the co-operation. In terms of simple non-computerized communication Fig. 10.3 places traditional methods of communication on a time–space matrix.

In terms of CSCW, Nunamaker (1993) and Rodden (1991) investigate the environmental facets of group work and specify the *form of interaction*, or *time dimension*, which can be synchronous or asynchronous, and the *graphical dispersion*, or *spatial dimension*. Rodden (1991), Dix (1993), and Mallach (1994) all apply the idea of a time–space matrix to classify CSCW/GDSS systems and it is from these sources that Fig. 10.4 has been proposed. It emphasizes that there is no clear boundary between the different types of system. Co-authoring systems, for example, may include elements common to message systems which themselves overlap with electronic conferencing. We will examine each subgroup in turn.

Types of CSCW

Message systems Electronic mail allows users to exchange messages and files attached to messages across networks using some form of addressing to identify themselves and the intended recipient. The message is transferred from the sender's machine to the remote user's machine and is delivered to a *mailbox*. This is essentially an area of disk space allocated to each user and accessible only through the mail system software. One of the most convenient aspects of email is that all or some of the original recipients can be copied with a reply so that large groups can be kept informed without the need to stand next to a photocopier and then post pieces of paper into pigeon holes or envelopes. This provides a major saving in time compared to paper systems and

	Same place	**Different place**
Same time	Face-to-face communication	Telephone
Different time	Post-it note	Letter

FIGURE 10.3   *Non-computer methods of communication and a time–space matrix*

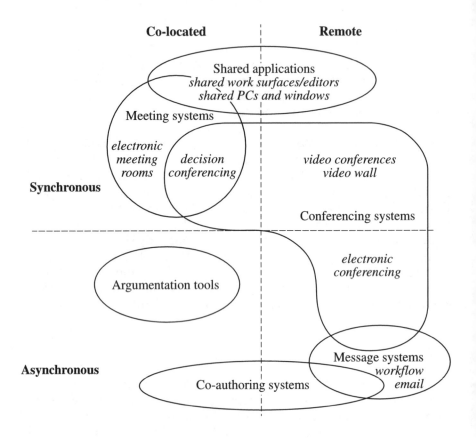

FIGURE 10.4   *CSCW and the time–space matrix*

improves communication within companies by keeping interested people informed with very little effort.

The interfaces for handling email can provide many facilities which users quickly find valuable. Being able to sort incoming mail according to subject, originator or date is a major advantage. Being able to save mail into folders or directories that the user can create means that the process of filing becomes fully merged with the process of saving. This manipulation allows users to handle large volumes of incoming mail with comparative ease and access the important items quickly. Sending a reply is usually possible at the press of an icon or selection from a menu.

Currently, wide area networks allow electronic mail to be exchanged world-wide primarily between companies, government agencies, and universities. Today domestic users are generally not part of these communications systems and need to use a modem or some other means to communicate with a computer that is connected to a wide area network. Economics mean that this situation is likely to continue for a long time to come and in addition there is user resistance to change to be overcome. Sending greeting cards, anniversary cards, or sympathy cards electronically would not carry the same emotional content as a card (Shay, 1995).

Email has also been the springboard for several more advanced groupware applications (Dix, 1993). Mallach (1994), for example, describes a *workflow system* as a form of intelligent electronic mail in which the system knows what the flow of information in a decision-making situation is supposed to be, and routes information accordingly. Bulletin boards are a further example of message systems, which, in terms of the time–space matrix are asynchronous and remote.

Meeting systems   In electronic *meeting room systems* a number of participants are situated in one room with his or her own networked computer. All participants are able to see, and through their computer, access a large electronic white board. The system operates under the WYSIWIS (what you see is what I see) principle: all participants have identical screens. Through the use of an appropriate floor control policy, often managed by a group leader or facilitator, individual participants are able to take control of the whiteboard. Through their computer and specialist software, often providing drawing tools, users can contribute to group working in a manner that mirrors the use of a traditional whiteboard. Meeting room systems tend to support brainstorming type activities. Kraemer and King (1988) distinguish between meeting room systems and decision conferencing systems in which enhanced task oriented tools are provided.

Shared applications   Shared work surfaces are similar in a way to meeting room systems, but operate in remote mode. They do not have the facility of an electronic whiteboard. When two or more computers work together and use mainstream application software we have a situation known as the shared PC. A refinement of this is the shared window system where individual workstation windows are shared between users.

Conferencing systems   There are a number of variants of the conferencing concept. Video conferencing facilities are commercially available products and, although based upon telecommunications, need not include a computer element. Video links are clearly synchronous whereas electronic conferencing without the video link can occur asynchronously. Decision conferencing systems are co-located and are discussed above as a subsection of meeting room systems.

Co-authoring systems Co-authoring systems allow controlled updating of documents by more than one person. They provide facilities to track the changes made and who is responsible for them, so that the process of multiple creation and maintenance of documents is facilitated in an orderly manner. Allied systems for document management offer a library repository for storage of documents. Once a document is placed under the system's control, access is regulated to allowed users, updates are restricted to users with modify privilege and when changes are made, a distribution list of interested parties is used to mail them that changes have occurred. Should the author decide to delete the document, other interested parties can be notified and their agreement sought before actual destruction takes place. For many company documents, such systems mean that all members of the organization can have read access to the latest version while management of changes occurs with automatic software support.

Argumentation tools Tools that aim to document the rationale and argument behind group working and group decision making, are known as argumentation tools. Systems can be based upon graphical methods similar to the documentation of design rationale as implemented in the design space analysis (QOC) technique described in Chapter 6.

Nature of functionality afforded

At a first level of refinement we can use the nature of the functionality afforded by the system to identify two board types of CSCW. Although in *enabling technology* systems an appropriate infrastructure is provided for users to undertake their task in group mode, no specific support is provided to actually perform the detailed task. Alternatively *co-operative development* systems, as we will call them, provide facilities to perform the core task with an anticipated improvement in group performance.

The framework for co-operation can itself be used as a tool for classifying and analysing CSCW systems (Dix, 1993). As shown in Fig. 10.5 it leads to three broad types of CSCW system:

1. *Computer-mediated communication*, an enabling technology that supports *direct communication* between participants.
2. *Meeting and decision support systems*, which capture common understanding, and are mainly an enabling technology.
3. *Shared applications and artefacts*, which are co-operative development systems and support the participants' interaction with shared work objects— the artefacts of work.

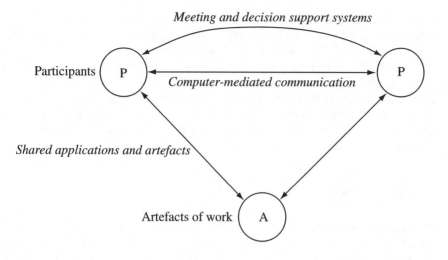

Meeting and decision support systems

Participants   P   *Computer-mediated communication*   P

Shared applications and artefacts

Artefacts of work   A

FIGURE 10.5   *Using the framework for co-operation to classify CSCW*

10.3.3   Effects of CSCW on the user role

Although CSCW systems may be at a relatively early stage in their development, they are already having a significant effect on the way users undertake co-operative work. As we have noted message systems have seen the greatest degree of implementation and it is with these computer-mediated communication systems, that most case study research has been carried out.

Electronic mail has been shown to change the culture of the organization in which it resides, it changes who talks to whom, what kind of person is heard and the tone of what is said. In the absence of feedback some users write asocial or emotive messages, which are often shocking, and upsetting to the recipient (Sproull and Kiesler, 1991). Galegher and Kraut (1994) compare computer-mediated communication with face-to-face communication. From their work we can identify three criteria with which we can make a comparison:

1. Project performance
2. Quality of output
3. Social experience

Effects on performance

Galegher and Kraut (1994) show that when compared with face-to-face communication, computer-mediated communication results in both an increased time to complete tasks, and a greater difficulty in co-ordinating the tasks. The basic difficulty with computer-mediated communication is that it places constraints on the nature of the communication. In face-to-face situations there is much more flexibility in the types of communication that can occur. Participants can switch from one-to-one to group discussion, and can work together in subgroups with individual artefacts (drawings, etc.) all in one session. While a range of CSCW systems offer support to each of these types of communication they do not offer the flexibility of all types at once.

Quality of output

In a study Galegher and Kraut (1994) found that groups undertaking a task using computer-mediated communication were able to produce work to a similar level of quality as groups which were able to meet face-to-face. Users engaged in computer-mediated communication were, by adapting their behaviour to the new situation, equally as effective as face-to-face groups, although they seemed to operate at a lower efficiency level.

Social experience

The inability to meet face-to-face means that communication is mainly textually based and as a result the interaction lacks the normal social cues inherent in group work. This greatly inhibits the capacity of participants to get to know each other and to identify the particular strengths that fellow workers can bring to the collaborative effort. It has also been suggested that the lack of face-to-face communication in CSCW groups leads to *polarization*: the fact that CSCW groups tend to generate more extreme decisions. Groups working together on important issues should not rely exclusively on CSCW systems.

10.3.4   CSCW and the design of user-centred systems

Until recently information systems have been developed centrally by the organizations IT department and have been based upon conclusions drawn from many interviews, observations and questionnaires with users. We have referred to this model of development as technical-centred design (Chapter 3). In the last decade this type of development process has been supported by the use of computer aided software (or systems) engineering (CASE) tools. There is no clear, or agreed, definition of CASE but Avison and Fitzgerald (1995) define a CASE tool as:

> any computer software and/or system which is specifically designed to support any sub-stage or stage or stages of the information systems development process of a computer based information system or any aspect of the management of these tasks and processes

and recognize that their definition would include tools and support environments such as workbenches, builder tools, project support environments, integrated project support environments (IPSEs) and system factories. CASE tools can be classified as Upper CASE (used in strategy , planning or logical design), Lower CASE (concerned with aspects of physical design, programming and implementation) or Integrated CASE which attempt to integrate both into a fully integrated support environment.

Although some CASE tools address strategic and planning issues informing information systems design, current tools focus primarily on providing support for technical centred design. In our study we are particularly interested in the user role. Within a commercial development project although CASE tools will be used by a number of developers, they have not in the past been seen particularly good at supporting interpersonal communication and co-ordination among the various groups of individuals involved (Avison and Fitzgerald, 1995), and certainly not in relation to user—developer communication.

It is perhaps through an integration of CASE and CSCW that design in general, and user-centred design in particular could be significantly enhanced. Yang *et al.* (1994) describe a CASE tool that supports a geographically dispersed collaborative development environment where teams can 'co-specify, co-analyse, co-code and co-debug information systems projects over a distributed, heterogeneous network of workstations and desktops'. When the design approach is extended from technical-centred to joint user-specialist design, *computer aided co-operative user-centred system engineering* tools should be able to offer a range of services to enhance user-centred design through:

- Partnership between users and developers (meeting and decision support systems).
- Communication between all participants working remotely (computer-mediated communication) thereby providing co-ordination between and within the *structures* of design (project steering group, main design team, local design teams).
- Provision of computer aided support (shared applications and artefacts) to a range of *processes*.
- Facilities to support (shared applications and artefacts) for the socio-technical nature, wide *scope*, of design.

10.3.5   CSCW: the future

As we have said CSCW systems are at an early stage in development. There is much that needs to be done if CSCW is to mature enough so that it provides the same degree of support that other information systems provide to the end user. Essentially CSCW will need to show that it can enhance both the infrastructure supporting groupwork and the performance of the core task itself.

Olson (1993), in a comprehensive exploration of the future potential development of CSCW systems, shows how researchers and designers are beginning to explore the special needs that groups have for technology support for group working and describe how they are beginning to design systems that fit these needs. According to Olson researchers need to:

*   Understand the fundamental nature of group activity that we are attempting to support.
*   Extend our understanding of the dimensions by which the important aspects of the situation, the task, the technology and the group composition affect work.
*   Begin to build laws of group-technology behaviour.
*   Design specific interaction styles and input output devices appropriate for groups of workers.
*   Produce special toolkits for the effective development of CSCW systems.

In essence until CSCW can offer support to all of the elements of generic co-operation, as outlined in page 329, they will remain limited to the enabling technology mode. Collaborative work is the core of our society, wrought with both difficulties and benefits. It is clear that technology can change group work and there is a good possibility that, given sufficient development effort, it will result in major enhancements to productivity (Olson, 1993).

10.4   Virtual reality information systems

Virtual reality (VR), once the dream of a few far-sighted visionaries (Sutherland, 1986) is now becoming a possibility as the result of a new generation of powerful, and increasingly low cost, processors. Virtual reality games, now prevalent in amusement arcades are only the public face of this development. VR technology is being used more and more in serious applications. A small but growing number of software houses and systems consultants are now offering VR solutions to business, managerial and scientific problems. As the introduction of VR solutions to mainstream business applications increases there will be major implications. Organizations that exist in cyberspace will make possible new forms of organizational structure, which will require new methods of management.

The development of virtual reality technology represents a major *paradigm shift* in human–computer interaction. The ability to *immerse* the user in a computer-generated reality of 3D images, sound and tactile feedback takes the user through the interface to interact directly with the objects in that reality. These objects can be anything, from simulations of real-world entities and systems, fantasies and games, to visualizations of abstract data spaces. Interface devices such as the data glove have been developed that allow users to grasp and manipulate objects in the virtual world, or send commands to the computer through gestures. Coupled with neural net technology, the system can even adapt to individual variations in gestures (Vaananen and Bohm, 1993).

In this new paradigm of HCI, the user becomes a *participant* in the virtual world (Bricken, 1991). The interface becomes *inclusion*, the interaction changes from mechanistic to *intuitive*, and the presentation of data changes from visual to *multimodal*. Of course, the interaction still has to be mediated by hardware (data glove, head-mounted display, etc.) as well as some form of operating system, but the technology is itself invisible, and carefully adapted to human activity so that participants can behave naturally. The technology makes possible truly user-centred systems design which should result in greatly increased rates of user acceptance and systems success (Smith and Dunckley, 1995). There are currently a number of levels of VR technology that we will now explore.

10.4.1   Virtual reality—variations and definitions

Full immersion VR

The description of virtual reality as a *full immersion* experience is what is generally taken to define the technology itself. Gigante (1993) characterizes VR as:

> the illusion of participation in a synthetic environment rather than external observation of such an environment

VR relies on three-dimensional, stereoscopic, head-tracked displays, hand/body tracking and biaural sound. It is an immersive, multisensory experience. Rheingold (1991) also defines immersion as an essential component of a VR system, combined with the ability to navigate through the computer-generated world.

Enhanced reality

There is another school of thought that regards the definition of a VR system as a full immersion system, as too strict, and this limits the potential applications of the technology. With *enhanced* or *augmented reality*, the computer-generated world is *overlaid* onto the physical world, allowing the participant to operate in both environments. The computer display typically presents information about the physical world that assists the participant in understanding or working in the real world. Examples of such applications would be wiring plans for a building, that allow maintenance workers to *see* the wiring inside the walls, or complex engine plans overlaid on the real engine to assist engineers in carrying out repair work.

Ultrasound images of patients, fed back to a surgeon in real time and overlaid on the patient would allow surgeons to see inside their patients, enhancing their ability to perform operations with the minimum risk. This technology can be used to *animate* inanimate objects. Kellog, Carroll and Richards (1991) describe the possibilities for an enhanced kitchen, and a Natural History Museum; many everyday objects could acquire (or appear to acquire) cartoon-like behaviours: a kettle that calls you when it has boiled, or a vacuum cleaner that complains when it needs emptying. Perhaps the ideal system is one in which the user can tune the display between full immersion and transparent mode, making possible the benefits of both systems.

Desktop VR

Desktop VR is emerging as a low cost alternative to full immersion VR. It provides the same benefits of 3D data representation and sound, while avoiding the problems that are experienced with immersion systems. While many may not regard this as true VR, these systems are increasing in popularity as a visualization aid in design, training, sales and communication. However, such systems should also be configurable to support head-mounted displays and other interaction devices such as the data glove and 3D mouse, if they are to be considered as VR systems (Blau and Yurica, 1994).

Telepresence

Telepresence refers to the experience of being at a remote site. Through sufficiently sensitive interface devices, the user's consciousness is projected to another physical location, or is able to operate a robot working in a harsh or dangerous environment. According to Stone (1993) telepresence is:

the ideal of sensing sufficient information about the teleoperator and task environment, and communicating this to the human operator in a sufficiently natural way, that the operator feels physically present at the remote site

Cyberspace

The term *cyberspace* was first coined by William Gibson in his novel *Neuromancer* (Gibson, 1984). It is generally taken to refer to a multi-participant environment, which may or may not involve devices such as head-mounted displays, datagloves and other interaction devices normally associated with VR. The Internet, for example, although screen and keyboard based, is regarded as a cyberspace.

10.4.2   Virtual reality and information systems

While the first generation of computerized information systems may have fulfilled many of their functional requirements they have yet to maximize their potential. To date they have generally been used to complement an existing way of managing people and processes and have tended to maintain a centralized structure of authority and control (Taylor and Katambwe, 1988). Some current information systems, however, are moving away from a centralized structure. Line and middle managers, and others in the field, now have the tools to input data, analyse information and make decisions. The powerful combination of graphical user interfaces (GUI), networks and databases present an almost infinite array of possibilities, but there is a problem in making best use of this complex technology (Greenguard, 1994). The problem of representing complex data to end users is being tackled by a number of organizations by turning to virtual reality technology.

Virtual reality is emerging from the realms of science fiction and hype to become a serious solution to many information management problems. With the vast amounts of information generated by today's systems, humans require new and innovative methods of retrieving knowledge from this information. Information of itself has little value unless it can convey meaning or enhance the knowledge of human beings. Virtual reality is being recognized as one solution to the problems of efficient knowledge management.

In a survey Leston (1996) found that more than 80 per cent of international companies are expecting to boost their investment in VR. According to Leston (1996) companies are now using VR in the following ways:

- *Design automation*, in which virtual prototyping is by far the most important area through which VR provides a digital alternative to building expensive physical models.
- *Sales and marketing,* to help customers visualize and select from a variety of options, be it a car or a kitchen.
- *Planning and maintenance*, to model what goes on inside a building or project, how it will work and how humans will interact within their physical environment.
- *Training and simulation*, including staff familiarization, equipment operation, assembly and production-line training.
- *Concept and data visualization*, which is likely to greatly increase the VR user base.

Three-dimensional databases

Virtual reality technology provides a natural extension to work being done on spatial databases. A spatial data management system (SDMS) represents a database in a graphical form that is presented spatially on a screen. This makes the organization of the data more obvious to the user, enabling the user to navigate the database more intuitively than text-based systems. Data surrounding the current data item is visible, which encourages browsing through related items (Herot, 1980). Such systems are typically provided with a graphical query language, in which queries are made by manipulating graphical icons (for example by manipulating an entity relationship diagram), rather than expressing the query in some form of text-based query language (Campbell, Embly and Ejdo, 1987).

These systems have typically been represented on 2D flat screens, however, there are obvious advantages for the introduction of 3D representations of data. In a 3D database, users are placed *within* the data and are able to *walk* or *fly* through the data space. The perception of distance allows the user to step back from the data to get an impression of the structure of the database, or spot areas of particular interest. The results of a query can similarly be represented spatially, with items most closely matching the query being visibly closer than less accurate matches (Mariani and Lougher, 1992).

This spatial management of data has been described as *cognitive space* because it emphasizes multisensory, multidimensional information-presentation capability. It offers a range of representational and presentational tools to the system designer and user. The 3D representation of data provides a more intuitive interface, which is therefore easier to remember and navigate, than 2D representations. According to Del Bimbo *et al.* (1993):

> the use of 3D interfaces provides a significant shift of quality in the user interaction with respect to 2D interfaces .... using 3D icons, the user

experiences a mental shift from the sensation of interacting with a schematic representation of reality, to the sensation of directly interacting with reality

The placing of icons in 3D space can convey the relative importance of those icons. Wexelblat (1991) discusses the application of these ideas in relation to program modules, showing how the evolution of different versions of modules can be represented by their relative placing in 3D space. He refers to this meaningful ordering of abstract relationships as *semantic space*.

It is possible that 3D databases will become a common management tool. In view of the considerable investment in relational database technology, the best opportunity for VR in this area may be to build upon and extend the existing technology. VR technology can provide user access to, user understanding of, and user interaction with, relational information in a way that has not formerly been possible (Coyne, 1993). Existing data can be visualized and manipulated in new ways. One business application that has used VR included large amounts of financial data that were rendered into a virtual world. Analysts could fly over stocks and market segments, and could understand the state of the stock from the shape, size, motion, spin, or colour of a stock symbol. The analyst could fly into a stock symbol and obtain data on the particular stock.

Management information and decision support systems

Management information systems provide managers and executives with relevant and timely information, enabling them to make better decisions, alternatively it permits the user to search for facts that may help in formulating policy making decisions. Many decision support or expert systems applications are designed to provide management with the opportunity to manage their organization more effectively. The increasing power of today's hardware, linked in vast global networks, is able to provide managers at all levels with a massive amount of data. The problem is representing that data in a way that can be easily grasped by the human mind. In order to deal with this complexity, many companies are turning to virtual reality technology.

Grantham (1991) approaches VR from an organizational and management perspective and is concerned with the application of VR to the organization and management of information flows within organizations. He claims that advanced visualization techniques can provide researchers, scientists and managers with a new methodology for analysis of complex systems. Smith (1991) explored the use of animation to simultaneously display up to 150 variables contained or derived from information in the profit and loss, balance sheet, and cash flow statements, thus permitting viewers to *see* business as an evolving living object. He claims that visualization techniques can be applied to many complex systems, providing more information to be conveyed and assimilated than is possible through numerical representations.

Cahill (1993a, 1993b) has discussed the potential of VR technology for accountancy management. He claims that this technology will revolutionize the practice of management accounting. Several ways in which the technology could be applied include the observation of data collection, the variation of data aggregation levels and the integration of financial and non-financial performance measures. Non financial performance measures could include the speed of customer order processing. The application of virtual reality to decision support systems has been examined by Coull and Rothman (1993). They argue that, as the flow of information available to organizations increases and becomes ever more complex, VR is emerging as one of the most important paradigms in the area of decision support and analysis systems. The multidimensional presentation of data, dynamic interaction with data, and multi-user networking all provide a powerful alternative to static 2D displays.

10.4.3   Organizational implications

The *technological imperative* theory of organizations regards information technology as the main causal agency in organizational change (Markus and Robey, 1988). While some writers argue that there is little empirical evidence to support this view (e.g. Taylor and Katambwe, 1988), others report significant changes as the result of the introduction of new technology (e.g. Foster and Flynn, 1984). These conflicting results are, as most of the above authors admit, probably dependent on the type of organization chosen for study. While new technology makes possible new forms of management and organizational structure, it has often been used to maintain already existing forms of power and control structures. Because of the power that the new wave of technology potentially gives to *all* individuals it is becoming increasingly difficult to protect the established order.

With the development of virtual reality and the possibility of networked multi-participant cyberspaces, the impact on organizational structure is likely to be greater than previously. New technology is bringing about a change in working practices (Arthur, 1994), the use of teleworking is becoming more prevalent, with many employees working at remote sights. Project development teams in the future are likely to consist of people who have been selected and brought together for the purpose of that particular project. The workforce of the future will be more fluid, with individuals working for the company on a temporary basis and who may only ever meet each other in cyberspace. The current challenge of human resource information systems is in developing systems that allow human resource personnel to manage the increased amount of rapidly changing information that these changing working practices inevitably involve.

In order for human beings to access and make effective use of the limitless forms of data that will be available through cyberspace, there needs to be certain structural conventions by which the cyberspace workers can orient themselves. The structures are fluid in the sense that individuals can choose the form of representation that has meaning and usefulness to themselves. It is likely though, that a number of cyberspace domains will develop, each with its own architecture and forms of representation that reflect the function of the activities carried out in that space. Some organizations may operate entirely in and through the cyberspace environment. Even enterprises that produce physical outputs, such as a car production plant, could have its entire managerial and organizational structure modelled in cyberspace with 'shop floor workers' operating industrial robots through 'telepresence'.

10.4.4 VR and information systems: the future

As has been discussed, the development of VR technology represents a fundamental shift in the relationship between humans and computers. This technology may have a profound impact on the form and structure of organizations and on the relationships between the people who are part of those organizations. As yet, the limitations of present network technology means that these images cannot be available to a wide audience, but in time it can fairly be expected that we will all have access to VR software across networks. VR technology can be defined as technology that enhances and extends the human intellect, making effective its inherent natural qualities with the means of exerting influence through the possession of force or power. It is in this capacity to imbue human beings with qualities and powers that would, in another age, have been considered magical that the technology has its greatest value.

The development of VR, and the collective experience of cyberspace, represents a natural evolution in the relationship between human and computer. It has been seen that, rather than supplanting the human being, VR technology extends and enhances human capacities and human intellect. This does not apply just to logical and rational capacities. Anything that can be imagined can be recreated within a virtual world. The possibility of experiencing physical interaction from a distance challenges established concepts of reality. Suppose you were operating a robot through telepresence, and walked into the room where you see yourself operating the robot. Where is your consciousness?

The new technology promises to reverse the trend of recent years. Automation has led to the loss of many jobs, as repetitive and mechanical activities have been replaced by computers and robots. Many traditional jobs have been replaced by software. VR puts the human back in the centre of things. It is an enabling technology that extends and augments human physical and intellectual capacities rather than replacing them. It is this ability to enhance and extend human capacities that gives VR its unique place within our study of human–computer factors. The ability to present information through intuitive metaphors and provide interaction through natural behaviours represents a fundamental shift in the relationship between human and computer.

10.5 Back to the future: the information age

As we have emphasized, predicting the future is not an easy game. At the turn of the century there were major concerns about the predicted growth in horse-drawn traffic and the resultant increase in the need for dung collection in the streets. Soon after this the invention of the internal combustion engine removed the necessity to solve the problem! With this analogy in mind we will look at a few ways in which technology is currently being predicted to affect the ways in which users and organizations access information systems in the new *information age*.

More information has been produced over the last 30 years than in the previous 5000 and the information glut is recognized as a real problem for many knowledge workers and managers. To reduce the chance of becoming overwhelmed by detail, it is important for users to prioritize information. Essentially, that means knowing what to remember and what to forget. A simple rule is to remember only what is of interest, and forget the rest. Interest means that the chances are greater that the information will actually be put to use. Other advice that has been identified is to avoid over analysis as it can lead to paralysis! It is necessary to select the best data available and use it, deleting and forgetting anything that does not meet the selection criteria exactly. 'So relax, prioritise, go with what you've got, and hit that delete key!' (*Investor's Business Daily*, May 1996).

The adage that knowledge is power is true in any age, but in the information age it is the power to transform the organization and its employees, and to adapt to rapidly changing environmental pressures. The increased amount of information which company staff have about products, process strategies and work flows will be the basis for efficiencies and competitive advantage, through the use of new forms of organization and new management technologies. Experimentation with new forms of organization and new management technologies is designed to reduce communication barriers between cross-functional units. This will be achieved by horizontal organizational processes that empower decision makers at the lower levels of the organization Firms that cannot make the transition will find themselves at a competitive disadvantage compared with the firms that do adapt. In the information age, competitive advantage can be achieved only 'by expanding and using an organization's information, knowledge, and learning capability, which can be accomplished only by sharing information, not containing it' (Tucker *et al.*, 1996).

Organizations are predicted to implement specialist *ad hoc* work teams, employed outside the company's existing organizational structure. Bridges (1996) goes further and predicts that in the 21st century, most work will be carried out by independent contractors, and that this will require the current work force to prepare itself and adapt to 'new expectations and the economic realities that have shaped them'.

What the full effect all the new types of information technology, such as the Internet, CSCW and VR will have on individuals and society is, as we have said, impossible to predict. They have the potential for eliminating many of the barriers and limitations of the past. Geographic location is no longer a limiting factor. They have the potential to eliminate the prejudices of the past and unite the planet as a truly global village. The Internet has been described as like a vast collective nervous system that is developing, growing new connections at an incredible rate. The effect could be to unite everyone on the net in a shared global consciousness, while at the same time providing the opportunity to develop individual qualities and uniqueness.

It was once believed that computers would eventually become sufficiently complex enough to become conscious beings in their own right, the ultimate goal of researchers in artificial intelligence. Science fiction writers even envisaged a time when human beings would become redundant and computers would *rule the world*. The truth is actually the reverse, because without humans, computers would become redundant. With hardware being modelled more and more closely on the human nervous system, and software reflecting more and more closely the activities of the human intellect, the computer extends the range of human experience of the physical world. If a machine should ever exhibit self consciousness it will be a human consciousness, projected into it through the experience of telepresence. The classic image of the cyberman is a human machine completely divorced from the feelings and emotions that make us truly human. What is more likely is the reverse, rather than the machines mechanizing their users, the users are humanizing the machines.

10.6   Back to the present: where are we now?

Card (1991) has characterized the growth in the study of the field of human–computer interaction as following four schematic stages typical of systems technologies in general. The four stages are:

Stage 1   *exploratory design or point systems*, an examination of what can be done to support working with computers and the construction of individual point systems.

Stage 2   *dimensions of design space*, an evaluation, comparison and review of different systems so that we understand the *dimensions* that seem to affect the success of systems.

Stage 3   *characterization*, in which we analyse the dimensions so that we can characterize the relationships in more detail.

Stage 4   *articulation of laws and behaviours*—a stage in which the models and laws that govern behaviour can be established.

The discipline of human–computer factors has largely followed this path and has now reached Stage 4. Throughout our study we have identified point systems (examples of user interactions with information systems), compared different approaches and systems, classified and characterized aspects of the whole socio-technical system, and articulated laws and behaviours that govern our domain. Although human–computer factor researchers are currently working at Stage 4, by no means do we understand everything about the discipline. If it was that easy then the only barrier to fully successful information systems development would be effective communication between researchers and practising developers. Unfortunately this is not the case.

As new aspects of human–computer interaction are identified, the four-stage process needs to restart. CSCW systems are one example. CSCW is far behind HCI in Card's four-stage approach. Many different CSCW systems have been built, only some have been evaluated and we are only beginning to understand the dimensions that seem to affect the success of systems. VR is at an even earlier stage in development. While we have made many predictions about the future impact of VR, they are just predictions.

Without having fully explored all systems, understood their

dimensions, and characterized and articulated their laws we are unable to rigorously evaluate the contribution that VR, or any other new aspect of information system technology will make to society, or to the individual users within it.

For probably the first time in history, society is currently discussing at great length the potential implications of an emerging technology before it has actually been developed. No doubt this is an indication that the potential social and political implications of this technology for the human race will be more profound and far reaching than any new technology to date. These issues need to be discussed and debated beforehand if we are to take full advantage of the potentials and opportunities that the technology will make possible, and not make the mistake of simply transferring outmoded and outdated attitudes, power structures and prejudices into a different environment. There is much yet to do in the arena of human–computer factors, and in the study of users and information systems.

Questions

10.1 In what ways does the introduction of computerized communication systems change the user role within the organization?

10.2 CSCW software is most appropriate when group members are required to perform different, but complementary tasks as opposed to the situation where all group members are performing the same task. Discuss.

10.3 Describe the relationship between the expansion in the use of CSCW systems and strategic planning and organization design.

10.4 In what ways can the use of VR technology be said to represent a paradigm-shift in human–computer interaction?

References

Arthur, C. (1994), 'The future of work: it's all in the mind', *New Scientist*, April.

Avison, D. E. and Fitzgerald, G. (1995), *Information Systems Development*, 2nd edition, McGraw Hill, London

Birenbaum, A. and Sagarin, E. (1976), *Norms and Human Behaviour*, Preage Publishing.

Blau, B. and Yurica, K. (1994), 'Designing VR applications for the desktop', *Virtual Reality World*, September/October.

Bricken (1991), 'Virtual worlds: no interface to design', in M. Benedikt (ed.), *Cyberspace: First Steps*, MIT Press, Cambridge, MA.

Bridges, W. (1996), *JobShift: How to Prosper in a Workplace without Jobs*, Brealey Publications.

Cahill, P. (1993a), 'True, fair, virtually real', *Accountancy (ACE)*, 112, 52–53.

Cahill, P. (1993b), 'Management accountants and virtual reality', *Management Accounting*, 71(8).

Campbell, D. M., Embly, D. W. and Ejdo, C. Z. (1987), 'Graphical query formation for an entity-relationship model', *Data and Knowledge Engineering*, 2, 46–48.

Card, S. (1991), 'Presentation on the theories of HCI', at the NSF Workshop on Human–Computer Interaction, Washington DC.

Clarke, A. A. and Smyth, M. G. G. (1993), 'A co-operative computer based on the principles of human co-operation', *International Journal of Man-Machine Studies*, 38, 3–22.

Coull, T. and Rothman, P. (1993), *Virtual Reality for Decision Support Systems*, AI Expert Aug.

Coyne, J. (1991), 'Relational databases and multimedia repositories', *Multimedia Review*, 2(2), 50–52.

Coyne, J. (1993), 'Virtual reality and relational databases', *Virtual Reality World*, November/December.

Del Bimbo, A., Campanai, M. and Nesi, P. (1993), 'A three-dimensional iconic environment for image database querying', *IEEE Transactions on Software Engineering*, 19(10), 997–1011.

Deutch, M. (1962), 'Co-operation and trust: some theoretical notes', Nebraska Symposium on Motivation.

Dix, A., Finlay, J., Abowd, G. and Beale, R. (1993), *Human–Computer Interaction*, Prentice-Hall, London.

Dunckley, L. and Zajicek, M. (1996), 'How useful is the Internet— usability concepts and the Internet— a task-based approach', in A. Ozok and G. Salvendy (eds), *Advances in Applied Ergonomics*, USA Publications.

Ellis, C. A., Gibbs, S. J. and Rein, G. L. (1993), 'Groupware: some issues and experiences', in R. M. Baecker (ed), *Readings in Groupware and CSCW, Assisting Human-Human Communication*, Morgan Kaufman, San Francisco.

Fitzgerald, J. and Dennis, A. (1996), *Business Data Communications and Networking*, 5th edition, Wiley.

Foster, L. and Flynn, D. (1984), 'Management information technology: its effects on organizational form and function, *MIS Quarterly*, December.

Galegher, J. and Kraut, R. E. (1994), 'Computer-mediated communication for intellectual teamwork—an experiment in group working', *Information Systems Research*, 5(2), 110–138.

Gibson, W. (1984), *Neuromancer*, Ace Books.

Gigante, M. A. (1993), 'Virtual reality: definitions, history and applications', in R. A. Earnshaw, M. A. Gigante and H. Jones (eds), *Virtual Reality Systems*, Academic Press.

Grantham, C. E. (1991), 'Visual thinking in organizational analysis', *Beyond The Vision: The Technology, Research and Business of Virtual Reality 1991*, Meckler.

Greenguard, S. (1994), 'The next generation', *Personnel Journal*, March.

Gupta, U. G. (1996), *Management Information Systems*, West Publishing, St Paul, Minneapolis.

Halsall, F. (1995), *Data Communication, Computer Networks and Open Systems*, 4th edition, Addison-Wesley.

Herot, C. (1980), 'Spatial management of data', *ACM Transactions on Database Systems*, 5(4), 493–514.

Kellog, W., Carroll, J. and Richards, J. (1991) 'Making reality a cyberspace', in K. R. Michael (ed.), 'The promise of VR for network management', *Virtual Reality World*, 1(2).

Kent, P. (1994), *The Complete Idiot's Guide To The Internet*, Alpha Books.

Kraemer, K. L. and King, J. L. (1988), 'Computer based systems for co-operative work and group decision making', *ACM Computing Surveys*, 20(2).

Krol, E. (1996), 'Spotlight', *Computer Bulletin*, 8(3).

Kyas, O. (1995), *ATM Networks*, International Thomson Publishing.

Leston, J, (1996), 'Virtual reality: the IT perspective', *Computer Bulletin*, 8(3), 12–13.

Mallach, E. G. (1994), *Understanding Decision Support and Expert Systems*, Irwin, Burr Ridge, Illinois.

McGrath, J. E. and Hollingshead, A. B. (1994), *Groups Interacting with Technology*, Sage Publications.

Mariani, J. and Lougher, R. (1992), 'TripleSpace: an experiment in a 3D graphical interface to a binary relational database', *Interacting with Computers*, 4(2), 147–162.

Markus, M. and Robey, D. (1988), 'Information technology and organizational change: causal structure in theory and research', *Management Science*, 34(5), 583–598.

Marwell, G. and Schmidt, D. (1975), *Co-operation—an experimental analysis*, Academic Press.

Nielsen, J. (1996), 'Effective Web design for current and future user needs', NPL Usability Forum Notes, May, National Physical Laboratory.

Nunmaker, J. F. *et al.* (1993), 'Electronic meeting systems to support group work', in R. M. Baecker (ed.), *Readings in Groupware and CSCW, Assisting Human-Human Communication*, Morgan Kaufman.

O'Leary, T. and O'Leary, L. (1996), *Internet*, McGraw-Hill, New York.

Olson, J. S. (1993), 'Computer-supported co-operative work: research issues for the 90s', *Behaviour and IT*, 12(2).

Rheingold, H. (1991), *Virtual Reality*, Summit Books, New York.

Rodden, T. (1991), 'A survey of CSCW systems', *Interacting with Computers*, 3(3), 319–353.

Shay, W. (1995), *Understanding Data Communications and Networks*, PWS Publishing.

Smith, A. M. and Dunckley, L. (1995), 'Human factors in software development—current practice relating to user-centred design in the UK', in K. Nordby *et al.* (eds), *Proceedings of INTERACT-95*, Chapman and Hall.

Smith, B. (1991), 'The use of animation to analyse and present information about complex systems', in *Beyond the Vision: the Technology, Research and Business of Virtual Reality 1991*, Meckler.

Sproull, L. and Kiesler, S. (1991), *Connections: New ways of Working in the Networked Organization*, MIT Press, Cambridge, MA.

Stone, R. (1993), 'Virtual reality: a tool for telepresence and human factors research', in R. A. Earnshaw, M. A. Gigante and H. Jones (eds), *Virtual Reality Systems*, Academic Press.

Sutherland, I. E. (1986), 'A head-mounted three dimensional display', in Fall Joint Computer Conference (FJCC), Washington, DC, Thompson Books.

Taylor, J. and Katambwe, J. (1988), 'Are new technologies really reshaping our organizations?', *Computer Communications*, 11(5), 245–252.

Tucker, M. L., Meyer, G. D. J. and Westerman, (1996), 'Organizational communication: development of internal strategic competitive advantage', *Journal Of Business Communication*, 33(1).

Yang, F., Shao, W. and Li, W. (1994), 'JadeBird/III: a collaborative multimedia case environment', in J. Zupancic and Z. Wrycza (eds), *Proceedings of the Fourth International Conference on Information Systems Development, Methods and Tools, Theory and Practice*, Moderna Organizacija, Kranj, Slovenia.

Vaananen, K. and Bohm, K. (1993), 'Gesture driven interaction as a human factor in virtual environments—an approach with neural networks', in R. A. Earnshaw, M. A. Gigante and H. Jones (eds), *Virtual Reality Systems*, Academic Press.

Wexelblat, A. (1991), 'Giving meaning to place: semantic spaces', in M. Benedikt (ed.), *Cyberspace: First Steps*, MIT Press, Cambridge, MA.

Further reading

Baecker, R. M. (1993), *Readings in Groupware and CSCW, Assisting Human-Human communication*, Morgan Kaufman, San Francisco.

Earnshaw, R. A., Gigante, M. A. and Jones, H. (eds) (1993), *Virtual Reality Systems*, Academic Press.

Preece, J., Rogers, Y., Sharp, H., Benyon, D., Hillard, S. and Carey, T. (1994), *Human–Computer Interaction*, Addison-Wesley, Wokingham.

CASE STUDY: PLUMBEST PLC

A.1 About the company

Plumbest plc is the major provider of plumbing services to domestic and commercial customers in the eastern region of the United Kingdom. A significant development opportunity currently exists for expansion as Plumbest seems set to secure a major contract from UK Gas, one of the new private sector gas providers, for non-street maintenance and emergency work within the eastern region.

Plumbest employs a number of plumbers, who have recently been renamed *mobile operatives* (MOs) to reflect their impending enhanced role. MOs operate from mobile vans and when the UK Gas contract is operational will provide services from routine central heating boiler maintenance contract work, through domestic plumbing leaks, to emergency domestic and commercial (non-street) gas leaks. At present, and even without the UK Gas contract, Plumbest are experiencing inefficiencies in their current operation, with long delays between job requests and job completions.

Plumbest currently operate a manual *job processing system* with mobile telephone communication to MOs for emergency work. This system is operated from a *central service centre* which is situated in the town of Bedford. MOs operate out of three regional *depots* in Luton, Northampton, and Colchester. The telephone link to MOs can be a problem, particularly in emergencies, as it is often difficult to make contact when the MO is carrying out repairs.

Access to a computerized distributed database inventory systems already exists at each depot. Invoicing, accounting and all other services are managed by the parent company in Kings Cross, London. A variety of Plumbest staff need to access these systems for data input and output purposes. The invoicing and accounting elements are part of a wider *management information system* which the directors and senior staff use to manage the organization at a tactical level. There is also a decision support system which is used by the marketing function to support company developments at a strategic level.

Plumbest are quite happy with the current computerized MIS, inventory, invoicing, marketing and accounting systems. The basic problem is the system which allocates jobs to MOs. Plumbest require a new computerized system on which they can rely. Any new computerized job allocation system (*JAS*) will be what is known as a *trusted* or *safety critical* system. Lives are at risk if MOs do not get to the site of emergency gas leaks in the correct time scale.

Plumbest say that they pay great attention to employee *participation* and feel that their organization will not succeed unless they maintain the support of staff in any new system that might be implemented.

A.2 About your role

You work for *Usersoft* which is a software house employing 80 staff, mainly analysts and programmers. At Usersoft you are one of two *programme managers* and report to the *software director*.

You have two *project managers* who work for you. One of these (Sunila Blake) has recently returned from a period abroad and is about to take over a new set of staff. Normally each project manager co-ordinates the work of a number of small teams of *analyst/ programmers* working on each project.

Usersoft have been recruited to advise Plumbest plc on its systems and, if approval is achieved, to design and implement the new JAS.

As Sunila has been away you have done some preparatory work yourself. After a meeting with the *operations manager* (Jenny Birch) at Plumbest, you have obtained some further information on the current manual job processing system. You have summarized these in a document titled 'Further Notes'. You have conducted initial interviews with the relevant stakeholders in the organization. You have summarized these in a document headed 'Summary of Initial Interviews'.

A.3 Further notes

A.3.1 Size and turnover

The operations manager looks after a unit with turnover in excess of £6m. This figure covers most of the costs relating to the service that the MOs provide. The exception is the use of spare parts and other equipment which might be consumed during jobs. These costs are added by each depot and billed directly by head office. Further data can be found in Sec. A.3.7. The £6m figure includes:

- MO salaries
- Service centre salaries
- Service centre overheads

- Van purchase and operation
- Purchase and repair of non-consumable equipment needed by MOs

It has been estimated that the UK Gas contract would be worth an extra 80 per cent of current turnover.

A.3.2   Current organization structure

The current organization structure is as shown in Fig. A1.1. The names refer to the people who have been interviewed (see Summary of Initial Interviews).

As may be clear from the organization chart there are two main organizational entities: the service centre and depot-based Foremen and MOs.

The majority of the Plumbest organization (MOs, radio operators and service administrators) work a rotating four shift system:

Shift 1	8.00 a.m. — 4.00 p.m.
Shift 2	2.00 p.m. — 9.00 a.m.
Shift 3	7.00 p.m. — 4.00 a.m.
Shift 4	2.00 a.m. — 10.00 a.m.

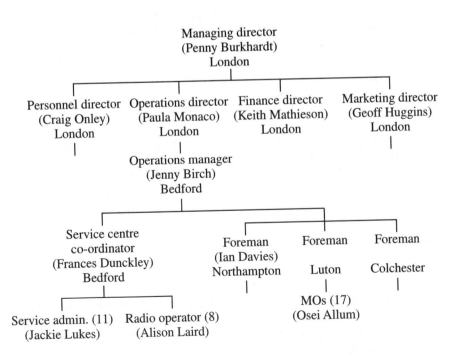

FIGURE A1.1   *Plumbest organization chart*

with overlap between each shift. MOs working Shift 1 (usually 8 per depot) are allocated to either *emergency* or *non-emergency* work, whereas those working Shifts 2 to 4 (usually three per depot per shift) only undertake emergency jobs such as water and gas leaks. There are two *radio operators* on duty at any one time. The majority of *service administrators* also work the shift system with a minimum of two on duty at any one time. In addition three further service administrators work a standard five day week with a 9.00 a.m. to 5.00 p.m. shift in order to complete administrative procedures within the service centre.

Plumbest is managed by a number of groups of personnel. A *board of directors* (comprising executive and non-executive directors) is responsible for overall strategy and planning within the business. Penny Burkhardt is a member of this group. In addition a *senior management board* which comprises the MD and the three directors, together with the operations manager and personnel at equivalent levels in the finance and personnel departments is responsible for implementing strategy and managing the business.

A.3.3   Unions

The majority of employees belong to a recognized trades union. Administrative staff are members of the *Union for Clerical Staff* (UCS) while the MOs mainly belong to *the Engineering Workers Union* (EWU).

A.3.4   Current system

There are two main documents used in the system:

* *Job instruction form* (**JIF**) which is used to record job details from the customer and, for non-emergency jobs, for the foremen/MOs to record parts raised for jobs.
* *Job completion form* (**JCF**) which is used by the foremen/MOs to record the result of all jobs and which is the source document for billing processes.

Job allocation

Telephone calls from potential customers are routed to service administrators in the service centre who also receive any fax or postal requests. If the service administrator decides that a visit is required details of the call, fax or postal request, are recorded on the JIF. All jobs are either:

- **Non-emergency**—In this case after completing the JIF, the service administrator files one copy while another copy is faxed to the relevant depot where the foreman orders any materials from store. The foreman maintains a diary of work pending for Shift 1 MOs for whom he or she is responsible and as a result is able to **allocate** the job for a future shift. The foreman then informs the service centre when the job will be done, which in turn tells the customer.
- **Emergency** (jobs that require immediate action) —In the case of emergencies the service administrator raises the JIF, passes it to a radio operator who telephones an MO. The MO will write details on a second JIF held in the van. At present it is not difficult, in theory at least, for the two radio operators to keep track of the MOs, and be able to allocate the job to an appropriate person. After contacting the MO, the radio operator will file the first copy of the JIF. MOs should have emergency parts for most jobs. If, however, parts are not available in the van the MO telephones the depot for fast delivery.

Job completion

When the work is completed (emergency or non emergency) the MO completes a JCF. These are sent, together with the JIF (for non-emergency jobs) to the relevant foreman. The foreman then checks and completes the paperwork and faxes the JCF back to the Bedford service centre. When the JCFs for completed jobs are received at the service centre in Bedford the service administrators complete the paperwork, and communicate with head office in London. The details of this part of the system are not relevant to the JAS.

A.3.5   An outline requirements definition

The general requirements are:

- Faster response to emergency jobs
- Prompter responses to non-emergency jobs
- Capable of coping with increased work load of UK Gas contract
- Improved customer service
- More efficient utilization of staff
- Ensure safety within the operation of the UK Gas contract

A.3.6   Two perceived options

It is thought within Plumbest that there are two potential computer-based solutions to their situation. These are often referred to as the *minimum solution* and the *pet plan*.

Minimum solution

The *minimum solution* would leave much of the overall system untouched. Communication to MOs would continue to be performed by the radio operators as now. A new computer system would be introduced within the service centre which would be used by service administrators to record customer details, job allocations and MO activities. The system would lead to the enhanced tracking of job progress.

Pet plan

The operations manager (Jenny Birch) has a pet plan to implement a much more extensive computerized automatic allocation system where data would be sent to remote mobile data terminals in each van. These would store a number of messages from the office and would circumnavigate the current communications system. Jenny is aware of the problems incurred in similar systems and would need to be persuaded about a fully automatic allocation system where the computer system decided which jobs to allocate to particular MOs. Such a system would allocate jobs without human intervention. A semi-automatic system, on the other hand, would prompt the user with a suggested MO after which the user would need to confirm the allocation.

A.3.7   Current data

Personnel

- 51 MOs
- 2 radio operators per shift
- 2 service administrators per shift
- 3 extra service administrators during normal working hours
- 3 foremen operate (1 from each depot) during normal working hours
- 1 service centre co-ordinator working during normal working hours
- 1 operations manager working during normal working hours
- Total salary bill c. £1 700 000

Volume of work—average data

- 12 telephone calls per hour (one every 5 minutes)
- 6 emergency jobs per hour (out of 12 calls)
- 32 emergency jobs completed per shift

- 128 emergency jobs completed per day
- 80 non-emergency jobs received and completed per day
- 4 jobs per MO shift
- c.200 jobs completed in total per day
- c.65 000 jobs completed per year
- Average cost of job (excluding materials) = £100
- Yearly turnover = £6 000 000

A.4   Summary of initial interviews

A.4.1   Operations manager (Jenny Birch)

Jenny is aware that the final decision on what type of JAS to implement will rest with the operations director but feels she (Paula Monaco) will take your advice. Jenny has a *pet plan* to implement a computerized automatic allocation system where data will be sent to remote mobile data terminals in each van. These would store a number of messages form the office and will circumnavigate the current communications system. Jenny is aware of the problems incurred at similar systems and would need to be persuaded about a fully automatic (i.e. one with no human intervention) allocation system— although this remains a possibility.

A.4.2   Foreman (Ian Davies)

Ian is aware of the operations manager's pet plan and is most concerned about the implication for the foreman role; will he, and all his colleagues be made redundant as a result? Ian considers that the problems with the current system lie within the manual clerical system at Bedford.

Ian is well respected within Plumbest. He has been a plumber/MO for many years now and gained a qualification in electrical engineering about 10 years ago. He has recently been "mugging up' in information technology. Jenny is aware that Ian has recently written a small end-user computer system to assist in stock re-ordering in one of the warehouses.

A.4.3   Service centre co-ordinator (Frances Dunckley)

Frances is aware of the operations manager's pet plan and has some support for it as she feels the MOs 'get away with murder' while 'on the job'. While she is aware of the inefficiencies in the current system she is largely unable to control the situation. Often jobs are not completed on time, or even undertaken at all, but there is no way at present of determining the efficiency within the system until complaints are received.

Frances feels an opportunity exits for enhancing the role of the service centre. It could lead to more staff, perhaps with higher grades. She has a distinction in a Higher National Certificate in business information technology which she obtained after studying part-time at the local university. She therefore feels quite comfortable with the idea of introducing computerized systems.

A.4.4   Operations director (Paula Monaco)

As operations director, Paula has a very wide ranging role and is happy to delegate the management of customer services to Jenny, the operations manager. However, she thinks that Jenny often has some strange ideas.

A.4.5   Service administrator (Jackie Lukes)

Jackie feels that her job is crucial to the system and always 'tries her best' to allocate the job to the most appropriate MO. This is often difficult as she relies on MOs telling the radio operators about the progress of their work. She is unsure whether she gets 'the full picture from the MOs'. The service centre co-ordinator has told Jackie about the operations manager's pet plan. Jackie agrees with her that it could be a good thing. She is, however, very concerned that it will not offer all she needs to do the job which is 'very stressful at times'. She might be persuaded as long as she get something out of it (i.e. promotion).

A.4.6   Radio operator (Alison Laird)

The service centre co-ordinator has told Alison about the operations manager's pet plan and she is very concerned. Although friends have told Alison about the potential for career development and promotion, she sees no place for her current job and does not know anything about computerization.

4.7   Mobile operative (Osei Allum)

Osei is quite happy with the current system as it gives him considerable independence during the day. He does not want 'some new computer system telling him what to do, keeping tracks on his every move'. He gets on well with his foreman but has heard that the operations manager's new system might involve him reporting to the service centre co-ordinator. He feels unhappy about this as she knows nothing about the technical nature of his job.

Plumbest plc

Water House, Gas Alley, Bedford

JOB INSTRUCTION FORM (JIF)

Part A - To be completed by Service Administrator   Emergency: Y   N

JOB NO   `_ _ _ _ _ _`   Date: `_ _ _ _ _ _`   Time `_ _ _ _`

Customer Name   ....

Customer Address   ....

....

....

circle   circle

Customer Type   *   Domestic   **Account?**   Y   `_ _ _ _ _ _`
                     *   Commercial   N

Description of Job

....

....

....

Part B - To be completion by Foreman / MO   MO Allocated   `_ _ _ _ _ _`

Parts raised:

Part No.	Description	Qty Raised	Qty Used (MO)
....	....	....	....
....	....	....	....
....	....	....	....
....	....	....	....

Part C - To be completed by MO

Comments   ....

Signed   ....

Plumbest plc
Water House, Gas Alley Bedford

JOB COMPLETION FORM (JCF)

Part A - To be completed by MO

Emergency: ☐Y ☐N

JOB NO [_____]

Date: [__ __ __]

MO Number [_____]

COMMENTS

....

....

....

....

Part B - To be completion by Foreman / MO

Parts used:

Part No.	Description	Qty
....	....	....
....	....	....
....	....	....
....	....	....
....	....	....
....	....	....

MO Hours [_ _ _]   Signed .... (MO)   Signed .... (Foreman)

Part C - To be completion by Service Centre

Administrative details for Head Office

GLOSSARY

analysis—the process of establishing the requirements for a software system

aspirational needs—the requirement of an information system to support the medium- to long-term personal goals of the user

attitude—a learned and organized collection of beliefs towards an individual, object or situation predisposing the individual to respond in some preferential manner

cognitive ergonomics—the study of the relationship between human information processing capabilities and technical information systems

computer supported co-operative working—the study of specific software systems to support group working

design—the process of developing a software system

design rationale—a representation for explicitly documenting the reasoning and argument that makes sense of a particular artefact

end user computing/system—the direct use, development, and maintenance of information systems by those whose primary role is to achieve a business purpose, rather than the indirect development and management through information systems professionals

engagement—a general term for the total set of user relationships towards information systems and their development, implementation and use

ergonomics—the design of appliances, technical systems and tasks in such a way as to improve human safety, health, comfort and performance

evaluation—a process in which the usability of a software interface is established

functional needs—the requirement for the information system to perform the specific tasks that the users require it to do in an operational situation

functional specification—a document which can be used as a basis for a contract between developer and client, also known as requirements specification

graphical interaction—an interaction style in which the user manipulates through button presses and movement of a pointing device such as a mouse, a graphic or iconic representation of the underlying data

human-computer communication—the dialogue between a user and a computer system

human-computer interaction—the processes, dialogues and actions that a user employs to communicate with a computer system, a discipline concerned with the design, evaluation and implementation of interactive computing systems for human use and with the study of major phenomena surrounding them

human-computer interface—the interface between software system and user

hypertext—a non-linear document based system with pointers from words or points in the document to other words or points

information system—an application of computing and communications technology to meet a defined need

information systems engineer—an IS specialist who applies engineering principles, founded on appropriate scientific and technological disciplines, to the creation, use and support of information systems for the solution of practical problems

interactive systems—a system which allows a direct two way flow of information between human and computer

interface—an imaginary plane across which information and power are exchanged

job enrichment—the process of redefining narrow, fragmented job roles into positions which encourage thinking and promoter personal growth

job satisfaction—the attainment of a good 'fit' between what the employee is seeking from his or her work (job needs, expectations and aspirations) and what he or she is required to do in his job (the organizational job requirements)

methodology—a collection of procedures, techniques, tools and documentation linked by a philosophical view of a system under analysis/design

network—a system that translates data to and from a number of locations which are geographically dispersed

norms of behaviour—legitimate socially shared standards or guidelines which must exist for acceptable and expected patterns of conduct

organizational user—any organization using information systems support of organisational objectives

participation—the observable behaviour of system users in the information systems development process

physical needs—the requirement of the information system to perform the tasks in a manner which is well suited to the physical characteristics of the user

physiology—the science of the functions of living organisms and their parts

processes—any activity within design in which users might be involved

process model—a framework in which a methodology is defined; representative of the sequence of stages through which a software product or information system evolves

prototype—a model that simulates or animates some, but not all, of the features of an intended system

psychology—the scientific study of

the human mind and its functions especially those affecting behaviour in a given context

requirements definition—a statement in natural language which is understandable by both client and technical specialists and which specifies the services which the proposed system will provide

requirements specification—a document which can be used as a basis for a contract between developer and client, also known as functional specification

scenario—a specific example of a user interaction with an information system

scope —the degree to which systems analysis reflects a socio-technical, as opposed to just a technical, solution.

social psychology—a study into how the thought, feeling and behaviour of individual is influenced by the actual, imagined or implied presence of others

socio-technical system—a system in which both technical (hardware and software) and social (people and procedures) issues are important

software interface—see human-computer interface

software methodology—a systematic approach to conducting at least one phase of software production and is concerned with software, analysis, design and implementation

stakeholder—those individuals who have an interest in the success of a new information system

strategy—a broad based formula for how business is going to compete,

what its goals should be, and what policies will be necessary to carry out those goals

structures—mechanisms which either support or inhibit the way in which the user is able to contribute to the design process

systems development life cycle—the stages involved in the analysis, design and implementation of an information system

systems methodology—a methodology (see above) which is concerned with the system itself, the procedures, people and organizational structures as well as possibly including software development

task analysis—the process of breaking down a user task into elemental actions

telematics—the application of communications technologies to information systems

teleworking—the ability to work remotely from the normal business location while maintaining, through telecommunication facilities, access to the data and information services of the organization

training—the systematic acquisition of skills, knowledge, and attitudes that will lead to an acceptable level of human performance on a specific activity in a given context.

usability—the effectiveness, efficiency and satisfaction with which specified users of an information system can achieve specified goals in particular environments

usability engineering—a life cycle of processes which need to be undertaken when designing for usability

usability engineering life cycle—the stages involved in the analysis, design and evaluation of a human-computer interface

usability metrics—quantitative measure of the usability of a system

user—any employee or customer of an organization who will be directly or indirectly affected by an information system

user-centred design—either: a development approach in which potential users have the opportunity of being actively involved, either directly or indirectly, in the whole analysis, design and implementation process, or: a development approach in which all types of user needs (functional, physical and aspirational) are addressed so that

usability (effectiveness, efficiency and satisfaction) is maximized in the end product

user needs—refer to functional, physical and aspirational needs

user specification—a specification of the user groups involved within an information system and their associated characteristics and needs

user support—enabling individual users to access a range of documentation, help and advice so that they can enhance their operational use of a specific application.

utility—the capability of a system to perform the functions for which it was devised

virtual reality systems—computer generated simulation of a world in which the user is immersed

AUTHOR INDEX

SUBJECT INDEX